# Innovations in NLP

# INNOVATIONS
## IN
# NLP

VOLUME 1

## FOR CHALLENGING TIMES

**L. MICHAEL HALL**

AND

**SHELLE ROSE CHARVET**

EDITORS

Crown House Publishing Ltd
www.crownhouse.co.uk
www.crownhousepublishing.com

First published by

Crown House Publishing Ltd
Crown Buildings, Bancyfelin, Carmarthen, Wales, SA33 5ND, UK
**www.crownhouse.co.uk**

and

Crown House Publishing Company LLC
6 Trowbridge Drive, Suite 5, Bethel, CT 06801-2858, USA
**www.crownhousepublishing.com**

*British Library Cataloguing-in-Publication Data*
A catalogue entry for this book is available from the British Library.

ISBN 978-184590734-1 (print)
     978-184590774-7 (mobi)
     978-184590775-4 (epub)

LCCN 2011938913

Printed and bound in the UK by
Henry Ling Ltd, Dorchester, Dorset

# Preface

*Innovations in NLP, Volume 1* is an impressive collection of articles, written by key innovators in the field, covering a range of significant recent developments in neuro-linguistic programming. A rare collaboration among leaders of the field, the book is the result of the vision and effort of two of the most dedicated and energetic figures in the field today. Michael Hall and Shelle Rose Charvet have worked hard to spearhead this inspired and inspiring contribution to NLP.

The list of contributors to *Innovations in NLP* is a veritable "who's who" of contemporary neuro-linguistic programming. Each author is an outstanding trainer and practitioner of NLP in addition to being a creative developer. I personally count many of them as close friends as well as valued colleagues.

Originated by Richard Bandler and John Grinder in the 1970s, neuro-linguistic programming is an approach to examining the deeper structure of human behavior, and a set of explicit models, applications, and tools derived from that approach. In our recent book *NLP II: The Next Generation*, Judith DeLozier, Deborah Bacon Dilts, and I point out that NLP has come a long way since its early days more than thirty years ago when it was essentially considered a new form of psychotherapy. Through the years, NLP has developed some very powerful tools and skills for communication and change in a wide range of professional areas including coaching, counseling, psychotherapy, education, health, creativity, law, management, sales, leadership, and parenting. Over the years, NLP has literally spread around the world and has touched the lives of millions of people.

One of the core values and characteristics of NLP as a field is its generativity—its ability to continue to produce new and creative models, applications, and tools. Like any successful field of study and application, NLP has grown far beyond the contributions of its original founders. New techniques and procedures have been presented in the ever-growing number of NLP books, recordings, and seminars.

As the fruits of this next generation of NLP developers spread into the world, it is important to have a way to acknowledge and showcase their creations and contributions. *Innovations in NLP* is that showcase, presenting an enriching overview of many of the most recent and important of these developments. Aptly subtitled *Innovations for Challenging Times* the book describes models such as Meta-States, LAB Profile®, Social Panorama, Clean Language, the RESOLVE Model, and Behavioral Remodeling.

Part II covers the ways in which NLP has enriched other areas of application such as coaching, entrepreneurial leadership, research, addictions, wealth management, and cancer treatment.

Part III presents innovative computer tools that can be applied toward developing emotional intelligence, assessing personality, and reaching personal goals and objectives.

Indicative of the new generation of NLP is the development of communities formed around these innovations that are described in a final section of the book.

I am deeply grateful to Michael and Shelle for taking on such a monumental project. It is a reflection of their devotion and commitment to the field. I cannot think of any two other people who could have successfully taken on such a major project. Congratulations on a job well done!

Robert Dilts
July 2011
Santa Cruz, California

# Contents

# Introduction

## What's New in NLP for Challenging Times?

*L. Michael Hall and Shelle Rose Charvet*

We live in a world where there are a great many challenges! Writing this in early 2011 it seems to both of us that life on planet earth today offers us tremendous challenges. What are we talking about? We are talking about climatic catastrophes, the rise of violent extremism in so many forms, incompetent or corrupt governments, widespread economic volatility that directly affects many millions of people, millions of people unemployed (the estimate is 200 million worldwide in February, 2011), entrenched armed conflict, along with the issues that continue to plague our planet—hungry people, oppression, and lack of access to basic necessities, including education.

And that's just the beginning. So with all of these troubles and challenges, many of us are wondering: What can I do? What can we together do? What can anyone do? Are there solutions at the individual level? Are there solutions at the community level? How can we in the field of neurolinguistic programming offer some answers and resources to these challenges?

As we all know, when NLP was first developed in the 1970s, it was created in a therapeutic context and the purpose was to help people overcome personal issues, to communicate more effectively, and to access further personal resources. Since that time, the field has been changing and evolving. It has been expanding the original modeling strategies to areas such as education, health, business applications, and sports achievement. And many contributors have developed new ways of thinking, new models, new applications, and new tools.

Over the past thirty-eight years, through the skillful and ethical efforts of practitioners, NLP has made a dramatic difference to the way in which many people lead their lives and their achievement of success. If there is anything that connects and unifies the worldwide NLP community, it is the singular desire of tens of thousands of people to make a difference in our world and to respond to the challenges before us.

NLP has also been moving out beyond dealing only with individuals. As it has moved into areas such as business, education, marketing, and sales, it has been developing models for groups, for communities, for leadership, for management. NLP has been expanding its realm of influence to empower the movers and shakers of our world. And NLP, as a model of subjective experiences, has been modeling organizations, cultures, and the variables that make a community of people operate effectively. As modelers, NLP thinkers and trainers have taken the foundational work of people modeling "good to great companies," self-actualizing leaders and companies, as well as the "tipping point" phenomena of how societies grow, develop, change, and transform. The result? We now know a whole lot more about how to influence our world for good.

## Making a Difference in a Troubled World

As the editors of this book we believe that now is the time to truly make a difference that makes a difference. That's one of the reasons why we have collaborated to create this unique book—*Innovations in NLP, Volume 1*. This book is premised upon the idea that the new things happening in NLP are valuable for solving important problems in our world and that the resources for creativity and innovation that we have in NLP ought to be applied more broadly to the challenges before us.

In this volume we have collaborated to bring together many of the key people in the field of NLP who share this passion and vision. The contributors not only believe in applying the rich and powerful tools in NLP to make a difference in our world, but they have created models, patterns, and tools to enable that to happen. The result is that we have a unique opportunity for collaboration, creativity, and innovation in the NLP community with the specific aim of looking at how what we do can help the world.

What is this book about? We have a three-fold focus:

First, it is about *what's new in NLP as effective innovations for communication, change, and leadership in our world*. If you are interested in the ongoing development of the NLP model, you will discover many of the new contributions to the field in this book. Some of these innovations go back to the 1990s and others began after 2000.

Second, and more important, it is about *applying these new innovations in NLP to the problems and challenges that trouble our world so that they can help solve the problems that confront all of us*. If you have an interest in how to make the planet a better place and to know about models, applications, and new ways of thinking for doing precisely that, this is the book for you. Obviously, we have not addressed every challenge, but this is a beginning and subsequent volumes will address other problems.

Third, *to offer an inspirational and educational look at the ongoing creativity and innovation in the field of NLP*. One of our aims is to let those in the field of NLP know what's been developed, what's being developed, and to encourage more people to engage in cultivating solutions that will give us new models, patterns, and tools for making a difference.

## Innovating New Things in NLP

What's new in NLP? How often we ask or have heard that question! Many of us ask it because we truly want to know what's new. We ask it also because NLP people tend to be curious individuals interested in what's being developed in this field and interested in what needs to be developed. We ask it because we are an optimistic people who believe in possibilities and in inventing new things to create more resourcefulness in individuals and organizations. And sometimes we ask it wondering if anything actually is new or just rehashed from things already developed.

If you have asked the question about what's new in NLP, this book will give you some solid answers. We have searched for practitioners who have created and innovated new techniques and have collected models, patterns, tools, and information about communities that are indeed new in the field of NLP.

A challenge in this field is that of *communication*; that is, the challenge of keeping people informed about what is happening in this sphere, who is developing new things, what they have developed, and what results they have obtained. Yes, it's paradoxical—NLP is a field that came into being as first and foremost a communication model, and yet we have difficulty communicating! We also are collaboratively challenged—as a field we do not have a good record of collaborating as colleagues.

To address these challenges we have invited two dozen people who have been contributing to the field, developing new things, and advancing NLP in the twenty-first century. There were others we invited and who will appear in subsequent volumes. And there are undoubtedly people who we should have invited, but we just didn't know who they were, where they were, or how to get in touch with them. Our hope is that with this publication, we will be able to identify other developers who are contributing to this field.

In this sphere, the problem is not *creativity*. Not at all! If we were to ask everybody with inspirational creative ideas to contribute, this would be a 3,000 page book. As a model and field, NLP inherently attracts creative people, especially highly individualist people who want to do it by themselves.

If there is a problem in NLP, the problem is one of *innovation*. One of the fathers of creativity, Abraham Maslow, who was a leading business expert in creativity in the 1950s and 1960s and who wrote extensively on creativity said, "Creative inspirations are a dime a dozen." The second part of creativity is innovation and, as Thomas Edison said, this is only 1% inspiration and 99% perspiration. It is innovation that is required for working out structure, procedures, details, testing the process, redesigning, testing again, and so on, until a model, pattern, process, or instrument is developed to the point that it is ready to be rolled out as an effective contribution. So it is exciting to gather actual innovations in this field and present them here.

## The Innovative Vision

The vision that we shared that has inspired this work is to create a book, and possibly a series of books, on innovations in NLP. Our desire is to provide communication worldwide about what is happening in this field, to collaborate with those who are developing new things, and to encourage more collaboration, creativity, and innovation.

The original inspiration that brought us together was the book that Robert Dilts, Judith DeLozier and Deborah Dilts published at the end of 2010, *NLP II: The Next Generation*. In it, the co-authors did an excellent job in describing the new developments that they have been creating and contributing to NLP. Then, after a book review by Michael of that book, Shelle suggested that we collaborate and bring together contributions from all of those that we know about who are working in a similar vein in the field of NLP so that we could supplement what Robert, Deborah, and Judith began.

## Criteria for Determining "What's New in NLP"

Our first challenge in creating this book was deciding what to include. That led us to set out some criteria for guiding our decisions and making them as objective as possible. From the beginning we knew that identifying what is within the category of NLP is a volatile area. Some people think that, "Everything is NLP." And to the extent that every subjective experience can be modeled by NLP, yes, that's true. But if NLP is everything, then it is also nothing. Then there are others who think that only things identified in the original 1970s model meet the criteria.

So from the start we realized that we needed some boundaries on the territory of what is NLP and what is not, as well as what we would consider an innovation in NLP. To that end we set out five criteria that would provide some rigor and that we have used for this first volume.

### *Criteria 1: The contribution grows out of the classic NLP models developed from 1972 through 1990*

The model, pattern, tool, or community uses the basic NLP communication models to develop another model or pattern. That is, it uses the meta-model; meta-programs; Test–Operate–Test–Exit (TOTE) strategies; sub-modalities; meanings (beliefs, understandings, concepts, etc.); Symptoms, Causes, Outcomes, Resources and Effects (SCORE); neurological levels, and so on.

### *Criteria 2: The contribution fits the basic essence of NLP; that is, modeling subjective experiences*

Ideally, the model provides a way to model some human experience and to therefore expand the essential NLP theme of modeling or mapping excellence in human experiences. The contribution operates from the basic NLP presuppositions: "The map is *not* the territory," "We construct our mental models of the world and operate from them," and so on.

## Criteria 3: *The contribution innovates a new model, pattern or process, tool, or community for the field of NLP*

We quickly realized that all "innovations" are not the same, that there are different kinds of innovations and that they fall into various categories. Consequently we have structured this book so that the innovations fall into four different areas. Now, while any of us have and certainly can take a model that has already been developed and then re-work it using NLP premises and tools, that is not what we have included here. So while that would be an innovation, at least in this first volume, we decided to stay away from the re-modeling of already existing models that actually belong to another discipline. This means that we have excluded such models as Bert Hellinger's Family Constellations; the Graves Model; Drive, Influence, Steadiness, Compliance (DISC); the Enneagram; the Myers-Briggs Type Indicator (MBTI), and so on.

## Criteria 4: *The contribution leads to effective practical applications of the models, patterns, processes, tools, and communities*

We included this criterion because from the beginning NLP has been highly practical and pragmatic. This principle maintains that distinction; namely, that the innovation has relevant and practical use for those working in therapy, coaching, business, leadership, health, parenting, and so on. If it doesn't have a practical use, then we have not included it.

## Criteria 5: *The contribution adds credibility to the field*

The model or pattern fits the scientific model in that it can be tested, falsified (i.e., proven or disproven), and it is a process others can use. It can be replicated and further improved and developed.

## Areas of Innovation

As mentioned, we have identified four areas or categories wherein an innovation may fall: models, patterns, tools, communities.

### *Innovative Models*

A fully-fledged model is a paradigm that addresses a specific area and that operates from an explicit theoretical understanding. Model (capital M) entails theory, variables, guiding principles (heuristics), and applications (see Appendix B for the requirements of a Model).

### *Innovative Applications*

Applications are the patterns and processes that result from a Model and, with the richness of the NLP Models, there are always several hundred patterns and the possibility for many more. A pattern is often called and considered a "model;" as such, however, it is model (with small m).

### *Innovative Tools*

Another form of application from a Model is a tool, typically a psychological instrument used for assessment, diagnosis, and pattern detection. A well-developed tool that has been refined over several years of use can offer what "using or running a pattern" often cannot provide—consistency in use.

### *Innovative Communities*

NLP as a field means that there are groups of people working together and collaborating, and so it is an innovation to create a community that can keep alive a particular NLP model, pattern, or tool, which can facilitate that community to be a learning organization and add credibility to NLP. While this has been a weak area in NLP, there are numerous collaborations occurring around the world keeping NLP alive. Communities include associations, conferences, support groups, practice groups, and so on.

## Innovations R Us

Our belief is that *NLP is, and ought to be, a highly innovative field*. If NLP is a highly creative field that enables and empowers people to model excellence, and if none of us have a corner on good ideas, then the more we communicate and collaborate in effective ways, the more we can make a larger and more positive contribution to our world. Actually, we see this book as the beginning of a series on innovations in NLP and trust that this first volume will inspire you and many others to tap into your own creativity and to innovate in your life, your town, and your community.

## On a Personal Level

When we began, we really didn't know how we would get along in working together. We had never done so before and so had no idea how this project would go or if our work styles would fit. What we both had, however, was a deep respect for the contributions of the other and we soon found out that we both had an "active" meta-program that enabled us to take on projects and get things done. The result has been a most delightful experience of daily emails, proofreading, sending back manuscripts, contacting lots of people, and working out the publication details with David Bowman of Crown House Publishing.

Early in the process we made a joint decision that all proceeds from this book would go to the NLP Research and Recognition Project. It was easy to make that choice because we both believe in the importance of supporting this field and in the quality work that Frank Bourke and Rich Liotta are doing.

There were several people that we sought out to contribute to this first volume but who for a variety of reasons did not. Our hope is that they will do so in subsequent volumes. May this book be the beginning of a new era here in the twenty-first century for NLP—an era of more collaboration, more credibility, and more influence on the challenges before us.

# Part I
# Innovative Models

If we are open to new models in the field of NLP and if we anticipate that additional models will be added to NLP that were not part of the models that existed in 1975 or 1985, then what criteria do we use to determine if something meets the conditions necessary to be considered a "new" Model?

In the following sections we distinguish *models, patterns (applications), tools, and communities*. And with each of these, we will present a description and a criteria to define precisely what we mean by each one.

So what makes something "a Model" (with a capital M)?

- **A theory**
  First there has to be a theory which establishes the theoretical descriptions— background, foundation, hypothesis, and so on—and which offers an explanatory model for how the model or system works. This explanatory model will involve the governing ideas of the Model and how to test and refine the ideas to create new applications. A Model will present ideas (hypotheses) that can be tested and falsified and can answer the why-does-this-work type questions. Does the Model have construct validity? A theory functions as a way of bringing together a multitude of facts into a comprehensive order so that we can make reasonably precise predictions. A theory is a tentative expression of a regular pattern. And in spite of protests to the contrary, NLP *does* have a theory. Its theory is hidden in the NLP presuppositions which establish NLP on the premises of constructionism, phenomenology, and cognitive psychology.

- **Variables and elements**
  If the theory comprises the over-arching frame, then the variables and elements of the theory are the pieces and parts that make up the components of the Model. This answers the question: What makes up this Model? What elements are absolutely necessary and sufficient to make the Model work? What processes are necessary? Variables enable us to experiment, to observe, to identify key factors, and to create factorial designs in research projects. Operational definitions mean that theoretical constructs should be stated in terms of concrete, observable procedures. What can be observed and tested? What are the variables of the NLP model? As a communication model, the variables are the sensory

systems, the representations (visual, auditory, kinesthetic (VAK)), language, sub-modalities, meta-programs, and so on.

- **The guiding and operational principles**

  After the theory and variables come the guiding principles or operational principles. The laws or principles define and articulate the mechanisms that make the Model work and how they are used in a methodological, systematic, and systemic way. This gives us the ability to keep refining the Model. Principles answer the *how* questions: How does the Model work? How do the processes and mechanisms govern it?

  In the NLP model, you can find guidance for how the Model works in the meta-model questions, in the principles for how to detect and use the representational systems, in the implications that result from the NLP presuppositions, in the processes for working with the Test–Operate–Test–Exit (TOTE) Model, with strategies, and with the hypnotic language of the Milton Model (e.g., "pace, pace, pace, lead").

- **The technologies or patterns**

  This refers to the specific tools that provide immediate application for using the Model to achieve something. Patterns answer the questions about *how to*: How do you anchor a state, calibrate to a person's non-verbals, reframe meaning?

  In the NLP model, there are some 200 to 300 distinct patterns. Each one provides direction for how to do something in order to achieve a specific outcome. With patterns, always look for information about its context—where it is useful and effective and where it is not—and the elicitation questions that a person can use to begin the process. Typically there are usually conditions that are noted as times for caution in using the pattern.

### References

Kelly, G. A. (1955). *The Psychology of Personal Constructs*. New York: Norton.

Pelham, B. W. and Blanton, H. (1999). *Conducting Research in Psychology: Measuring the Weight of Smoke*. Pacific Grove, CA: International Thompson Publishing.

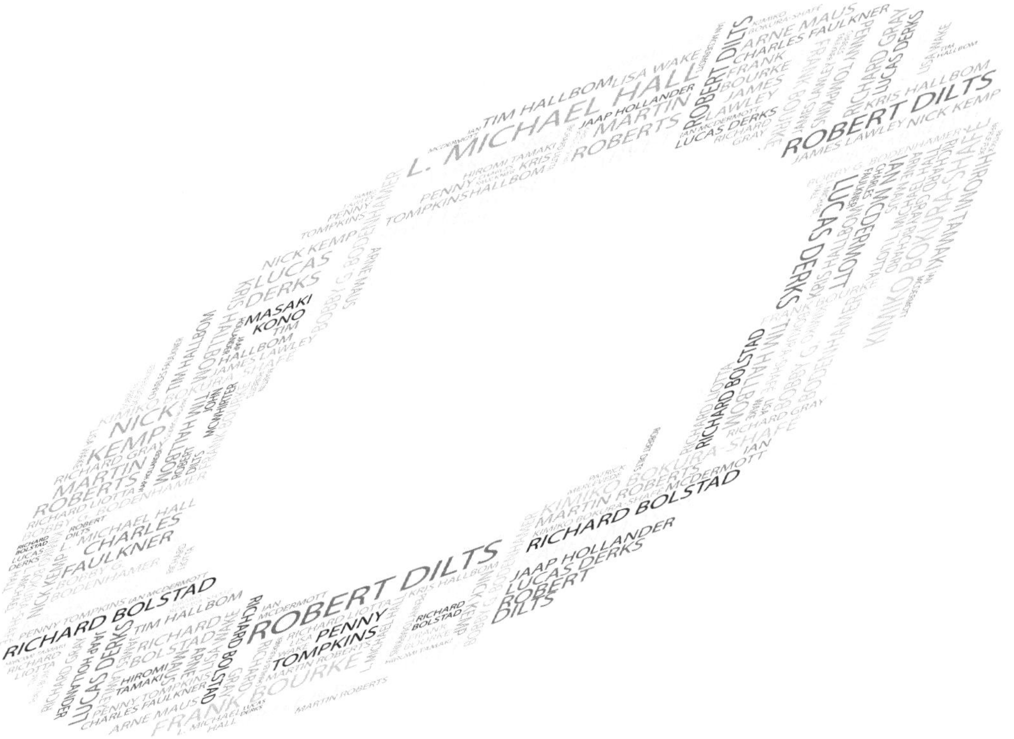

L. MICHAEL HALL
TIM HALLBOM
LISA WAKE
JAAP HOLLANDER
MARTIN ROBERTS
ROBERT DILTS
ARNE MAUS
CHARLES FAULKNER
FRANK BOURKE
JAMES LAWLEY
LUCAS DERKS
RICHARD GRAY
KRIS HALLBOM
NICK KEMP
HIROMI TAMAKI
PENNY TOMPKINS
IAN MCDERMOTT
KIMIKO BOKURA-SHAFE
BOBBY G. BODENHAMER
MASAKI KONO
RICHARD BOLSTAD
RICHARD LIOTTA
JOHN MCWHIRTER

 **L. Michael Hall, Ph.D.** is an international speaker and consultant who focuses primarily on modeling and researching self-actualization excellence. He worked for several years with Richard Bandler and wrote a number of books for and about him including *The Spirit of NLP* (1996) and *Becoming a More Ferocious Presenter* (1996). He co-founded the International Society of Neuro-Semantics with Bob Bodenhamer and the Meta-Coaching Foundation with Michelle Duval. Known for his prolific creativity, Michael has published over forty books on NLP, including eight on meta-coaching, and he has created more than a dozen NLP models. As a visionary leader, Michael pioneered the founding of neuro-semantics to "take NLP to a higher professional and ethical level."

email: meta@acsol.net
web: www.neurosemantics.com
 www.meta-coaching.org
 www.self-actualizing.org

# 1 Meta-States
## Modeling Self-Reflexive Consciousness

*L. Michael Hall*

## Why the Meta-States Model?

If NLP is to truly be "the study of the subjective structure of experience" then it has to have a model of the most challenging feature of human consciousness—*self-reflexive consciousness*. NLP began by modeling the *representational* mind, yet there's more to our mind–body consciousness than what and how we represent things. In the living mind–body system, there is a self-referential feature that needs to be modeled. That's what the Meta-States Model does.

Meta-States takes the exploration of structure to the next level as it models the structure of our complex layer states. These higher states are not simple primary states, but richly textured states that involve the most unique kind of consciousness that we have—our self-reflexive awareness. It is those highest, richest, and most complex states that empower people for unleashing their best potentials and for making a real difference in any and every area of life. For example, one such meta-state is when a person feels annoyed about something and at the same time is amused by his or her annoyance.

As a model, Meta-States goes beyond the basic Strategy Model to map complex states which extend over time. These include states such as the *transformational leadership* Nelson Mandela demonstrated when he took a nation through a radical change without a civil war. With Meta-States I modeled the *wealth creation strategies* of those who create wealthy minds, hearts, lifestyles, etc.[1] We can also model *attitudes*—like seeing opportunities, seizing them, being resilient in the face of difficulties, of realistic optimism that refuses to cave in to the negativism of the daily news.[2]

The Meta-States Model enables us to model how a great leader may use anger effectively in confronting those not living up to their promises or responsibilities. An effective leader can use anger by expressing it from the higher state of being *kind*, *calm, and respectful.* Via meta-stating she can now demonstrate *honorable anger.* And this kind of anger will have an entirely different quality than someone who is "out-of-control," using insulting or attacking anger.

Unlike the linear Strategy Model, which is great for smaller behaviors like spelling and getting out of bed in the morning, Meta-States maps how your self-reflexive consciousness creates complex layered states. Now you can model behaviors that occur over long-periods of time like entrepreneurship.[3]

The Meta-States Model can unpack most of the "magic" of NLP because it identifies the governing frames. When you set one state *about* a previous state, that second state (now at a higher level), operates as the *frame* for the first state. Because higher frames invisibly govern the lower ones, a self-organizing process is created. This is the magic of NLP. To that end, I have applied Meta-States to all of the meta-models of NLP: modeling and meta-programs,[4] sub-modalities,[5] sleight of mouth patterns,[6] and so on, and remodeled them to uncover the layered frames that make them work.[7] Meta-States has been so prolific in generating creative ideas that I have used it to develop more than 200 patterns and numerous other models—the Matrix Model, Axes of Change, Meaning–Performance Axes, Self-Actualization Quadrants, and so on.[8]

The Meta-States Model enables this by detailing more than the sequential steps of a person's thinking–emoting responses, but also a person's responses to his or herself, layer upon layer. As you go upward you can detect and work with your belief frames, value frames, intention frames, and so on. This exposes a whole matrix of frames making up the governing meanings of your experience.

With the Meta-States Model, you can track what's "in the back of the mind" that sets the frame for a person's reality. You have access to *the leverage points for sustainable change* instead of working merely with symptoms. As this complexity is unpacked, you can track and model how a person has constructed the frameworks of the experience and make it available to others. Very few of our highest and best "states" are simple states—they are richly textured with layers of frames. Meta-States can open up the secrets to these high quality states.

## What Does the Meta-States Model Innovate in NLP?

In 1994, the Meta-States Model created for NLP a model of the special and unique kind of consciousness of *self-reflexive consciousness*. This added to the foundational NLP model of "mind"—the representational mind.

NLP began when the founders identified *representational consciousness* and gave us the languages of the mind. Gregory Bateson said this was a tremendous step forward in his introduction to Bandler and Grinder's *The Structure of Magic*.[9] It identified that we think using the representational sensory systems of sights, sounds, sensations—the VAK (visual, auditory, kinesthetic) model of mind. We do *not* literally have a theater in our brain where we run movies, yet phenomenologically we experience our thoughts *as if* we are seeing, hearing, feeling, smelling, and tasting things.

While the representational mind is one level of mind, it is not the *unique human kind of mind*. The animals with higher intelligence can represent and remember what they see, hear, feel, and so on. What makes us truly unique is our ability to *reflect* on our mind. We can as it were step back, notice, and transcend to reflect on our representational processing and so add a new layer of thoughts. We can also continue to step back and reflect layer upon layer upon layer.

In noting this exceptional quality of human consciousness, Alfred Korzybski said that it is an infinite, never-ending process. Whatever you think and feel about something, you can always step back and transcend that level of consciousness and add yet another thought-or-feeling upon it. And it is this process that creates what we call "logical levels."[10]

Logical levels (a phrase made of two nominalizations) refers to how we *layer* level upon level ("levels") of thoughts and feelings as we use our internal logic to *reason* ("logical"). Layering-and-reasoning are the *process verbs* inside the convoluted double-nominalization, "logical levels." We are really talking about how we reflexively layer our thoughts-and-feelings (states) upon each other. In so doing, the next level up becomes the context frame of the previous level. We *transcend* our current state of thinking-and-feeling-and-experiencing and *include* that one in the next higher one as a member of a class. Korzybski and Bateson describe this as how we create our unique "logic" and how that logic is "psycho-logical." It "makes sense" to us, on the inside, given the kind of reasoning we used to construct it.

## Meta-States as States-about-States

Understanding meta-states begins with understanding "states," a holistic term for all of the thoughts, feelings, and physiological events that together make up an experience. A state is holistically a state of mind, body, neurology, and emotion. It is holistic in that it does not separate "mind" and "body" and "emotion" as distinct elements.

A meta-state emerges when you apply one state to another state. If you are in a state of fear, what do you think-and-feel *about* your state of fear? Do you fear it? Shame yourself for it? Enjoy it? Love it? Dread it? Whatever you reflexively think-and-feel about the first state (the primary state) generates a second level state (a meta-state). This now gives fear-of-fear, enjoyment-of-fear (like those who go to Stephen King movies to be scared and have fun being scared), anger-of-fear, hatred-of-fear, and so on.

Your self-reflexive meta-states are your interpretations, conclusions, and constructions of meaning *about* your first states. So if you love-learning or experience joy-of-learning, this meta-state indicates that you have made "learning" a member of the class of "Things to Enjoy" or "Things to Love."

The structure of a meta-state refers to your mind *reflecting back onto itself*, and so going *up*. So with each meta-stating of a state or experience, you create layers of frames—"logical levels." You create a matrix of beliefs, values, and identities. Take the example of *joyful learning*—is that a belief? Do you believe that learning can be joyful? Is it a value? Do you value learning because you have fun and enjoy it? Is it an identity? Do you identify yourself as a learner, a joyful learner? Is it part of your self-definition? Is it a decision? A memory? An imagination and expectation of your future?

Given the holistic nature of meta-states, *every meta-state is, at the same time, every other logical level*. It is simultaneously a belief, value, identity, decision, memory, imagination, expectation, intention, permission, and so on. All of these are just different words, different ways of describing the meta-level construction of a meaning-frame that you have created as you transcended your primary state and included it in a higher frame. All of these frames are just elements of the same thing—*the experience*. The experience, like a diamond, has many facets and names.

In NLP states are usually *primary states*—the states of mind, body, and emotion that we experience *about* something that happens in the world, something that happens to us interpersonally, or something that happens within our body to which we respond. The Meta-States Model introduces two more kinds of states: meta-states and gestalt states. A *meta-state* is simply any state that is *about* some other state: fearful anger, playful seriousness, curious sincerity, cruel silliness, and so no. The *about-ness* of the referent event completely changes from primary to meta-states. The first is *about* the world "out there," the second is *about* a previous inner experience, a thought, a feeling, a memory, and so on.

A *gestalt state* occurs when several meta-states layer an experience. Take courage. What's at the primary level? Fear. You are afraid of something that holds some danger or threat which you may not be prepared for. Which meta-states texture the experience and transform it into "courage"? Typically it requires several resources: transcend the fear to a strong objective, passion, determination, a sense of responsibility, and so on. When you layer all of these states, something more than and different from the sum of all of those parts emerges—a gestalt state. It's almost impossible to unpack "courage" to find the elements that make it up. It is something "more than all of the parts."

Many meta-states are actually gestalt states—seeing and seizing opportunities, forgiveness, unconditional self-esteem, ego-strength, and so on. These are not simple states, not even simple meta-states; they are richly textured and layered meta-states that have now become something more.

What is a meta-state? It is not only a layered state, a transcending and including of a state; it is how you respond to yourself. It is a reaction to your first reactions. It is your self-reflexive consciousness at work as you step back from yourself and your experiences to construct new layers of awareness. That is why meta-states texture primary states. If you bring calmness to your anger, you can create *calm anger*. Bring respect of persons and you have *respectfully calm anger*. Add kindness and you have *kind, respectful, calm anger*. Each meta-state adds new qualities and texture to your primary state.

Your layers of frames are also mostly unconscious—*outside of your conscious awareness*. You mostly live within these frames, this matrix of frames, and operate from them without an awareness of your installed frames. That is why sometimes awareness *per se* is curative. Sometimes becoming mindful of your meta-states enables you to run the higher levels of your mind and to set the frames of mind that will make you more effective and joyful.

## How Does the Model Work?

The Meta-States Model describes the structure of how a state-upon-state process textures and qualifies experiences. This is done by *meta-stating*, a process that you have been doing since childhood. You have been *constructing* meta-states about a thousand things. The process is profoundly simple: access and apply one state to another. These five steps for meta-stating provide a simple conscious process for creating state-upon-state structures.

1. **Access a state (Y) for which you want to texture or qualify a primary state (X)**
   What is the experience or state (Y) that you want to use to texture another state? Example: What quality might you want your sadness to have? What qualities do you want your learning to have? As you decide upon the state (Y) with which to meta-state, then access that state by using the basic NLP state elicitation processes. (Memory: Remember a time when you experienced that state. Imagination: What would it be like if you fully experienced that?)

2. **Amplify the state (Y) so that it is sufficiently strong and robust**
   How much do you now feel that state? Is it sufficiently strong? Do you need to make it stronger? If so, then what do you need to do to increase it? What representation? What physiology to adopt?

3. **Apply the state now to the primary experience (X)**
   As you *feel this* (fire an anchor for the chosen state of Y) feel this *about* X (the first state or experience) and notice what happens. (Link the second state to the first state so it now operates as *the frame category* of the first one.)

4. **Appropriate the state into the context**

   As you now apply the Y state into the X experience, notice how it qualifies it. How is that? Does it provide the resources you want so that your X experience is now ecological for you? What other resources might you need?

5. **Analyze the overall impact of state-upon-state structure**

   If you imagine taking this into your work or home context, is this ecological? Does it support the health and well-being of your relationships, health, career, spirituality? Is it realistic, useful, empowering?

Conversely, you can start with an experience that does not have the qualities that you want, that may actually have qualities that make your life miserable and diminish you as a person. Holding that state, you can invite an exploration into the meta-states as beliefs, meanings, values, identities, and so on that hold it in place. To do that, take the meta-levels distinctions and ask them as *meta-questions*.

1. **Access the unresourceful experience**

   What is the experience that you find troubling and troublesome? What do you call the state you experience in that event?

2. **Transcend to explore the structure of that experience**

   Are you ready to explore this state to understand it? What do you believe about that experience? If that's so, then what do you think about that? And let's say that's true, what does that mean to you? (Continue to do this level upon level; be sure to keep track of the levels you elicit.)

3. **Step back and do a quality control about the set of frames**

   When you have fully moved up the levels and identified the frames that are holding the primary experience in place and texturing it, meta-state by stepping back to gain the perspective of the whole. Ask quality control questions such as: Does this serve you well? Does it empower you as a person? Does it bring out your highest and best?

## Using Meta-States to Qualify Anger

**LMH:** What would you like to achieve in this conversation that would be the most transformative thing for you today?

**John:** I would like to work on my anger. Sometimes it just flares up and I really don't know why; and sometimes it is very intense and I've had some people tell me that they are afraid of my anger.

**LMH:** Who says that to you?

**J:** My wife and sometimes even my son.

**LMH:** When? When are the times when this happens? How often are we talking about?

**J:** When? When I'm upset or stressed.

**LMH:** And when do you get upset or stressed? What events trigger your response?

**J:** Oh, like when I have had to work late, and had too many things to do, and then there's more demands when I get home.

**LMH:** When was the last time that happened? Any time recently?

**J:** Yes, last week I had an outburst, and I really don't know where it came from.

**LMH:** OK, so you have grounded the context of your anger, now just welcome in the memory of that event so that you recall it as clearly as possible, and when you do, if you now step back in your mind to that anger, what's your next thought?

**J:** Next thought? Well, I don't like it.

**LMH:** Yes, I figured that! You don't like it. And you don't like it because …? [Pause] What does it mean to you? [Moves up a level]

**J:** [Pause] It means that I'm out-of-control, that I'm … not able to think very clear.

**LMH:** Is that true for you? Are you out-of-control? Can you not think very clear when you are in an angry state?

**J:** Well, I definitely cannot think very clear. And yes, I'm kind of out-of-control.

**LMH:** Let's say that's true—you are out-of-control and unable to think very clearly. If that was true, what does that mean to you?

**J:** Means? Just that I'm out-of-control.

**LMH:** OK, what do you believe about it? What are your thoughts and/or your feelings about being out-of-control and unable to think very clearly?

**J:** I believe it is dangerous, that it will ruin things, that I'll end up saying stupid things, and I feel afraid of my anger.

**LMH:** So you're afraid of your anger—that it will lead you to say stupid things and ruin things.

**J:** Yes!

**LMH:** Let's say that's so, that your anger will move you to do those things, so what? What would it mean or what do you believe if that happened?

**J:** I shouldn't get angry!

**LMH:** That's about doing—does that mean that you don't allow yourself to feel anger?

**J:** Yes, I try really hard to hold it in, or if it arises to swallow it and not let it show.

**LMH:** So does that mean that you forbid and taboo your anger because it holds all these meanings, and that's why you have become afraid of it?

**J:** Well, yes, although I never thought of it like not-allowing or making it taboo.

**LMH:** So if you go inside and give yourself permission to feel the anger without tabooing it, what happens? If you go inside and say to yourself, "I give myself permission to feel the anger and just feel it without needing to misuse it"—what happens? [Pause as John does that] So how well does that settle?

**J:** It's kind of okay, but ... I am still afraid of it.

**LMH:** And you are afraid of what? What will the emotion of anger cause or mean?

**J:** I'm afraid that my anger will get out of hand.

**LMH:** And what will you be doing when it gets out of hand?

**J:** I will be hurtful.

**LMH:** OK, now give yourself this permission, "I give myself permission to feel my anger, notice what seems to be violating something important, to notice without being hurtful." Now what happens?

**J:** It is much better; it is settling much better.

**LMH:** What other resource do you need? Would you like to bring calmness to your anger and create calm anger, or respect for respectful anger, or thoughtfulness, curiosity, learning, acceptance, appreciation ...? What resource would give your anger the quality you would really like?

**J:** I'd like calmness and respect.

**LMH:** OK, as you access each of these states ... fully, strongly, and then apply them to your anger state ... notice what happens.

## Caveats

First, meta-stating should not be confused with "dissociating." The kinesthetic feeling quality of the meta-state depends on the state you are accessing as you "go meta." If you go into "witnessing" or "mere observation" there will be little emotional intensity. Yet if you go into *fear-of-your-fear*, you will have immense emotional intensity, so also with *passionate learning*. The meta-states you create will be very emotional.

Second, meta-stating is not the same as collapsing anchors. These are two entirely different processes. In meta-stating you hold the primary state and include it within a larger state. So instead of collapsing or making it go away, in meta-stating, the higher state *coalesces* into the lower and textures it.

## How Did You Create the Model?

Upon learning NLP, I set out to do several modeling projects. In 1990 I began modeling *resilience*. I wanted to know how some people were so resilient that nothing seemed able to knock them down. As soon as they suffer a setback or knock-down, they bounce right back. I wanted the strategy for that level of buoyancy of attitude and spirit. After interviewing more than a hundred people who had "been to hell and back," I put together a workshop for the NLP Conference in Denver in September 1994. The title was, "Go For It—Again!"

In preparation I read Korzybski's classic *Science and Sanity* and Bateson's *Toward an Ecology of Mind* and many other works. I especially used the work of Elisabeth Kübler-Ross on the grief stages[11] and Martin Seligman on learned pessimism and learned optimism.[12] In the workshop I presented the basic stages of resilience: knock-down, cognitive shock, emotional roller coaster, coping with the losses and challenges of putting life back together again, mastering the challenges, being back. Then during a demonstration, I interviewed a participant "who had been to hell and back."

When he identified how he went through the stages, I asked him at one point, "How did you know to go from this stage to the next?" In answer, he sat back in his chair, looked up and said, "It was like I had this higher state and I knew that I would get through it." "You knew you would get through it!" I mirrored back. Then one of us, and I don't remember if it was he or I, said, "It's like a meta-state about my state and I just knew that I'd get through this. This too would pass."

That's when the heavens opened and the light bulb went on and suddenly I had a new understanding of resilience—a layer of awareness *about* the primary level states of the stages. That week I wrote a forty-page paper on meta-states and sent it to the International Association of NLP Trainers. Later Wyatt Woodsmall called me to let me know that I had won the contest on "The most significant contribution to NLP in 1995."

## Summary

The Meta-States Model is much more extensive than what I have presented here. The meta-stating process operates by framing and out-framing and so establishes the interpretative contexts by which we "make sense" of things. The meta-stating process also innovates in NLP a model for how each of us reflect on our responses which then textures our everyday states with qualities that can empower and unleash new potentials.

### Notes

1.  See Hall (1999a, 2009, 2010).

2.  See Korzybski (1994/1933) and Bateson (1972).

3. For books on modeling that resulted from the Meta-States Model, see Hall (2002) and my training manuals, Hall (2001, 2004). For wealth creation, see Hall (2010).

4. Hall and Bodenhamer (1997).

5. Hall and Bodenhamer (1999).

6. Hall and Bodenhamer (2005).

7. Graham Dawes noted this remodeling of NLP with Meta-States in his book reviews of *Meta-States* and *Dragon Slaying* in 1996 in *Anchor Point* magazine in 1996 and *NLP World* in 1997.

8. See Hall (1995), as well as the training manual, Hall (1999d).

9. Grinder and Bandler (1989).

10. For more on "logical levels," see Bateson (1972) and Hall (1995, 2002).

11. Kübler-Ross (1969).

12. Seligman (1975, 1991).

## References

Bateson, G. (1972). *Steps to an Ecology of Mind*. New York: Ballantine.

Burton, J. (2000). *State of Equilibrium*. Carmarthen, UK: Crown House Publishing.

Goodenough, T. and Cooper, M. (2007). *In the Zone with South Africa's Sports Heroes*. Cape Town: Zebra Press.

Grinder, J. and Bandler, R. (1989). *The Structure of Magic. Vol. 1: A Book about Language and Therapy*. Palo Alto, CA: Science and Behavior Books.

Hall, L. M. (1995). *Meta-States: Mastering Your Mind's Higher Levels*. Clifton, CO: Neuro-Semantic Publications.

Hall, L. M. (1996). *Dragon Slaying: Dragons to Princes*. Grand Junction, CO: E.T. Publications.

Hall, L. M. (1999a). *Games Business Experts Play*. Carmarthen, UK: Crown House Publishing.

Hall, L. M. (1999b). *Secrets of Personal Mastery*. Carmarthen, UK: Crown House Publishing.

Hall. L. M. (1999c). *Winning the Inner Game*. Clifton, CO: Neuro-Semantic Publications.

Hall. L. M. (1999d). *Resilience*. Clifton, CO: Neuro-Semantic Publications.

Hall. L. M. (2001). *Cultural Modeling Using Neuro-Semantics*. Clifton, CO: Neuro-Semantic Publications.

Hall. L. M. (2002). *NLP Going Meta: Modeling with Meta-States*. Clifton, CO: Neuro-Semantic Publications.

Hall. L. M. (2004). *Advanced Modeling with Neuro-Semantics*. Clifton, CO: Neuro-Semantic Publications.

Hall. L. M. (2009). *Unleashing Leadership: Self-Actualizing Leaders and Companies*. Clifton, CO: Neuro-Semantic Publications.

Hall. L. M. (2010). *Inside-Out Wealth: Holistic Wealth Creation*. Clifton, CO: Neuro-Semantic Publications.

Hall, L. M. and Bodenhamer, B. G. (1997). *Figuring Out People: Design Engineering Using Meta-Programs*. Wales, UK: Anglo-American Book Co. Reprinted in 2007 by Neuro-Semantic Publications.

Hall, L. M. and Bodenhamer, B. G. (1999). *Sub-Modalities Going Meta*. Clifton, CO: Neuro-Semantic Publications.

Hall, L. M. and Bodenhamer, B. G. (2002). *User's Manual of the Brain*. Vol. 2: *The Master Practitioner Course*. Carmarthen, UK: Crown House Publishing.

Hall, L. M. and Bodenhamer, B. G. (2005). *Mind Lines: Lines for Changing Minds*. Clifton, CO: Neuro-Semantic Publications.

Korzybski, A. (1994/1933). *Science and Sanity: An Introduction to Non-Aristotelian Systems and General Semantics*, 5th edn. Lakeville, CN: International Non-Aristotelian Library Publishing Co.

Kübler-Ross, E. (1969). *On Death and Dying*. New York: Simon & Schuster.

Seligman M. E. P. (1975). *Helplessness: On Depression, Development, and Death*. San Francisco: W.H. Freeman.

Seligman M. E. P. (1991). *Learned Optimism: How to Change Your Mind and Your Life*. New York: Knopf.

See www.neurosemantics.com for more than 5,000 pages of articles on NLP and Meta-States.

**Shelle Rose Charvet** has been learning NLP since 1983 and became a Certified NLP Trainer in 1992. She has been exploring Rodger Bailey's Language and Behavior Profile (LAB Profile®) since she encountered it at Institut Repère in Paris in the mid-1980s. Today she is known in the NLP community as the "Queen of LAB Profile" because of her books—*Words That Change Minds* (1997) and *The Customer is Bothering Me* (2010)—and the LAB Profile training she delivers to NLP institutes around the world. She also works with businesses and organizations to help them transform communication with customers and solve other influencing and persuasion challenges. Shelle speaks English, French and Spanish and is currently learning German.

email: shelle@wordsthatchangeminds.com
web: www.WordsThatChangeMinds.com
     www.labprofilecertification.com

# 2

# LAB Profile®
Decoding Language and Behavior to Improve
Communication between People

*Shelle Rose Charvet*

## Why the LAB Profile?

I discovered NLP in Paris in 1983 with Josiane de St. Paul and Alain Cayroll on the second NLP Practitioner course offered in France. The next year I did my Master Practitioner at Repère and, with Lynn Conwell, discovered the meta-programs. There were over sixty different distinctions for identifying the things to which people were paying attention or ignoring, how they evaluated different situations and made decisions. These were the NLP patterns that grabbed my heart. For the very first time I encountered a detailed understanding of how one person is different from another.

The problem was that there was no methodology for applying the patterns. Even figuring out who was operating from which patterns was nearly impossible. Then I discovered Rodger Bailey's LAB Profile, based on the original NLP meta-programs developed by Leslie Cameron-Bandler. Rodger created a straightforward methodology which made possible the systematic detection and use of these patterns.

First, he reduced the patterns to a manageable number and divided them into two distinct types: *motivation traits* (what someone needs to be motivated in a given situation) and *working traits* (how they process information, respond to their environment, and make decisions). Second, he designed questions to ask a person to elicit the patterns. Lastly, he created the influencing language that matched each pattern.

These developments made it possible to apply the meta-programs to make significant improvements in areas such as recruitment, people management, marketing and sales, coaching, conflict resolution, and interpersonal communication. Suddenly there was a methodology to uncover people's hidden motivations and thinking patterns. This changed my world.

**Note to Reader:** Now that you have read my answer to the "Why?" question, do you recognize my LAB Profile Pattern? In structuring the chapters in this book, Michael and I decided to start with *why*. Then after I wrote that section, I realized I answered this why question with a story, which indicates a Procedures Pattern. If I had given a list of reasons, that would have been the Options Pattern.

## What is the LAB Profile?

The LAB Profile is short for the Language and Behavior Profile, a behavioral profiling instrument that detects what people need to be motivated, how they think, and how they make decisions. Because the LAB Profile is a profiling tool that works with *behavior, not personality*, people's patterns can change from context to context. Sometimes the patterns can be different even if someone merely changes the person to whom they are speaking.

The LAB Profile has proven to be so practical that three tools have been developed based on Rodger's work—iWAM, Identity-Compass (see Chapter 16), and MindSonar® (see Chapter 17).

## LAB Profile Patterns

Here is a list of the categories and patterns measured by the LAB Profile with their definitions.

### *Motivation Traits*

What a person needs to be motivated and maintain their interest level.

- **Level:** Does a person need the initiative or would they prefer to think and wait?
  - **Proactive:** Likes to jump into action; motivated by doing.
  - **Reactive:** Motivated to wait, analyze, consider, and respond.

- **Criteria:** These are the exact words that describe what is important to a person in a given context. They create a positive physical and emotional reaction.

- **Direction:** When a person is motivated by what they want or by what they want to avoid, prevent, or solve.
  - **Toward:** Motivated by goals and the benefits of achieving them. Focus on what they want and may not notice issues and problems; may not be motivated if there are no goals or benefits to *move toward*.
  - **Away from:** Motivated to *move away* from what they do not want. Focus on problems to be prevented or solved and may not focus on goals.

- **Source:** When a person evaluates based on external sources or by using their own internal standards.
  - **Internal:** Judges based on his or her own internal standards; motivated to judge and decide for him or herself.
  - **External:** Evaluates based on outside sources or guidance; motivated by feedback.

- **Reason:** When a person prefers alternatives or would rather follow the established procedure.
  - **Options:** Motivated by having many choices, likes creating procedures and systems; little interest in following them; enticed by bending or breaking rules.
  - **Procedures:** Motivated to follow and complete a logical process; interested to know the next step and wants to know how to do something.

- **Decision Factors:** The way someone reacts to change and the frequency of change he or she needs.
  - **Sameness:** Motivated when things stay the same; needs major change every 15–25 years.
  - **Sameness with exception:** Motivated by what is improved and in incrementally evolving situations; needs major change every 5–7 years.
  - **Difference:** Motivated by what is new, by constant change; needs major change every 1–2 years.
  - **Difference and sameness with exception:** Motivated by a combination of evolution and revolution; needs major change about every 3 years.

### Working Traits

How a person processes information, the type of tasks, the environment they need to be most productive, and how he or she goes about making decisions.

- **Scope:** The size of the "chunk" of information with which a person is comfortable.
  - **Specific:** Focuses on specific details and may not see the overview.
  - **General:** Focuses on the overview, big picture; can only handle details for short periods.

- **Attention Direction:** Does a person pay attention to non-verbal behavior or on the content of the communication?
  - **Self:** Focuses on the words; tends not to notice other's behavior or voice tone; little use of tone changes, facial expressions, or gestures when communicating.
  - **Other:** Notices and responds to the non-verbal behavior of others and uses non-verbals when communicating.

- **Stress Response:** How a person reacts to the "normal" stresses of a given environment.
  - **Feelings:** Emotional responses to normal levels of stress; stays in feelings.
  - **Choice:** Moves in and out of feelings voluntarily; can be empathetic.
  - **Thinking:** Responds rationally; may not establish rapport or show empathy easily.

- **Style:** The preferred human environment to enable a person to be most productive.
  - **Independent:** Alone with sole responsibility.
  - **Proximity:** In control of own territory with others around.
  - **Cooperative:** Together with others in a team, sharing responsibility.

- **Organization:** The preference for paying attention to people and relationships or to tasks, ideas, systems, and tools.
  - **Person:** Focuses on people, experiences, feelings, and relationships.
  - **Thing:** Focuses on tasks, systems, ideas, tools, and material objects.

- **Rule Structure:** The rules a person has for him or herself and for others.
  - **My/My:** My rules for me/My rules for you; able to tell others what they expect.
  - **My/.:** My rules for me/I don't pay much attention to others.
  - **No/My:** Don't know what the rules are for me/I have rules for others.
  - **My/Your:** My rules for me/Your rules for you. Sees both sides; so may be hesitant to tell others what to do.

- **Convincer Channel:** The type of information a person needs to start the process of convincing themselves about something.
  - **See:** See evidence.
  - **Hear:** Oral presentation or hear something.
  - **Read**: Read something.
  - **Do:** Do something.

- **Convincer Mode:** The way in which the information previously gathered is processed to enable a person to become "convinced" of something.
  - **Number of examples:** Need to have the data a certain number of times to be convinced.
  - **Automatic:** Convinced immediately and rarely change their minds.
  - **Consistent**: Never completely convinced. Every day is a new day and they need to get re-convinced.
  - **Period of time:** Need to a certain duration to be convinced.

## How to Use the LAB Profile

Rodger originally designed the profile to be used conversationally one on one. This questionnaire makes it very simple to learn. Here are the questions to ask and the indicators for each pattern.

### Identify the context and ask each question about that context

| Question | Category | Patterns | Indicators |
|---|---|---|---|
| No question | Level | Proactive | Short, active sentences |
| | | Reactive | Passive voice, thinking, considering |
| **What is important** to you (about context)? What do you want? | Criteria | | Exact words and phrases used |
| **Why is that important** to you in (context)? | Direction | Toward | What the person wants |
| | | Away From | What they want to prevent or avoid |
| **How would you know that you have done a good job** at (context)? | Source | Internal | Knows inside self |
| | | External | Knows from external sources |

(continued)

| Question | Category | Patterns | Indicators |
|---|---|---|---|
| **Why did you choose** your current (context)? | Reason | Options<br>Procedures | Gives a list of reasons why<br>Tells a story (as in my introduction to this chapter) |
| **What is the relationship between** X and the one before it? | Decision Factors | Sameness<br>Sameness with Exception<br>Difference | Stays the same, no change<br>Same but, improved, increase, decrease (words on a sliding scale)<br><br>Didn't understand question, new, different |
| No question | Scope | General<br>Specific | Overview, few words<br>Detail, detail, detail |
| Use a gesture to test | Attention Direction | Self<br>Other | Doesn't notice gesture, few non-verbals<br>Notices and displays non-verbal behavior |
| Tell me about a (context) **situation that caused you trouble**? | Stress Response | Feelings<br>Choice<br><br>Thinking | Goes into feelings and stays there<br>Goes into feelings and chooses to stay or come out<br>Doesn't go into feelings |
| Tell me about a (context) **situation that was** (Criteria from first question)? | Style | Independent<br>Proximity<br>Cooperative | Alone with responsibility for activity<br>Responsible with others around<br>All together, shared responsibility for the activity |
| **What did you like** about it? (from above) | Organization | Person<br>Thing | People, relationships, emotions<br>Things, results, ideas, methods |
| **What is a good way for you to increase your success**? | Rule Structure | My/My<br>My/.<br>No/My<br><br>My/Your | My rules for me and you<br>My rules for me/I don't care about you<br>I don't know the rules for me/My rules for you<br>My rules for me/Your rules for you |
| **How would you know that someone else is good at** (context)? | Convincer Channel | See<br>Hear<br>Read<br>Do | |
| **How many times would they have to** (insert answer from previous question) **for you to be *convinced*** they are good? | Convincer Mode | Number of examples<br>Automatic<br>Consistent<br>Period of time | Number of times<br><br>Knows right away<br>Never completely convinced<br>Needs a duration of time |

To practice asking these questions, and decoding the answers, identify the context prior to asking the questions since the patterns can vary as the context changes. I do this before asking each question (e.g., "Talking about your work as a plumber … what is important to you?").

One problem with this interview technique comes from listening to someone's patterns without an awareness of our own patterns. When I first began doing LAB Profiles, the vast majority of people had an Away From pattern in their work context. It took me a while to realize that I was somehow imposing my own preference on other people. To prevent this from occurring, I developed the following process.

### *The Rigorous, Empirical, and Scientific Methodology*

1. Guess.
2. Test.

First ask your client each of the questions and guess which of the patterns they have as you go along. Once you have completed the profile, test it by describing each pattern you "guessed." If you guessed that your client had an Away From pattern, you would test by describing the behavior associated with that pattern: "When you are taking a vacation (context), it seems you like to get away from your normal activities and not have to deal with the problems at work," or "When you are at work (context), one thing that motivates you is preventing and solving problems."

Instead of using the pattern name "Away From," describe the behavior and phrase it as an affirmation rather than a question. Offer your client a hypothesis and test by watching and listening for reactions. If your guess is correct, your client will likely acknowledge it, provided it does not sound "bossy." If you are perceived as overly directive, the client may simply reject your guess because they do not like the way you said it.

If you use the name of the pattern to give someone feedback, the client may become confused because of the difficulty of trying to apply oneself on an abstract label. It is much easier for a person to respond to a behavioral description. Once you have confirmed the patterns, you can then use the appropriate Influencing Language for the pattern.

## Beyond the Question and Answer Routine

It has been many years since Rodger developed the original model and much of the practice using it has changed. One of the first things we do in the LAB Profile Consultant/Trainer program is to eliminate asking the LAB Profile questions. You can identify the patterns just from listening to normal conversations. This was an exciting development because the LAB Profile was no longer restricted to an interview format.

You can therefore use the LAB Profile in many other ways. When I am giving a presentation, I can tell which patterns are operating for the audience at a given moment. If I were to emphasize results, methods, and ideas—in other words Things—and I noticed that the audience seemed bored or frustrated, or if the audience asked questions concerning relationships, emotions, and how these ideas generally affect people, I would know this audience had more of a Person pattern.

The first time I taught LAB Profile in Mexico, I completely misread the group. The classroom was full of formally dressed businessmen, chins up, looking at me through semi-closed eyes. I concluded that, as a group, they were both Internal (decides for oneself) and Thing (which is an indicator that they need me to be credible). To establish my credibility, I mentioned all my credentials (Thing) and all of the very important organizations (Thing) for whom I had worked. They remained impassive. Suddenly one gentleman cocked his head to the side, smiled, raised his hand and asked: "Do you have any children?" Everyone in the room smiled and looked at me with interest. I took off my jacket and told them about my family and showed them a picture of my children.

## The Many, Not the One

While my original book, *Words That Change Minds* discussed each pattern one by one, it has become apparent through our research that individuals, groups, and even whole cultures operate with complex sequences of combination patterns. When most people go to the supermarket, they tend to walk up and down the aisles in a set way (Procedures) as they choose the items they wish to buy. They have Criteria for choosing items, and may or may not be influenced by the advertising/packaging (Internal or External).

Once they are ready to check out, this becomes a new sub-context, where many people switch to Options, Internal and they want the whole process to go quickly. They search for the shortest queue, become annoyed when it doesn't move fast enough, jump to a different queue, and generally look and sound impatient. In order to keep these customers happy, many North American supermarkets open up new cash registers as soon as the line exceeds two or three people.

When you can decode the sequences of Combination patterns for large groups of people, you can design the experiences you would like them to have.[1]

## Where Else Can You Use the LAB Profile?

I have decoded the generic structure of conflict in LAB Profile terms, and identified different types of conflicts by their LAB Profile Patterns. In conflicts, each party adopts Internal + Away From patterns with regards to the other party. This kind of analysis enables me to train high-stakes negotiators to understand the motivations of their counterparts and to use the right language and behavior to create lasting agreements.

In *The Customer is Bothering Me*, I describe how customer attitudes have changed.[2] Prior to the easy access to information afforded by the Internet, customers tended to be more External to their suppliers. In other words, once a supplier had credibility with the customer, they could pretty much tell them what to do and the customer would comply. Then the Great Customer Attitude Shift happened.

| Compliant Customers | LAB Profile Patterns | Shift in Behavior | LAB Profile Patterns | Challenge to Suppliers |
|---|---|---|---|---|
| Do what they are told | **External** (influenced by outside factors) | Won't do what suppliers want; insist on what they want | **Internal** (decides for self) | Customers are difficult to influence, they are skeptical |
| Will follow the supplier's process | **Procedure** (follows a step-by-step method) | Insist on breaking the rules, want a special deal, individualized service | **Options** (want choices, alternatives, an exception to the rule) | Difficult to cater to individual requests |

(continued)

| Compliant Customers | LAB Profile Patterns | Shift in Behavior | LAB Profile Patterns | Challenge to Suppliers |
|---|---|---|---|---|
| Wait for supplier to respond or initiate | **Reactive** (waiting, thinking) | Insisting, confronting, demanding | **Proactive** (taking initiative) | Customers difficult to predict, feeling attacked |
| After a few Good sales or service experiences, they believe the supplier is good | **Convincer Mode: Number of Examples** (+/−3, the number of positive or negative interactions needed to convince) | Each experience is evaluated separately | **Convincer Mode: Consistent** (every day is a new day, difficult to convince) | Customers believe: "You are only as good as the last thing you did," no trust |

In January, 2011, much of the world was following news about the uprisings in the Arab world. At that time significant shifts in LAB Profile Patterns were occurring for large groups of people:

### Protestors' LAB Profile Pattern Shifts

| Behavior Before | LAB Profile Patterns | Behavior Now | LAB Profile Patterns | Implications and Needs |
|---|---|---|---|---|
| Decades of submission | **External** (needs direction from the outside) | Protesting, demanding | **Internal** (decides for oneself) | Won't be told what to do or intimidated; need to invite consultation, explore their demands, and negotiate |
| Willing to follow the expected procedure | **Procedures** (motivated to follow a step-by-step process) | Want alternatives, choices, options | **Options** (motivated to break rules to have more choice) | Demand to break with the process of the past to create new alternatives |

(continued)

| Behavior Before | LAB Profile Patterns | Behavior Now | LAB Profile Patterns | Implications and Needs |
|---|---|---|---|---|
| Doing the same thing | **Sameness** (motivated to keep things the same) | Wanting change | **Difference** (driven to create change) | Don't want leaders from the *same* old regime to lead the transition; want *new* leaders |
| Not taking initiative, waiting | **Reactive** (preference for waiting, thinking) | Taking the bull by the horns, not waiting | **Proactive** (need to take initiative) | Want to be in charge of what happens next; need to be involved in taking action and making decisions |
| No movement | Neutral | Resisting authority | **Away From** (Moving away from what they do not want) | Highly motivated to notice and respond vociferously to events considered undesirable |
| Little collective movement, people acting as individuals | **Independent** (preference to operate alone) | Collective consciousness, working together | **Cooperative** (acting as a group) | Prepared to stand together, want to be taken seriously as a group |

Why is it useful to decode such large group behavior into LAB Profile terms? Once one understands their patterns, it becomes easier to communicate with them.

## Conversational Coaching with the LAB Profile

Coaching associations around the world are interested in the LAB Profile, particularly because of the dichotomy between how coaches work and what motivates people to seek coaching. Coaches help people identify their objectives and how to reach them, working *Towards* something. However, many people want to get away from an undesirable situation, to solve issues or to prevent problems from occurring (Away From). Once a coach is familiar with the LAB Profile, they can identify the patterns in the client's Present State and uncover how they are similar or different in the client's Desired State to develop easier ways to attain the objectives while respecting what motivates the client. I have developed a coaching methodology based on the

LAB Profile called Conversational Coaching,[3] which can help a coach detect the LAB Profile Patterns within how a client thinks about issues and the desired state.

Here is the Conversational Coaching Process:

1. **Get in state:** Preparation for the coach to receive a client. The state I use is "Calm and alert, grounded and centered," which I call my *state of grace*.

2. **Establish framework—rapport and credibility**: Let the client know that while you are on the same wavelength (Rapport), you are also confident in your skills to be able to be of help to them (Credibility). This is best communicated non-verbally. See Michael Grinder's work on approachability and credibility.[4]

3. **Get permission and anchor resources:**
   - Permission vs. Healitis: Make sure that the client has really said yes to the whole intervention, even if you are in an official coaching session, otherwise there is a risk of trying to help someone who is not committed to doing the work.
   - Create faith: There *is* a solution. When many people are in a problem-state, they do not believe there is a way out. They sometimes view their issues as much larger than they are. As their coach, you can use language to create a more resourceful state and shift the belief that they will find a solution: "When you have figured out the solution to this, what will that be like?" "Once you have gotten this to where you want it ..." "I suspect that you are sufficiently frustrated (use the emotion he or she has expressed) to solve this now, and get what you want instead."
   - *I* can help you. Saying "I can help you" is very reassuring and will help the client be ready to do what is needed to reach their desired state.

4. **Agree on "problem" and outcome.**

5. **Present state:**
   Description of problem—put in past tense
   Criteria
   LAB Profile Patterns
   Cause-Effects

   **Desired state:**
   Description of outcome—
   present and future
   LAB Profile Patterns
   Cause-Effects

This step is the messiest. It is about going back and forth and around to discover how the client puts together both the issue/obstacles in the Present State and how they think about the Desired State. The key is to identify which LAB Profile Patterns are different in the Present and the Desired States.

6. **Intervention—overlapping LAB Profile Patterns into from the present to the desired state:** If the difference is that the client tends not to change their mind even if others disagree in the Present State (Internal), and is more responsive to feedback in the Desired State (External), overlapping based on a previous dialogue with the client, may sound like this:

> You had already decided (Internal) that the right thing to do is to continue with your process the way you've been doing it? And you know yourself (Internal) when your business has been working well or not? And you decided (Internal) that your clients' experience was also important (slight shift to External) to you?
>
> So as you speak with your clients, now and in the future, holding the decision that what they experience (External) is important to you (Internal), you find yourself really paying attention to what they say and show you (External). And adapting what you provide them, based on what they want and don't want (External).

This is an example of using the LAB Profile language of the Present State, gradually overlapping into the LAB Profile language of the Desired State. Once you have done this let the client process this and watch as they integrate the shift into their Desired State. The example above incorporates the objectives and criteria from the client. The coach only adds in the LAB Profile language from the Desired State.

7. **Ecology check and sanity check—the former is standard NLP:** The latter simply asks the client to check if it is indeed a good idea.

8. **Future pacing**: Test for commitment and ease of accomplishment, the "Done Frame." If you hear the LAB Profile language for Proactive, Toward, Internal, and Procedures, then the client is committed to applying what he or she said they would.

## Summary

As you pay attention to the language and behavior (Thing) of yourself and others (Person), you can gain (Toward) real insight into what motivates them, how they think and how they make decisions (Procedures). The possibilities are endless (Options).

### Notes

1.  For more examples of decoding mass communication or large group situations check out my blog: www.theshelleblog.com especially the following entry: "The Psychology of Mac vs. PC."

2.  Rose Charvet (2010a).

3.  To learn the process, please see "Conversational Coaching with the LAB Profile," part of the Advanced LAB Profile series available in CD or MP3 from www.theshellestore.com.

4.  See Grinder (1997).

### References

Bailey, R. (c.1979). *The LAB Profile* (learning manual, out of print).

Grinder, M. (1997). *The Elusive Obvious*. Battle Ground, WA: M. Grinder & Associates.

Hall, L. M. and Bodenhamer, B. G. (2007). *Figuring Out People*. Clifton, CO: Neuro-Semantic Publications.

Rose Charvet, S. (1997). *Words that Change Minds: Mastering the Language of Influence*, 2nd rev. edn. Dubuque, IA: Kendall/Hunt.

Rose Charvet, S. (1998). *Understanding and Triggering Motivation*. Audio CD/MP3. Burlington, Ontario Canada: Success Strategies.

Rose Charvet, S. (2002). *Presenting Ideas to Skeptical People*. Audio CD/MP3. Burlington, Ontario Canada: Woodsmall, W. and James, T. (1988). *Time Line Therapy and the Basis of Personality*. Capitola, CA: Meta Publications.

Rose Charvet, S. (2004). *Building Long Term Relationships with Clients. Decode What Your Customers Really Want*. Audio CD/MP3. Success Strategies. Burlington, Ontario Canada: Success Strategies.

Rose Charvet, S. (2005). *Solving Communication Problems with the LAB Profile*. Audio CD/MP3. Burlington, Ontario Canada: Success Strategies.

Rose Charvet, S. (2006). *Conversational Coaching with the LAB Profile*. Audio CD/MP3. Burlington, Ontario Canada: Success Strategies.

Rose Charvet, S. (2008). *The LAB Profile Learning Manual*. Burlington, Ontario Canada: Success Strategies.

Rose Charvet, S. (2010a). *The Customer is Bothering Me: How to Change Attitudes, Improve Results and Grow Your Bottom Line*. Dubuque, IA: Kendall/Hunt.

Rose Charvet, S. (2010b). *How to Increase Business in Tough Times*. MP3. Burlington, Ontario Canada: Success Strategies.

For further resources visit www.wordsthatchangeminds.com or www.labprofilecertification.com

 **Lucas A. C. Derks** is a social psychologist, researcher, and trainer, working mainly with psychotherapists, mediators, conflict coaches, managers, and dentists. Lucas was born the Netherlands where he studied art and psychology. During the 1970s he taught drawing and painting at De Werkschuit in Utrecht, during which time he developed a strong interest in psychology. He went on to complete a masters degree in social psychology and pragmatism and became acquainted with the work of Bandler and Grinder. He later trained at the New York Training Institute for NLP and the Institute for Eclectic Psychology in Nijmegen, Holland. He teamed up with the Dutch NLP trainers Jaap Hollander and Anneke Durlinger during the 1990s and developed the "social panorama model" as a tool to analyze and improve human relations. The connection between the pragmatic field of NLP and social psychology has become his major activity over the last decade. He has written seven books on psychology.

email: info@sociaalpanorama.nl

# 3 Social Panoramas
## How to Change Unconscious Landscapes to Improve Relationships

*Lucas Derks*

People, like all things, exist in space. Human beings begin to represent the space around them probably in the womb. Cognitive linguists gave the name "mental space" to the representation of physical space in the mind. *Mental space* is like a three-dimensional unconscious blackboard on which the cognitive map of reality is drawn.

The physical reality of humans living on earth naturally coincides with a diversity of spatial situations between them. A person's *model of the social world* is constructed from generalizations about where the person believes he or she is situated relative to others. The way an individual positions him/herself in regard to others in mental space governs the better part of social behavior and is the foundation of the social side of personality. That is why the spatial characteristics of social imagery provide an effective tool for psychotherapeutic diagnosis and intervention.

## Creating the Model—The Why

Being a social psychologist, I have searched for NLP extensions for the social part of subjective experience. Early clues came from witnessing the great influence of the imagined size of authority figures. When large images of authorities were shrunken by the subjects, they felt immediate relief. During the development of the Social Panorama Model, I was inspired by NLP's model of the experience of time, the Time-Line. This model shows how time is generally represented spatially with the past, the present, and the future being projected at different locations in mental space.[1]

After experimenting with therapy clients for several years, it all became very obvious—social experience is primarily the result of spatial constructs. Social Panorama captures the idea that people live within an imaginary landscape filled with social images. The locations where these social representations appear in this panorama determine the emotional quality of the relationships. In brief: *relation equals location*. I saw the great potential of this concept and since 1995 I have been traveling around the world educating people in the application of these ideas.

### Why Is This Important for NLP?

The strength of the Social Panorama Model is primarily found in how it simplifies all kinds of social relationships, and in the tools it provides to improve people's social lives. The model is built on the work of Bandler and Grinder,[2] but is not the result of the modeling of single outstanding experts.[3] It is built from exploring the patterns in the *subjective experience* in a population (thousands) of ordinary people (*population modeling*). I believe that population modeling is one of the ways that will enable NLP to develop.

## The Scope of Applications: Why It Is Relevant

Because almost all human problems have something to do with relationships (i.e., have social components), the Social Panorama Model is highly applicable to personal development. Its systematic nature clarifies even the most complicated relational themes. It is an NLP instrument that can, in an often surprisingly simple way, be used to work with relationships with loved ones, friends, colleagues, children, parents, strangers, groups, teams, the deceased, ghosts, and gods. It is also applicable in cases where lack of self-worth and self-confidence are problems. It is also a very useful approach when the subject is relationships between groups, tribes, peoples, political parties, departments, and organizations.[4]

### Why Is It an Innovation in NLP?

The Social Panorama Model fits in the NLP tradition of working with sub-modalities, parts, and resources.[5] The central idea is that when people feel troubled about relationships, this is the result of how they have unconsciously placed themselves and the others in mental space. This implies that when one's relationship with someone is bad, the mental representation of this person is sited on a *bad spot* in one's social panorama.

As simple as this may sound, it opens the way for *single-sided changes* where the client improves his side of the coin by moving his representation of the other to a better location. The place where a person is projected creates an expectation about how they will interact with each other. A change in location implies a shift in that expectation. A relocated social image causes instant emotional changes and will result in different unconscious non-verbal behavior. This generally helps to break the limiting feedback loop between those involved.

For example, if Peter hates John, then Peter has represented John in an unfavorable location in his social panorama. With the aid of special techniques, Peter moves John's image to a better spot in his mental space. Now Peter immediately feels different about John. When he meets John in reality, Peter will automatically behave in a more relaxed and tolerant way. John senses this on an unconscious level and may also become less tense. This can cause John to change his attitude toward Peter.

Work with the social panorama forces one to focus on the role of self-concept in social life. A relationship always has two sides: (1) the representation of the self in combination with (2) how the other is seen and felt.[6] One of my discoveries is the spatial structure of the self-concept.

The first step for working with the Social Panorama Model is to distinguish between *real flesh and blood people* and the *mental representations of people*. The latter I started to call "personifications" to clarify the difference.[7] The Social Panorama Model aims directly at changing these personifications. They make up one's model of social reality and so can be used as a tool to help change someone's model of the social world. This work done in the imagination may have a strong and immediate effect on people's lives. How do we find the personifications and their locations in a reliable way? Help initially comes from natural language.

## Description of Use: Accessing the Locations of Social Images

Many people describe their relationships in terms of *high, low, in front of, behind, beside, between, close,* and *distant*. Example: "Our children came *between* us." They are expressing themselves in terms of location. George Lakoff and Mark Johnson's early work *Metaphors We Live By* (1980), calls these expressions "metaphoric." In their more recent work *Philosophy in the Flesh* (1998), they point out that most of our abstract thinking results from generalized bodily experience. In other words, as a child we have seen and felt many large, strong, close, distant, and warm people. We generalize these experiences into relational concepts that everybody intuitively understands because we all share these same basic experiences. For instance:

- *Distance*: The proximity of personifications has a tremendous influence. People can represent others from galaxies away to within the center of their bodies. Externally referenced people tend to have more close social representations while internally referenced people tend to have the others at some distance. To feel lonely, one has to represent people far away. Loved ones are not only seen but also felt very near.

- *Vertical*: The size of a personification is easily measured by whether their eyes are seen above or below one's own eye level. Size translates into importance. For the experience of power and authority the balance between the size of the self-image and the size of the image of the other is decisive.

- *Horizontal*: Many people use left/right to differentiate between good/bad, nice/nasty.

- *Side by side*: Most people experience side by side as cooperative and, as one might expect, opposed to each other as conflicting. Nose to nose with a smile may be positive but nasty with a serious expression.

## How the Model Works: Techniques for Finding the Location of a Personification

In the context of psychotherapy, most clients follow instructions quite easily. The two approaches below are reliable ways for finding the locations of problematic personifications. When people are not able to follow these steps, it is wise to check other aspects of the cooperation. However, some individuals are just trying too hard; they don't trust the validity of the vague unconscious knowledge that comes into awareness this way. They need to be educated first. For instance, let them imagine they are seated in their living room, and then ask them to point out the location of a piece of furniture. When they can do that, ask them to move it to an unfavorable place: "Put the piano in front of the TV." Their reactions will help to identify what it is they need to do when working with the social panorama: "How do you know that the piano stands there ... and should stay there?"

## Ways to Find the Location of a Personification

We reduce what we want to know about a personification to its *direction*, *distance*, *eye level*, and *the direction in which it is looking*, all from the perspective of the subject.

1.  **From *the feeling* that belongs to a relationship:**
    a)  Have the client evoke the feeling that belongs to the relationship that is being explored.
    b)  As soon as the client is associated in the feeling, ask him to point at the direction in which he *senses* the person involved (or "sees with his eyes closed," or "where he notices the person," or "where is the picture in your mind of that person").
    c)  Ask the client to point out the exact distance, the eye level, and the direction in which the eyes are looking.

2.  **From *all the people* in the world:**
    a)  Ask the client to think about humanity in his own way and then invite him to feel himself in the middle of all the people in the world, in an associated manner.
    b)  Ask the client to name the personification with his inner voice and then point out where, among all those people, the person involved is located.
    c)  As soon as the client points out the location, ask about eye level and eye direction.

## Changing Relationships Unilaterally

### Moving a Personification

The formula *relationship=location* implies that a personification with whom the relationship is not satisfactory should be moved to a better spot. The central question then is: Where to? The simplest approach is to ask the client *where* he thinks the personification should move, but experience shows that this does not always give the best results. In that case a consultant can *suggest* and *test* locations on the basis of "universal patterns."[8]

These are:

1. The intensity of social feelings increase the closer a personification comes, and attenuate as it moves away.

2. The higher above eye level a personification rises, the greater its influence. Lower it and the influence decreases.

3. The direction in which a personification is looking means attention.

4. Personifications that are straight in front get more attention and have a greater influence.

5. Personifications that are straight in front mean confrontation or intimacy depending on the facial expression.

6. Personifications that are straight in front may interfere with the self-image.

7. Personifications with the same eye direction have shared attention.

8. Personifications at the back, who look in the same direction as the subject, are either supporting or controlling.

9. Shared locations (two personifications on the same spot) often result in identity confusion.

10. Bi-locations and tri-locations cause uncertain relationships and show role conflict.

11. Domination and authority are present when the other appears higher, closer, broader, and/or lighter than the self-image.

A coach or therapist can assist a client to find a suitable location for a personification with the help of the above directions. Quite often this may not be precise enough. For finding the *exact* spot one may use the following technique.

## *Using Reference Personifications*

1. Determine the location of the problematic personification.

2. Determine the location of a reference personification: "Do you know someone with whom you have a relationship similar to what you *would like* with the problem person?" When the client identifies someone, find his or her location in the

client's social panorama. Ask if the two *real people* know each other. (If they know each other, one needs to make sure that both the problem personification and the reference personification end up at a suitable location. If they don't know each other, then the reference personification is from a different *social context* and can go to "sleep," since we only need the reference to identify the appropriate location.)

3. Have the client shift the problematic personification in the direction of the place of the reference personification: "How far did the problem personification manage to move?"

4. Check if this new position is satisfactory.

5. If it is, then go on the closing procedure (see below).

6. If not (and this usually happens), add any lacking abilities to the problematic personification (see the enrichment technique below).

## Enrichment with Missing Abilities

1. Establish the *target location* to which the problem personification must be moved.

2. Ask what *ability* the problem personification *lacks* that prevents him/her from being able to reach this target location. Ask the client to name this capability.

3. Next, remember a time when he strongly and clearly applied this capability to him/herself and let him/her associate in that experience.

4. When the client is intensely associated in using this capability, ask him or her to attach a color to it and to imagine being surrounded by this color.

5. Now use the color as an imaginary medium to send the ability to the problem personification. (If there is more than one capability involved, repeat Steps 2–6.)

6. Check if the problem personification has reached a satisfactory location.

7. If he has not, go back to Step 5. If he has, complete the closing procedure (see below).

## Closing Procedure

1. Ask the client to imagine *fixating* or *locking* the former problem personification by "mouse clicking" in its new place.

2. Test the ecology: "Imagine that this is how you must relate to this person for the rest of your life. What would you lose?" and/or "Imagine that you meet this person and he behaves in the same old rotten way. How would you react?" and/or "Come on help me out, be creative—think of an objection to this change!"

3. Deal with all objections with appropriate NLP processes.

## Framing the Transfer of Resources to Others

Many NLP techniques transfer resources to the others in one's mind. In most such procedures a capability that is naturally used in context X, but not in context Y, is transferred from context X to context Y. In the Social Panorama Model, you transfer resources from the client A, who has the ability, to the personification B who lacks it. This is based on the idea that the client A and the personification B are both *parts* of the same human mind. For the human psyche there is no such thing as real people; the mind knows only personifications and social representations. To help clients to grasp this point we may try the following framings:

1. You give your ability to the imperfect copy of the other that you have made in your mind. In that way you improve your hated copy.

2. The ugly image that you had of the other person was not accurate and neither is the improved one that you have created depicting reality. It is immaterial whether or not it is real; the point is that you now can deal with each other.

3. If you believe that someone lacks a capability, the way you interact with him will keep him from showing that he can do it at least a little bit.

## Psychosomatic Symptoms Caused By a Personification

Chronic physical symptoms can be the result of the influence of personifications. Usually the feelings toward these personifications are strong (hate, fear, love) and they are perceived in/or near the client's body—usually close to the physical symptoms. It is possible that the client is not aware of their existence. This personification can cause continuous tension in the muscles, skin, or organs with chronic symptoms as a result. Such a personification can be moved by the social panorama techniques presented here.

## Deep Rooted Social Personality Traits

With countless clients, my colleagues and I[9] explored what we call the *family pano-rama* and the important role of family ties and intimate relations in mental health. We presumed that early family ties had great influence on social development and so explored the spatial configuration of families through regression. With the aid of simple hypnotic techniques, we assisted clients to go back in time to revive their childhood. They are stimulated to explore the locations of mum, dad, their siblings, and other family members.

Supported by developmental psychology,[10] one can state that the configuration of the family in early childhood forms the blueprint for the social side of personal-ity. Disturbing social personality traits—unproductive patterns that people main-tain with other people—are often rooted before age 6 within the family panorama. Working with the family panorama from childhood has proven to be one of the most effective and elegant approaches to personality change.

## The Spiritual Panorama

The representation of the social world is not limited to living people. With the same principles of personifications in mental space, people represent virtual comrades, imaginary creations like the characters in novels, death, ancestors, spirits, gods, saints, angels, aliens, and ghosts.

In 1996 this resulted in the so called *spiritual panorama*, a tool that enables thera-pists to approach religious issues in a content-free, process-oriented, and secular way. With the increasing popularity of the spiritual level in NLP, this is a useful instrument to prevent NLP from slipping away into new age religiosity.

## Exploring Self-Awareness

It is often difficult to find the right vocabulary to speak of our "selves," mainly because much of the experience is inaccessible to reason. When it comes to express-ing our true self we find refuge in metaphor. If we stop trying to talk about it, then we are left with the sensations, images, and internal voices.[11]

The Social Panorama Model concentrates on the "speechless" non-lingual side of the self, the awareness that precedes the use of language. How do you know that you are someone? What do you feel, see, smell, taste, and hear? This search brings people to their *social core* and at the same time helps them and us to escape from philosophizing about the exact meaning of terms like identity, self, ego, myself, me, and so on. Because the self is always present wherever one goes, it operates like a steady habituated background experience. In other words, we are always ourselves but that is so normal that we only notice it when there is something unusual about it.

## Conclusion

NLP is the study of the structure of subjective experience and its applications.[12] There has been a large focus on modeling in NLP but the distinctions and concepts by which the subjective experience is described in NLP are far more fundamental for the social panorama. The NLP sub-modalities, parts, and resources became the main building blocks of the Social Panorama Model.

The social panorama rests on the concepts of *parts* and *personifications*. It shows how space is more than just another sub-modality, but the very heart of cognition. Beyond all of that, the social panorama opens one's eyes to the overwhelmingly sophisticated social skills that most humans possess. And it brings the huge part of our unconscious mind that is occupied with social calculations to light. These highly intelligent unconscious resources are extremely powerful.

### *Where Does It Not Work? Where Or How Could It Be Misused?*

The Social Panorama Model makes use of the existing unconscious social potential of the subject. It cannot go beyond the range of the client's social competencies. However, the model does offer guidelines for how to train socially challenged (e.g., autistic, sociopathic) individuals to improve their skills. The model has a great potential to be misused in the hands of exploiting personalities.

## Case Study: Motherly Love—A Shared and a Bi-Location

Beatrice, a 45-year-old mother, had the outcome of *letting go of her 18 year old son William*. Most therapists would ask what exactly she meant by "letting go." How is their current relationship? What does William's father think about it? What did she fear would happen if she kept him with her?

From the point of view of the Social Panorama Model the relevant questions are: When you think about William, and your wanting to let him go ... Where do you sense him? In what direction is he looking? What is his eye level in comparison to yours?

Beatrice seemed unsurprised by these questions. But it took a while before she said that he was in two places. William appeared to be standing two meters away facing away from her and at equal level *and also* halfway in her right shoulder and torso, looking forwards and slightly up to her. She could easily point it out with her hands.

Technically it was a *bi-location* and *shared location*, which means that a personification shared the same space as another personification and was represented in two different places. In this case William shared a part of Beatrice's body space—her shoulder and side. A shared location generally causes identity problems—and bi-locations can cause confusion about who the person really is—in the sense of is he A or B?

Beatrice confirmed that she had worries and emotions that belonged to William and that she was not clear whether he was a man or a boy. "I feel feelings as if I were him in trouble. These feelings are a warning to me and make me pay extra attention to my child, because otherwise something might go wrong for him." She confirmed this had happened in the past.

This was enough information to do an intervention. In such cases two techniques can be combined into one—the shared location pattern and the bi-location technique can be integrated.[13] And that is what I did.

I helped Beatrice to create a monumental self-image (the *sovereign self* in the Social Panorama Model), which consists of a two-and-a-half times real size and shiny self-image at about five meters away and that is held straight in front. This great self-image is needed to fill the empty hole in the client, which might exist after taking a personification out of their body. Beatrice could construct this huge self-image with little effort and smiled when she stared at it.

I asked Beatrice to imagine William as a toddler. She lit up while doing that. "Take him on your lap for a while and cuddle him," I suggested. Next I asked Beatrice what capability William had failed to learn in his later life, of which the lack caused him to stay *with her* and also be in this *double representation*. Or, in other words, what withheld him from being on the *outside* of her as just *one* image. Questions of this complexity are frequently asked when working with the social panorama. While they may be too complex for the conscious mind, they seem to match the capacity of the unconscious social intelligence.

Beatrice did not need to think about this very long: William should be able to live healthily and to take care of himself, she said. It is about *loving himself*! This resource was found in Beatrice's own life: she loved herself, lived healthily, and took care of herself very well. She associated in a strong experience of doing so. The color red/yellow helped to symbolize these capabilities.

When she signaled the experience was intense, she was ready for the next phase of the work. She was asked to take her large (sovereign) self-image into her body at the same moment as she sends the resources of loving oneself, living healthily, and taking care of oneself to the personification of William as a small boy. This transfer of the resource to the young boy takes care of the bi-location, which in fact represents an inner conflict in Beatrice. The taking in of the sovereign self at the same time of the transfer of the resource is the standard procedure for dealing with shared locations.

It took only a few seconds before Beatrice showed all the non-verbal signs of an emotional shift. Spontaneously she told me that William had moved out of her and had found a spot beside and in front of her. And now he was sensed at only one location. We explored this new spot and made sure the old place was now filled with her self. She smiled in the way people do who sense their sovereign self within themselves.

We tested and fine-tuned this new situation, and stabilized and installed this repositioned relationship for the future. We could not find any objections. This session was complete very quickly! As fast as it was, the result has lasted ever since. Now Beatrice does not worry about her son's well-being. She can be very straightforward to him and does not feel what he might suffer. It was a typical case for working with the social panorama.

As simple as it may sound, it took about fifteen years to come to this solution for cases like this. It is important to note that in fact this is the NLP procedure for exorcising infestations with disturbing entities of any kind, be it ex-partners, children, ancestors, spirits, or punitive dissociated parts. This solid and ecological procedure has been shown to provide great help in cases that were too complex before.

## Notes

1. Fauconnier and Turner (2002).

2. Bandler and Grinder (1979).

3. Bostic St. Clair and Grinder (2001).

4. Derks. L. (2005).

5. Bandler and Grinder (1982); Bandler, R. (1985).

6. Augoustinos and Innes (1990).

7. Derks (2005).

8. Derks (1995).

9. Walker (1996).

10. Greenspan (1998).

11. Andreas (2001).

12. Andreas et al. (1994).

13. Derks (2005).

## References

Alstadt, D. and Kramer J. (1993). *The Guru Papers: Marks of Authoritarian Power*. Berkeley, CA: Frog Press.

Andreas, S. (2001). Building self-concept. *Anchor Point* 15(7): 4–13.

Andreas, S., Faulkner, C., and McDonald, R. (1994). *NLP: New Technology of Achievement*. New York: William Morrow.

Augoustinos, M. and Innes, J. M. (1990). Towards an integration of social representations and social schema theory. *British Journal of Social Psychology* 29: 213–231.

Bandler, R. (1985). *Using Your Brain for a Change*. Moab, UT: Real People Press.

Bandler, R. and Grinder, J. (1979). *Frogs into Princes*. Moab, UT: Real People Press.

Bandler, R. and Grinder, J. (1982). *Reframing: Neuro-Linguistic Programming and the Transformation of Meaning*. Moab, UT: Real People Press.

Bostic St. Clair, C. and Grinder, J. (2001). *Whispering in the Wind*. Scotts Valley, CA: J&C Enterprises.

Derks, L. (1995). Exploring the social panorama. *NLP World* 2(3): 28–42.

Derks, L. (1997). Family systems in the social panorama. *NLP World* 4(1): 21–38.

Derks, L. (2005). *Social Panoramas, Changing the unconscious landscape with NLP and psychotherapy*. Carmarthen, Crown House Publishing.

Derks, L. and Hollander, J. (1996a). *Essenties van NLP*. Utrecht: Servire.

Derks, L. and Hollander, J. (1996b). Exploring the spiritual panorama. *NLP World* 3(2): 55–69.

Fauconnier, G. and Turner, M. (2002). *The Way We Think: Conceptual Blending and the Mind's Hidden Complexities*. New York: Basic Books.

Fiske, S. T. and Taylor, S. E. (1991). *Social Cognition*. New York: McGraw-Hill.

Greenspan, S. J. (1998) *The Growth of the Mind and the Endangered Origins of Intelligence*, Jackson, TN: DaCapo.

James, W. (1890). *The Principles of Psychology*. New York: Dover Publications.

James, W. (1956/1897). *The Will to Believe; and Other Essays in Popular Philosophy*. New York: Dover Publications.

Kunda, Z. (1999). *Social Cognition: Making Sense of People*. Cambridge, MA: MIT Press.

Lakoff, G. and Johnson, M. (1980). *Metaphors We Live By*. Chicago and London: University of Chicago Press.

Lakoff, G. and Johnson, M. (1999). *Philosophy in the Flesh*. New York: Basic Books/Perseus.

Lawley, J. and Tompkins, P. (2003). Clean space: modeling human perception through emergence. *Anchor Point* 17(8).

Tomasello, M. (2003). The key is social cognition. In D. Gentner and S. Kuczaj (eds), *Language and Thought*. Cambridge, MA: MIT Press.

Walker, W. (1996). *Abenteuer Kommunikation. Bateson, Perls, Satir, Erickson und die Anfaenge des Neurolinguistischen Programmierens (NLP)*. Stuttgart: Klett-Cotta.

**James Lawley and Penny Tompkins**

NLP has been a significant part of James and Penny's lives since 1991 when they met on a practitioner training course in London. They were even married by Todd Epstein at NLP University in Santa Cruz at the end of their trainer's training!

Their lives took an unexpected turn when they decided to model David Grove. It took them four years and resulted in *Metaphors in Mind: Transformation through Symbolic Modelling* and a training DVD *A Strange and Strong Sensation*. They've also produced "Modelling Robert Dilts Modelling" which includes nine short videos. This and many more articles are available on their website.

They have been neurolinguistic psychotherapists registered with the United Kingdom Council for Psychotherapy (UKCP) since 1993 and recognized Neuro-Linguistic Psychotherapy and Counselling Association (NLPtCA) supervisors since 1995. Recently the Association of Coaching Supervisors (AOCS) made them honorary members. They have a private practice in London—except in winter when they slip off to the sunshine of Australia and New Zealand. In recognition of their contribution to the field, Penny and James have been awarded lifetime memberships of the Canadian Association of NLP (CANLP), and were the first to be appointed Honorary Certified Trainers of the International NLP Trainers Association (INLPTA). In addition to their work with individuals, they have provided consultancy and conducted modelling projects for organizations as diverse as GlaxoSmithKline, Yale University Child Study Center, NASA Goddard Space Center and the Findhorn Spiritual Community. They are leaders in the field of using metaphor, modelling and Clean Language.

email: james@cleanlanguage.co.uk
      penny@cleanlanguage.co.uk
web: www.cleanlanguage.co.uk

# Symbolic Modelling
Emergent Change through Metaphor and
Clean Language

*James Lawley and Penny Tompkins*

## Why Is This Model Important?

Before we introduced David Grove's work into NLP, metaphors were mostly used to tell Milton Erickson-style stories. There was little use of autogenic metaphor—metaphors generated by the client.[1] When we stumbled upon David Grove we realized he had devised a new way to "study the structure of subjective experience"—the *raison d'être* of NLP.[2]

David Grove is best known for Clean Language—a questioning model designed for working with the metaphoric and symbolic domain of experience.[3] In 1995 we decided to model his innovations which led us to write *Metaphors in Mind: Transformation through Symbolic Modelling*. While we incorporated many of Grove's ideas we also drew upon recent findings in cognitive linguistics, self-organizing systems theory, and evolutionary dynamics. Our aim was to create a model that could be applied to a range of contexts in addition to psychotherapy—in education, management, research, and so on.

When we recently reviewed our model we saw that the process has a central core—Symbolic Modelling *Lite*—which is presented here for the first time.[4] Mastering the Lite version means you will be able to facilitate people to identify, develop, explore, and evolve their metaphors using the basic Clean Language questions. If you want to go further you will need to acquire the skills of a symbolic modeller; which will take somewhat longer.

## Using Symbolic Modelling in a Troubled World

Just about everyone uses metaphor all the time—often six times a minute! We are surprised by this figure because most metaphors are constructed, spoken, and received out of awareness. Research over thirty years has shown that we not only speak and gesture in metaphor; we think and act on the basis of our metaphors. Your clients, colleagues, customers, friends, and enemies will all use metaphor—and not just occasionally, but much of the time.[5]

Metaphors can be a source of creativity but they can also specify and constrain ways of thinking, thereby maintaining unproductive and self-destructive patterns of behavior. Knowing how to listen and observe a person's metaphorical words and gestures gives great insight into how their inner world works, and Clean Language is tailor-made for modelling the process and structure of that world.

Symbolic Modelling has been used successfully as a change, creative, and educational process in settings as diverse as a maximum security prison, the NASA Space Center, and an elementary school. There is a growing recognition of its value in business, life, and sports coaching. While it is highly effective for working with "everyday" issues, it is particularly suited to:

- The big issues of life—e.g., finding a sense of purpose.
- Ill-defined feelings—e.g., something is wrong, fearful, unsafe, or missing.
- Identity and spiritual levels.
- Internal conflicts.
- Intractable and double-binding patterns.
- Trauma work.

While Symbolic Modelling has traditionally been used to facilitate individuals to develop themselves, it has also been applied in large-scale environmental projects, such as creating a strategy for European-wide sustainable land management; using hydro-thermal water to heat ex-mining communities in Holland and Scotland; and responding to rising sea-levels by re-visioning the Dutch attitude from "holding the ocean back" to "living with water" and "water cities." The Modelling Shared Reality process used in these projects provides a snapshot of the current collective experience of those involved and a communal voice for those not usually engaged in decision-making—thereby turning metaphors into action.[6]

## What is Symbolic Modelling?

All change processes require a *medium*, a *method*, and a *means*. In Symbolic Modelling these are: metaphor, modelling, and Clean Language. Together they can be used in three ways: to model successful strategies and states of excellence; to facilitate change; and to facilitate individuals and groups to create new metaphors (see Figure 1).[7]

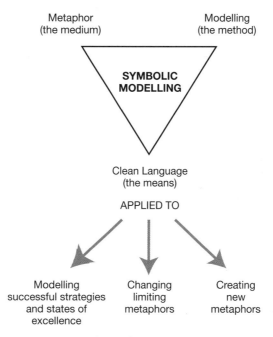

**Figure 1.** *Three ways of applying the components of Symbolic Modelling*

Unlike the majority of psychology which aims to discover generalities about humans, Symbolic Modelling seeks out the distinctive and idiosyncratic organization of each individual's map of the world. For example, a client says they are "at a crossroads" in life. This is quite a common metaphor. However, after a few Clean Language questions it becomes clear that this crossroads is unique. It involves train tracks, an approaching train, barren land on one side of the tracks and lush nature on the other. Also, while the desire in the client's chest wants to take the small leap across the tracks, their legs are stuck because of the hands of responsibility in their stomach holding them back. The idiosyncratic is important because as Aristotle said, "There is no science of the individual."

## Metaphor—The Medium

As George Lakoff and Mark Johnson observe, "The essence of metaphor is understanding and experiencing one kind of thing in terms of another."[8] Research shows that the majority of our metaphors and similes are derived from our understanding of the body and the workings of the physical world.[9] When a client says they feel like a fish out of water we instantly grasp how they perceive their situation. Because we already know the nature of "fish," "out of," and "water" we can carry across our experience of the physical into the abstract mental realm.

Metaphor makes the intangible tangible, it embodies relationships and patterns, and it captures the essential nature of an experience. Metaphor provides a number of advantages:

- It allows a client to work content-free.
- It makes it easier to work at the process and structural level.
- It operates at multiple levels simultaneously.
- It is like a gift that keeps on giving. In the session a process unfolds which can continue for days, weeks, and sometimes years. A good resource metaphor can last a lifetime.

## Modelling—The Method

Symbolic Modelling differs from other forms of modelling in three ways. The first two are obvious: we model the organization of people's metaphors, and we use Clean Language to do it. The third is more subtle, our primary aim is for the client to *self*-model.

The entire focus of Symbolic Modelling is an exploration of the client's metaphoric model of the world from *their* perspective, within *their* perceptual time and space, using *their* words and non-verbals. Instead of a conventional dialogue there is what David Grove called "a trialogue" between facilitator, client, and their "metaphor landscape"—the four-dimensional, psychoactive world that emerges within and around the client. The facilitator sets aside their own perceptual space so that only one metaphor landscape occupies the physical space—the client's.

### *Four Fundamental Modelling Processes*

Having studied hundreds of Clean Language sessions we have concluded that experienced facilitators make maximal use of just four modelling processes: Identify, Develop Form, Relate over Time, and Relate across Space:

1. **Identify:** To establish, recognize, or distinguish what something is; to name and give something an identity; to individuate an element or characteristic. At each level a different kind of something can be identified: an attribute, a symbol, a relationship, a pattern, a context.

2. **Develop Form:** To elaborate what has been identified; to identify enough attributes of something that its nature becomes apparent; to bring a (symbolic) perception to life—like a pre-digital photograph emerging from developing solution.

3. **Relate over Time:** To identify a sequence of events (Before–During–After); to identify temporal relationships such as cause, effect, contingency, precondition, provenance, and expectancy.

4. **Relate across Space:** To identify relationships between separate things, places, perceptions, frames, contexts, and so on.

The four modelling processes are fundamental because they are so widely applicable. We have used them to model resources, desired outcomes, problematic situations, changes, the structure of excellence, conflict, corporate metaphors, and so on. Figure 2 shows how the four processes relate to each other.

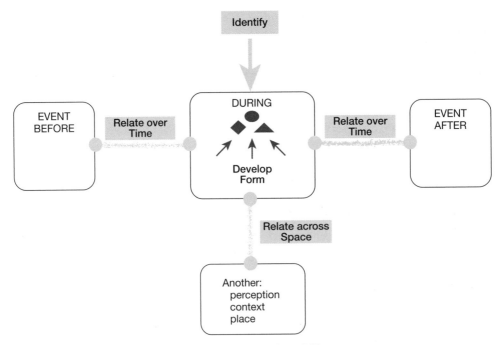

**Figure 2:** *Four fundamental modelling processes*

At first it may seem strange that a process based on modelling—with no intention by the facilitator for the client to change—can produce significant and long-lasting development.[10] That's the mystery of self-organizing systems. As a client's metaphors are identified, developed and explored, their system learns from itself. As the landscape evolves they discover new ways of perceiving themselves and the larger system of which they are a part. In doing so, their everyday thinking, feeling, and behavior correspondingly change.

## Clean Language—The Means

The three functions of Clean Language (to acknowledge, orientate, and send on a quest) and its four components (the syntax, vocal qualities, gestures, and clean questions) have been well documented and are freely available on the web, so we have not repeated them here.[11]

To be clear, Clean Language influences and directs attention—it wouldn't be useful if it didn't. However, unlike other uses of language, Clean Language is "clean" because it is sourced in the client's exact vocabulary, it is consistent with the logic of their metaphors, and it only introduces universal metaphors of time, space, form, and perceiver.[12]

There are nine basic questions which form the beating heart of Symbolic Modelling because they are asked so often.[13] Over the years we have devised a number of ways of organizing the questions.[14] Below they are arranged according to the four fundamental modelling processes:

**Identify:**
*And what would [you/X] like to have happen?*
*And that's [ ] like what?*

**Develop Form:**
*And what kind of [ ] is that [ ]?*
*And is there anything else about (that) [ ]?*
*And where/whereabouts is [ ]?*

**Relate over Time (within and between events):**
*And then what happens? or And what happens next?*
*And what happens just before [event]?*

**Relate across Space (within and between perceptions):**
*And when/as [X], what happens to [Y]?*
*And is there a relationship between [X] and [Y]?*

[ ] = A client's exact word or phrase.

## How Does Symbolic Modelling Lite Work?

Symbolic Modelling is an outcome-orientated approach. By making a client's desired outcome the focus of the four fundamental modelling processes, a simple framework for change is created. Figure 3 illustrates the six phases and the iterative loops involved.[15]

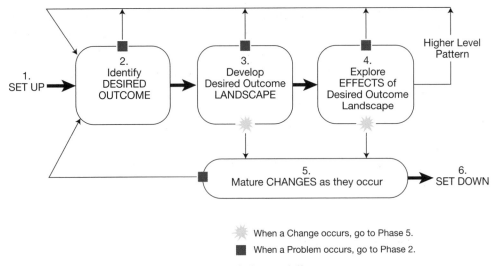

When a Change occurs, go to Phase 5.
When a Problem occurs, go to Phase 2.

**Figure 3:** *Symbolic Modelling Lite*

## Phase 1: Set Up[16]

Setting up a clean process itself needs to be clean. We want to offer the client a chance to align their inner perceptual world with the outer physical world where the session takes place. Thus the client decides where they want to be, and where they want the facilitator to be:

> With both client and facilitator standing: "And where would you like to be?" When the client has positioned him or herself: "And where would you like me to be?"

## Phase 2: Identify a Desired Outcome—The Problem-Remedy-Outcome (PRO) Model

Once the client has arranged the seating just as they would like, they are asked the opening question:

> And what would you like to have happen?

A person will invariably respond to this question in one of three ways—with a statement of: (1) a problem, (2) a proposed remedy, or (3) a desired outcome. To cleanly facilitate a client to identify a desired outcome we created the Problem-Remedy-Outcome (PRO) Model.[17] The PRO model has two stages. First we use the client's precise language to determine whether they are attending to:

A Problem—a current difficulty they do not like; or
A proposed Remedy—a desire for a problem to not exist, be reduced, solved, or avoided; or
A desired Outcome—a desire for something new to exist.

When the client responds with a problem or a remedy (which will also refer to a problem), the problematic aspect is acknowledged and noted for later use. In the second stage we respond with a question that invites the client to shift their attention to a desired outcome. Depending on how committed the client is to problem-thinking or to problem-solving, he or she may need to iterate round the loop a few times before they settle on an initial desired outcome.

When the client gives a desired outcome statement we ask a question that keeps their attention on that aspect of their experience. Figure 4 shows the PRO model in its entirety.

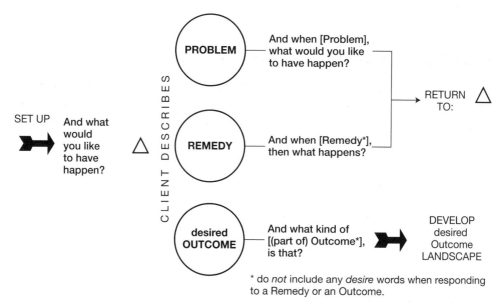

**Figure 4:** *The Problem-Remedy-Outcome model*

The following transcript shows how the nine basic questions are used during the developing, exploring, and maturing phases of Symbolic Modelling Lite. All words introduced by the facilitator are highlighted in italics. This makes it easy to see the syntax of the questions and to distinguish between client- and facilitator-introduced words:

**F:** *And what would you like to have happen?*

**C:** I feel like a fish out of water. [Problem]

**F:** *And when* you feel like a fish out of water, *what would you like to have happen?*

**C:** I want to stop suffocating. [Remedy]

**F:** *And you* want to stop suffocating. *And when* you stop suffocating, *then what happens?*

**C:** I can be at home with myself. [Desired Outcome]

Since a client can express a problem, propose a remedy, or desire an outcome at any time, we run PRO continuously in the back of our mind so that we are always paying attention to what the client is paying attention to, and are ready to respond with the relevant P, R, or O question accordingly.

## Phase 3: Develop a Desired Outcome Landscape

Once a client has identified a desired outcome we facilitate them to develop that statement into an embodied metaphor landscape. As Grove put it, "to make words physical." We do this by repeatedly asking the three classic developing questions:

**F:** *And when* you are at home with yourself, *what kind of* home *is that?*

**C:** It's comfortable.

**F:** *And when* it's comfortable, *where is* it comfortable?

**C:** In my heart [touches chest].

**F:** *And whereabouts* in your heart?

**C:** Right at the core.

**F:** *And* it's comfortable right at the core, in your heart. *And is there anything else about that* comfortable *there* [gesture to client's chest]?

**C:** It's flowing.

**F:** *And when* it's comfortable and it's flowing, it's comfortable and flowing *like what*?

**C:** Like a river.

Metaphors comprise a number of interacting symbols (in this case, "fish," "water," "home," "heart," "river"). Symbols exist in a client's perceptual space when they have a location and their attributes can be described. This usually means the client can point to the symbol and could, if asked, draw or enact it. While symbols are being identified, located, and described the client will usually mention the relationships between them. These too can be developed with the same clean questions.

Symbolic Modelling is entirely additive.[18] We aim to facilitate the client to retain everything relevant to their desired outcome in one perception. Developing a desired outcome landscape is not something to be "got through." It is central to the whole process and encourages the conditions under which change is the natural response. In other words, the client's self-modelling is preparing them to evolve in ways they are not yet aware of.

### Phase 4: Explore Effects of Desired Outcome Landscape

Once the ground is prepared, the client can explore the effects of their desired outcome happening (the "ecology"). This is done in two ways. We invite them to attend both to what happens after their desired outcome occurs, and how the desired outcome handles the problematic situations previously described (this is why we noted the exact words for the client's problems in Phases 2 and 3):

**F:** *And as* a river is flowing at the core of your heart, *then what happens*?

**C:** It's my destiny.

**F:** *And when* it's your destiny, *what happens to* a fish out of water?

**C:** It's trying to get to the spawning grounds but it's been frozen in mid-jump.

In Symbolic Modelling we are always on the lookout for what surprises the client about their inner world. Rather than trying to solve a problem or to make something happen we remain vigilant to the out-of-the-ordinary, and make that the focus of attention. Then we "follow the white rabbit," just like Neo did in the film *The Matrix*.

Should a new problem arise at any phase (such as, "frozen in mid-jump") we apply the PRO model and return to developing the enhanced outcome landscape:

> **F:** *And when* it has been frozen in mid-jump, *what would that* fish *like to have happen*?
>
> **C:** To get back in the water where I belong.
>
> **F:** *And what happens just before that* fish gets back in the water where you belong?
>
> **C:** I trust myself—it always comes back to trust.
>
> **F:** *And when you* trust yourself, *where is that* trust?
>
> **C:** In my heart again.
>
> **F:** *And is there a relationship between* trust *and* flowing river at the core of your heart?
>
> **C:** Yes, I can trust myself when the river flows.

We facilitate the client to keep going round their iterative loops until one of two things happen: they notice a pattern or a change occurs.

When a pattern is indicated (in this case by the client saying "it always comes back to") we continue as before but now use the client's metaphors to address the pattern in its entirety. Then, when the client makes a change, they are not just resolving the presenting problem but the class of experience of which the problem is just one example. In the future, when life presents similar but different problematic situations they will handle them in new ways.

> **F:** *And* you trust yourself when the river flows at the core of your heart, *and you'd like to* be at home with yourself, *and that* fish *would like* to get back in the water where you belong, *and* it's your destiny ... *and then what happens*?

**C:** I realize I've been fighting who I am. I have to accept it's a struggle but I am meant to be in the water. That's the only way I am going to get upstream.

**F:** *And when* you are meant to be in the water, *and* that's the only way you're going to get upstream, *what happens to that* fish out of water?

**C:** She completes the jump.

A change is indicated by the client's multiple realizations and because the fish "completes" the jump. When a change occurs at any time we immediately move to Phase 5—maturing the change.

### Phase 5: Mature Changes As They Occur

Figure 5 depicts a beautiful symmetry; the same four processes used before a change occurs are used after a change—but for a different purpose.

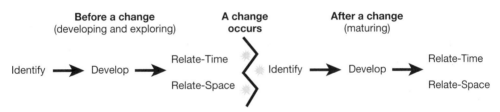

**Figure 5:** *Four modelling processes in change work*

Our aim during the maturing phase is for the client to find out whether the change starts a contagion which creates a new or reorganized metaphor landscape, or whether it invokes doubts, concerns, or fears. A problem reaction is not a sign of failure—quite the opposite. It indicates the client's system is revealing more of its complexity and is acknowledging its "current reality."[19] This increases the chance that the client's system will reorganize in a way that is more than relief of a symptom, more than a remedy. Rather it will be a generative change—a robust, resilient change that keeps on giving.

Maturing is also not a phase to "get through" as quickly as possible. We were amazed to see David Grove devote up to a third of a session to what happens *after* the first change occurs. Just as a desired outcome landscape was developed and explored in Phases 3 and 4, so each change is matured in Phase 5 using exactly the same questions:

> **F:** *And as* she completes that jump ... *then what happens*?
>
> **C:** I can continue.
>
> **F:** *And* as you continue *what kind of* continue *is that*?
>
> **C:** I'm comfortable in my own skin.
>
> **F:** *And when* you're comfortable in your own skin, *what happens to* a flowing river at the core of your heart?
>
> **C:** I can trust myself even when it's difficult.
>
> **F:** *And that* fish completes *that* jump, *and* you're comfortable in your own skin, *and that* river flows, *and* you trust yourself, *and then what happens*?
>
> [and so on]

The maturing process helps consolidate the evolving landscape and gives the client ample opportunity to model how they now respond to the previous problems ("suffocating," "frozen," "fighting who I am"), and to find out what happens next.

## Phase 6: Set Down

We know the process is finished when:

- The changes come to a natural conclusion or resting place.
- The logic of the new landscape is complete, coherent, and consistent.
- No new problems surface and the new metaphors can handle the previously problematic situations.
- The client says "no" to the question: "And is there anything else you need right now in relation to [their original desired outcome statement]?"

If there is limited time left in the session we invite the client to continue the process between sessions by drawing their metaphor landscape and saying, "And get to know more about ... [list their key metaphors], and to find out what happens next ..." To finish we ask something like, "And is it OK to leave it here?"

## Caveats about the Use of Symbolic Modelling

Symbolic Modelling is inherently rapport-ful, forgiving, and robust—as long as you stay clean and connected to the client's desired outcome. Even so, we recommend people only use it within their sphere of expertise. If you are a coach, use it in coaching; not with someone who suffers from a severe mental disturbance.

If a client gets into difficulties the first thing to remember is that most people have experienced their problematic patterns for many years, and while the pattern might be painful they know how to cope with it. Many facilitators step in too quickly and disrupt the client's process. Your first response should be to stay within the metaphor and do as little as possible. In the rare case that a client does not naturally transition to a different state you can ask clean questions to invite them to attend to a resource symbol, their desired outcome, or a meta-perspective.

Often a facilitator has said to us that their client was "stuck", when in fact it was *they* who were stuck. It is important not to confuse your state with what is happening for the client. When you don't know what to do (and it will happen, it's all part of bottom-up modelling[20]), it is best to let the client set the next direction. You can:

- Just wait.
- Ask: "And is there anything else?"
- Ask: "And what would you like to have happen *now*?"
- Go back to the exact wording of their desired outcome, and ask about that.
- Invite them to draw their metaphors.

## Conclusion

Even after fifteen years of facilitating people with Symbolic Modelling we are still in awe at the unexpected and creative ways people find to change themselves. One client found that not only was her anxiety like butterflies in the stomach but that one particular butterfly had to open its wings and fly out of her mouth—but it couldn't. You can probably think of several ways to help that butterfly, but we doubt you would ever come up with what worked for *this* client: all the other butterflies had to stand in a line and on the signal "go" flap their wings in unison to create sufficient updraft to propel the particular butterfly up and out of her mouth!

A clean approach encourages conditions whereby what changes fits the uniqueness of each client's system. These changes are ecological because they are self-generated. We have found that these conditions are encouraged less by an expert magician and more by a facilitator who is an expert at getting out of the way.

**Notes**

1.  Notable exceptions were Faulkner (1991); Hejmadi and Lyall (1991).

2.  Dilts et al. (1980).

3.  Less well known are his other innovations such as Clean Space and Emergent Knowledge. What unites all Grovian processes is the notion of working "cleanly." See Tompkins and Lawley (2003), Harland (2009) and Grove and Wilson (2005).

4.  "Lite" is less about food with fewer calories and more about fully functioning computer software aimed at entry-level users. Extra features require an upgrade and a more skillful operator.

5.  For a very readable and up-to-date account of the importance of metaphor see Geary (2011).

6.  The late Dutch environmentalist Stefan Ouboter and his colleagues devised "Modelling Shared Reality" which incorporates a clean approach in a number of innovative ways. See Tompkins and Lawley (2006c).

7.  Examples of Symbolic Modelling and Clean Language used to model excellence (Tompkins and Lawley, 2010); to create new metaphors (Lawley, 2001); and as an academic research methodology (Lawley et al., 2010).

8.  Lakoff and Johnson (1980), p. 5.

9.  Kovecses (2002).

10.  We coined the phrase "therapeutic modelling" to distinguish between modelling for change, and "exemplar modelling," which aims to replicate and codify excellence. See Lawley and Tompkins (2006).

11.  Tompkins and Lawley (1997, 1999).

12.  Philip Harland elegantly presents "the case for achieving healing, change, and self-knowledge with minimal outside intervention" (Harland, 2011, p. 10).

13. Other more specialized questions, which are only used when the logic of the client's metaphors permit, are available in Lawley and Tompkins (2000) and Sullivan and Rees (2008).

14. For our other models see Lawley and Tompkins (2004).

15. Iteration is a process that repeatedly applies a rule, computation, or procedure to the result of the previous application of the rule, computation, or procedure. See Tompkins and Lawley (2007).

16. "Set up" and "set down" are terms borrowed from McWhirter (2000).

17. Tompkins and Lawley (2006a).

18. Thanks to Steve Andreas for making this point explicit. See Andreas (2006, pp. 130–135), with prepublication comments in Lawley (2005).

19. "Current Reality" means the entirety of what is true for a client at that moment in time. The term is borrowed from Fritz (1989).

20. In top-down approaches, such as a step-by-step procedure, the facilitator has an idea of where the process is going and their job is to guide the client toward that end. In a bottom-up systemic outcome-orientated approach, like Symbolic Modelling, the end result is not known until the client gets there. See Tompkins and Lawley (2006b).

## References

Andreas, S. (2006). *Six Blind Elephants*. Vol. 1: *Understanding Ourselves and Each Other*. Boulder, CO: Real People Press.

Dilts, R., Grinder, J., Bandler, R., and DeLozier, J. (1980). *Neuro-Linguistic Programming*. Vol. 1: *The Study of the Structure of Subjective Experience*. Capitola, CA: Meta Publications.

Faulkner, C. (1991). *Metaphors of Identity: Operating Metaphors and Iconic Change*. Audiotape and booklet. Lyons, CO: Genesis II.

Fritz, R. (1989). *The Path of Least Resistance*. New York: Ballantine.

Geary, J. (2011). *I Is An Other: The Secret of Metaphor and How It Shapes the Way We See the World*. New York: HarperCollins.

Grove, D. J. and Panzer, B. I. (1989) *Resolving Traumatic Memories: Metaphors and Symbols in Psychotherapy*. New York: Irvington.

Grove, D. with Wilson, C. (2005). Six degrees of freedom: intuitive problem solving with emergent knowledge. *ReSource Magazine* (Summer). Available at www.cleanlanguage.co.uk/articles/articles/44/ (accessed August 12, 2011).

Harland, P. (2009) *The Power of Six: A Six Step Guide to Self Knowledge*. London: Wayfinder Press.

Harland, P. (2011). *Trust Me, I'm the Patient: Clean Language, Metaphor, and the New Psychology of Change*. London: Wayfinder Press.

Hejmadi, A. V. and Lyall, P. J. (1991). Autogenic metaphor resolution. In C. Bretto, J. DeLozier, J. Grinder, and S. Topel (eds), *Leaves Before the Wind*. Bonny Doon, CA: Grinder, DeLozier & Associates, pp. 99–122.

Kovecses, Z. (2002). *Metaphor: A Practical Introduction*. Oxford: Oxford University Press.

Lakoff, G. and Johnson, M. (1980). *Metaphors We Live By*. Chicago, IL: University of Chicago Press.

Lawley, J. (2001). Metaphors of organisation, Part 2. *Effective Consulting* 1(5). Available at www.cleanlanguage.co.uk/articles/articles/20/ (accessed August 12, 2011).

Lawley, J. (2005). Steve Andreas on Symbolic Modelling. Available at www.cleanlanguage.co.uk/articles/articles/253/ (accessed August 12, 2011).

Lawley, J. and Tompkins, P. (2000). *Metaphors in Mind: Transformation through Symbolic Modelling*. London: Developing Company Press.

Lawley, J. and Tompkins, P. (2004). Clean Language revisited: the evolution of a model. *Rapport* 64. Available at www.cleanlanguage.co.uk/articles/articles/28/ (accessed August 12, 2011).

Lawley, J. and Tompkins, P. (2006). What is therapeutic modelling? *ReSource Magazine* 8. Available at www.cleanlanguage.co.uk/articles/articles/121/ (accessed August 12, 2011).

Lawley J., Meyer, M., Meese, R., Sullivan, W., and Tosey, P. (2010). More than a balancing act? Clean Language as an innovative method for exploring work–life balance. Available at www.surrey.ac.uk/management/people/paul_tosey/ (accessed August 12, 2011).

McWhirter, J. (2000). Re-modelling NLP. Pt 6: Understanding change. *Rapport* 48. Available at www.sensorysystems.co.uk/RemodellingNLPPart6%20.pdf (accessed August 12, 2011).

Sullivan, W. and Rees, J. (2008). *Clean Language: Revealing Metaphors and Opening Minds*. Carmarthen, UK: Crown House Publishing.

Tompkins. P. and Lawley, J. (1997). Less is More ... The Art of Clean Language. *Rapport* 35. Available at www.cleanlanguage.co.uk/articles/articles/109/ (accessed August 12, 2011).

Tompkins. P. and Lawley, J. (1999). Clean Language without words. *Rapport* 43. Available at www.cleanlanguage.co.uk/articles/articles/8/ (accessed August 12, 2011).

Tompkins. P. and Lawley, J. (2003). Clean space: modelling human perception through emergence. *Anchor Point* 17(8). Available at www.cleanlanguage.co.uk/articles/articles/24/ (accessed August 12, 2011).

Tompkins. P. and Lawley, J. (2006a). Coaching for P.R.O.s. *Coach the Coach* (Feb.). Available at www.cleanlanguage.co.uk/articles/articles/31/ (accessed August 12, 2011).

Tompkins. P. and Lawley, J. (2006b). Modelling: top-down and bottom-up. Available at www.cleanlanguage.co.uk/articles/articles/240/ (accessed August 12, 2011).

Tompkins. P. and Lawley, J. (2006c). Using Symbolic Modelling as a research and interview tool. Available at www.cleanlanguage.co.uk/articles/articles/226/ (accessed August 12, 2011).

Tompkins. P. and Lawley, J. (2007). Iteration, iteration, iteration. Available at www.cleanlanguage.co.uk/articles/articles/191/ (accessed August 12, 2011).

Tompkins. P. and Lawley, J. (2010). Modelling Robert Dilts modelling. Available at www.cleanlanguage.co.uk/articles/articles/266/ (accessed August 12, 2011).

 **Richard Bolstad** is a Registered Nurse, a trained Teacher and a member of the New Zealand Association of Psychotherapists. His doctorate is in Clinical Hypnotherapy. With his partner Julia Kurusheva, Richard teaches NLP certifications, conflict resolution and NLP models of secular spirituality, in New Zealand, Asia, Europe and the Americas. He particularly teaches NLP techniques for use in areas of the world where there has been major trauma either from natural events (the 2011 tsunami in Japan, the 2009 tsunami in Samoa, the 2011 earthquake in Christchurch, New Zealand) or from war (Bosnia-Herzegovina in the 1990s, the Caucasus region near Chechnya early this century). A nurse with a clinical and teaching background in the health professions, Richard has tested what he is doing in the most challenging situations imaginable, in situations of significant cultural difference, and where NLP and psychotherapy are unheard of. In such situations "getting it right" can be a life-or-death matter, preventing the self-harming or escalating violence that sometimes follow such severe community disruptions. His RESOLVE Model was developed in response to these demands.

# 5 The RESOLVE Model
## Facilitating Generative Change

*Richard Bolstad*

## Why Use RESOLVE?

I like to take the magic of NLP to the challenges with which only it can deal. I have and continue to train psychiatrists, psychologists, and emergency service staff in places such as Bosnia (after the 1992–1995 Bosnian War), the Caucasus (after the 1999–2000 Chechen War), Samoa (after the 2009 tsunami), and Christchurch and Japan (the 2011 earthquakes). In these crisis situations, we don't have weeks to get helpers able to use NLP elegantly and magically.

To cope, I decided to utilize the latest research from the broader field of psychology about what truly works in NLP. Why does the same NLP process work magically at one time and not work at all at another? Can you show a new practitioner how to get the "magic" from their first day? There are hints in psychological research. For example, studies by James Prochaska and Carlo Diclemente make it clear that the success of coaching interventions depends on understanding the stage of change that the client is at.[1] The same NLP process that succeeds amazingly later in a session may not work if offered *before* the client feels that you understand their problem or before they have defined an outcome that they truly want.

What the coach does *after* the official NLP change process is also crucial. Scott Miller's research shows that simply asking the client a question that presupposes success, "What has changed positively as a result of that last process?" increases the client's self-report of successful change from 33% to 60%.[2]

It is also important to notice that the same NLP process cannot be applied equally to clients with fundamentally different meta-programs, a fact explored by Shelle Rose Charvet in her work with the LAB Profile (see Chapter 2). To state the case more strongly, NLP processes do not in themselves "work."

RESOLVE shows you how to transform a textbook technique into a clinical success. The secret of achieving seemingly magical results is not in the processes themselves, but in what happens before and after them.

## What Is RESOLVE?

The hundreds of techniques and models that make up NLP present an overwhelming collection for new practitioners. For me, one thing initially missing in Bandler and Grinder's work was an overview. NLP trainer Steve Andreas says:

> I think that someone who uses the NLP methods exceptionally well has several ways of gathering all the different skills and techniques under a single overarching framework of understanding.[3]

This is also important because by and large it is the skilled presentation of the therapist's underlying expectations and attitudes that make change work, more than the mere choice of a specific NLP technique. NLP author Joseph O'Connor prefaces my book *RESOLVE* (2002) by affirming that successful NLP coaches "are real people working with love from a grounded methodology to help the client mobilize their powers to heal." In parallel to Michael Hall's reworking of NLP discussed elsewhere in this book (see Chapter 1), the RESOLVE Model gives a structure for sequencing and selecting NLP interventions to create success.

## Using RESOLVE

RESOLVE is an acronym which I developed to teach helpers to quickly access NLP in challenging situations. RESOLVE provides a checklist for new practitioners as well as a series of layered NLP interventions to enhance advanced practice. The acronym helps practitioners become fluent with a useful sequence of interventions, meta-frames, and techniques in a few short days of training. These are not merely a series of steps leading up to and closing "the process"—each of the seven steps has the potential to create change in itself.

**R**esourceful state for the practitioner
**E**stablish rapport with client
**S**pecify an outcome
**O**pen up client's model of world
**L**eading (NLP change technique)
**V**erify change
**E**cological exit

The best way to explain the seven steps is to take an example. In Sarajevo in 1998, my partner Margot and I worked with a woman I'll call Fatima. When we met, everyday sounds such as a car backfiring triggered Fatima's memories of gunfire and gave her frequent panic attacks. Her sleep was filled with terrifying flashbacks where she relived her family being killed in the war. I'll use her case as an example as I explain the RESOLVE Model step by step below.

## The Resourceful State

Milton Erickson established in his research that a hypnotist who does not expect their client to demonstrate a particular trance phenomenon cannot elicit that phenomenon, and Robert Carkhuff showed in the 1950s that a client's success is linked to the personal functioning of their counselor.[4] Part of the practitioner's resourceful attitude is knowing that, just as in the sports situation where the "coaching" metaphor comes from, change is the client's job and not the coach's. This requires a skill in dissociating rather than in getting caught up in the client's horror of what happened to them.

Another part of creating a resourceful state is creating powerful resource anchors for yourself, based on times when you knew beyond doubt that something was working. We began working with Fatima in Sarajevo by explaining that her panic attacks were simply a result of an "anchored response" and could be quickly changed.

## Establish Rapport

Research on "mirror neurons" since 1995 has explained the neurological basis of what NLP calls "rapport"—a feeling of shared understanding, trust, and empathy which emerges when you synchronize your verbal and non-verbal communication with your client (pacing).[5] Verbally, this involves restating the client's initial comments to convey your understanding and using their sensory language (matching sensory systems). Matching another person's breathing, pulse rate, gestures, and tone of voice have all been demonstrated to increase their positive responses to suggestions and personal change.

In his study of intimate relationships, John Gottman has shown that by identifying such synchronization during a five-minute video, he can predict whether or not a couple will stay together for the next decade (predicting divorce with 95% accuracy and the precise year of divorce with 80% accuracy).[6] We created this rapport non-verbally with Fatima as she described her feelings of fear and anger about the war. Just listening and using reflective and clean language (as described by Penny Tompkins and James Lawley in Chapter 4) in itself often allows a person's problem to be transformed.

## Specify the Outcome

The most common way that new clients state their outcome is to say what they don't want (e.g., "I don't want my business to fail," "I don't want to feel anxious when I'm in a group"). Scott Miller and the other researchers in the solution focused therapy movement have shown that simply focusing people on what they want instead of what they don't enhances both commitment to coaching and success.[7]

Richard Wiseman did a very large study showing the same result.[8] He tracked 5,000 people who had some significant goal they wanted to achieve (everything from starting a new relationship to beginning a new career, from stopping smoking to gaining a qualification). Dramatic and consistent differences in goalsetting made the mere 10% who were successful stand out from the other 90%. Most of all, successful goalsetters described their goal in positive terms, and considered carefully what challenges they would face actually doing the work to achieve it ("ecology" in NLP).

Guiding the person to do this involves using meta-model questions to help the person shift from general nominalizations ("I want happiness") and unspecified verbs ("I want to nurture myself more") to sensory specific descriptions ("I will take ten minutes each day to focus on what I have done well and write three examples of actions I'm pleased with in my diary"). Prior to the war, Fatima had been a medical student, and she wanted to recover from her panic so that she could be relaxed enough to successfully complete her studies.

## Open Up the Client's Model of the World

Clients change when they believe they can change and that there is a reason to change. New clients frequently feel as if they are suffering as a result of events and responses they cannot control, and they hope that an NLP coach will magically "fix" their brain. My aim is instead to give them charge of their brain. I utilize their own motivation style (especially Towards–Away From) to create a compelling reason to change.

I also want to demonstrate that they *can* change. Scott Miller's collation of solution focused research suggests that all successful personal change is preceded by a change in the "locus of control" from external to internal. In their study of NLP psychotherapy, Martina Genser-Medlitsch and Peter Schütz in Vienna also found this characteristic shift to clients experiencing themselves as in charge of their life ("at cause" in NLP terms).[9]

This meta-level change can be elicited linguistically by asking the client to demonstrate how they do the problem and (eliciting the strategy they use to create the problem) pointing out that if they change that, they will have achieved their outcome. For me, this step of the RESOLVE Model, more than any other, is the key to transformative change. It is done with a series of metaphors, reframes, sleight of mouth patterns, and presuppositional questions.

We asked Fatima if she could get the feeling of panic just by thinking about the war. She could, and we pointed out "So that means that the feeling is a result of the way you think about that. You'd know if thinking about those experiences felt different in twenty minutes time wouldn't you?" Our question presupposed that her thinking strategies generate the problem and could be changed within twenty minutes in order to generate the solutions she wanted. In nodding her agreement, she accepted the reframing of her feelings as generated by her thinking, and accepted her changing quickly as a possibility.

## Leading

Leading is the step in the RESOLVE Model where the official "NLP change process" is done. In selecting which process to use, I assess the depth of the issue using Robert Dilts's neurological levels.[10] As a generalization, interventions work best when done at a deeper neurological level than the issue itself.

- When a person states that they want something external to change (environment level), we at least help them change their behavior or anchored responses.

- When they state that they want to behave differently, we at least help them install new skills and strategies (capability level).

- When they say they want new capabilities, we at least help them change their beliefs about the situation and the possible responses.

- When they say they want to change their priorities (values) or let go of old beliefs, we at least help them to change their sense of who they are and what their overall purpose is.

- When someone wants to change at that deeper (identity) level, we help them connect with a sense of what is greater than them that can give their life meaning (spirituality).

Another important aspect of selecting from the hundreds of NLP processes is to notice what "personal strengths" the client has and match these with NLP processes. Significantly, some clients describe their problem as an internal feeling response (demonstrating a "skill" with anchoring) while some describe their problem in a more detached way (demonstrating a "skill" with what NLP calls the sub-modality of dissociation). Some clients talk about their problem globally (using the Milton Model language patterns of trancework) and some talk in intricate detail (using the meta-model language of detailed planning).

In the RESOLVE Model I recommend beginning with what clients are already good at, and then shifting to the opposite pole (NLP "pacing and leading"). For example, Fatima was already good at anchoring herself into a panic attack using sounds, so we had her remember the enjoyable sounds of a party in her pre-war life, and anchored that good feeling with a touch on her arm. This "resource anchor" created a safe state of mind for her to begin the simple NLP Trauma Process, in which we teach the person's brain to dissociate or step back from the traumatic memories. Dissociation is the opposite skill from anchoring. This technique is currently the subject of an extensive research study by Frank Bourke and others, referred to elsewhere in this book.

Leading is distinguished from manipulation by what happens *before* opening up the model of the world and leading occur. The key components of ethical leading are:

- The practitioner is not trying to make themselves feel comfortable or benefit from the client's change; they are available simply to help the client (resourceful state).

- The practitioner gains an understanding of the challenges, intentions, beliefs, and values of the client, and aligns with these (establish rapport).

- The practitioner creates a sense of clear contract with the client about the outcome that will be used as a measure of the appropriateness of each intervention (specify outcome).

## NLP interventions

| Examples of interventions | Chunk up/ associate (e.g., depression, joy) | Chunk up/ dissociate (e.g., psychosis, awareness) | Chunk down/ associate (e.g., anxiety, fun) | Chunk down/ dissociate (e.g., borderline Personality Disorder, goals) |
|---|---|---|---|---|
| **Spirit** | Core transformation | Dis-identification | Drop through | Mind backtracking |
| **Identity** | Parts integration | Time-Line Therapy | Reimprinting | Core questions |
| **Values–beliefs** | Meta-stating | Sub-modality belief change | Mind to muscle | Values elicitation |
| **Capabilities** | Chain anchors | Swish | Strategy installation | Ideomotor signals |
| **Behavior** | Resource anchor | Trauma cure | Collapse anchors | Plan towards outcome |
| **Environment** | Community involvement | Move to retreat center | Tidy up environment | Move to new environment |

The above table does not seek to categorize NLP processes, but merely to give examples of where they could be used in terms of this model.

## Verify Change Has Happened

A new, more positive response pattern can sometimes be "anchored" in place during the NLP session without the person's conscious mind realizing; just as at times a panic response happens when the person's conscious mind doesn't expect it. The conscious mind is the reality testing component of the brain, and after changing response patterns it is important for it to reality test and confirm the change.

Asking the person to notice and even celebrate the difference installs a solution focused pattern which allows change to continue. As mentioned, simply asking, "What has changed positively as a result of that last process?" increases reports of successful change from 33% to 60%. After doing the NLP Trauma Process, we had Fatima think of the most disturbing situations that she had experienced in the war. A little surprised, she smiled and said, "I'm seeing the pictures and it's as if they're just over there and I'm here." We test the change using the client's own convincer strategy.

## Ecological Exit Process

Finally, it is important to have the client plan for the situations in which their new response will be useful and for situations which may challenge it or even temporarily evoke the old response. Prochaska and Diclemente say, "Just as one swallow doesn't make a spring, one slip doesn't make a fall." [11]

Planning for such challenges also allows us to check if anything else needs to change to make the new response fit ecologically (in a way that works for the person's life as a whole system). This involves both future-pacing and tasking. With Fatima, we had her think into the future and notice that she could relax and still keep safe. When we met her again a year later she'd had no further panic attacks or nightmares, and was amazed to remember how disabling they had been. Her life was back on track.

## Another Personal Example

RESOLVE is based on the idea that often how we frame something is more important than the thing itself. One case that brought this home to me dramatically was a demonstration case I worked with while training psychiatrists in Bosnia. I expected to demonstrate using an example from the war, but the man asked that we use another example. When he was 18 he went on his first date and met his young woman friend in the old town of Sarajevo. It was a romantic moment and she told him she had something to show him. She reached under her blouse and brought out … a pet white mouse. He was startled, and then embarrassed lest his startle be seen as fear. In humiliation, he ran from the scene and never dated the woman again. He had since developed a phobia of mice.

Years later, the war broke out. As the bombs fell on Sarajevo, sirens would sound urging people to head immediately into the nearest house and into the safety of the cellar. But this man could not go. Instead he stood out in the street, surrounded at times by the wounded or dead … because there might be a mouse in the nearest cellar. He would rather die than face that terror. It is not what happens to people that scars them. The mouse did him no harm at all. It is how we *code* what happens that shapes our lives. And similarly, it is not what technique I use that heals my client. It is how they code that technique.

## Does It Work?

I frequently tell my clients that neither NLP nor any specific NLP process "works" in some context-independent way. Human beings work, and NLP is just a way of explaining *how* you work so perfectly, even when the results you are getting are not those you would choose.

Panic attacks and compulsions, for example, are not merely problems; they are successful programs that your brain may be running in inappropriate situations. An anxiety response when a venomous snake is nearby or a compulsion to wash your hands whenever you go to the bathroom are examples of healthy applications of these natural skills. RESOLVE is just a map; it neither works nor doesn't work by itself. Experienced practitioners will of course shift more fluidly between steps and make more "intuitive" decisions once they know the territory of coaching.

## Another Example

A man I'll call Robert came to me saying that for eight years he had suffered from Obsessive Compulsive Disorder (OCD). He became anxious whenever he needed to go through a door. He had a persistent fear that if he did not open and close the door repeatedly, someone he cared about (either a friend or a family member) would be harmed. A number would come into his head (he would hear it spoken as if as an instruction) and that would be the number of times he felt compelled to open and close the door. As a result, just going down to the supermarket was a challenge, and certainly he was unable to hold down a job. Although he understood that this fear was irrational, he had also developed an interest in new age thinking, and had come across the idea of manifestation. His fear was that, even though it was irrational to believe that, merely thinking about it might cause his thoughts to "manifest" the feared result (as claimed in *The Secret*[12]). This meant that even his conscious mind was now convinced of the danger to his loved ones.

After listening to this story, I checked the ecology of a goal to be able to walk through doors. After all, if he could walk through doors, then he would lose his sickness benefit. I pointed out that he may decide to maintain the arrangement to get the benefit until he was confident that he could change.

In opening up his model of the world, I asked Robert if he had ever tried to manifest anything else, like $1,000,000. He said he had, and I checked that he had been unsuccessful, and asked him why he thought he had been unsuccessful. He explained that manifestation only worked if you congruently wanted the goal of manifestation. If you feel ambivalent about earning money, then the universe will return only this ambivalence. I asked Robert next if he had ever congruently wished for his friends or family to die, without simultaneously worrying and hoping they lived. Of course he had always worried at the same time as imagining them dying. This opening up of Robert's model was the crucial step in designing a solution which matched his personality skills.

The change technique I recommended was to practice the same type of skill as required by the problem Robert experienced. He thought in detail until he was so associated into his fear that he had to act (so obsessed that he felt compelled to repeat his ritual). I told him that to keep his loved ones safe, it was most important that he worry as much as possible, and so when he next came to a door, he should deliberately worry as much as he could. The more he worried, the safer they were. He appeared puzzled but agreed that this was true.

Since the only reason for Robert to worry was if his friends or family were in danger from his thoughts, the moment he tried to worry, they were safe and there was nothing to worry about. If he doubted it, he had only to worry again for a moment to reassure himself. The next week he came back to see me and told me he had been walking through doors without a thought all week. The solution was now in his hands. He had proved that he was able to "overcome" OCD. The reframe I used was very simple. I said, in effect, "Worry doesn't mean that your friends are going to die (which would justify even more worry). Worry means your friends are safe (which means the worry itself is no longer necessary)." Our second session involved dealing with some of the background issues related to OCD, and future-pacing further change sessions to support him creating a lifestyle which would need to be radically different to the last eight years.

## Where Else?

So far I've discussed RESOLVE only as a model for coaching. It also sheds light on the structure of NLP applications such as training or business consulting. Checking that students are motivated to a learning outcome before beginning a lecture, and providing them with evidence that they will now be able to use their new skills in the real world, are just as essential in classroom education as in personal change.

### Notes

1. Prochaska, Norcross, and Diclemente (1994).

2. Miller et al. (1996), pp. 255–256.

3. Andreas (1999) (2002b), p. 3.

4. Carkhuff and Berenson (1997), p. 5 and p. 35; Bolstad (2002b), pp. 122–123.

5. Rizzolatti, G. and Craighero, L. (2004).

6. Gottman (1999), p. 27.

7. Miller et al. (1996).

8. Wiseman (2009), pp. 88–93.

9.  Miller et al. (1996); Genser-Medlitsch and Schütz (1997).

10. Dilts (1996) pp. 18–23.

11. Prochaska, Norcross, and Diclemente (1994) pp. 227.

12. Byrne (2006).

## References

Andreas, S. (1999). What Makes A Good NLPer? *Anchor Point* 13(10): 3–6.

Bolstad, R. (2002a). *Transforming Communication*. Auckland: Pearsons.

Bolstad, R. (2002b). *RESOLVE: A New Model of Therapy*. Carmarthen, UK: Crown House Publishing.

Byrne, R. (2006). *The Secret*. London: Simon & Schuster.

Carkhuff, R. R. and Berenson, B. G. (1997). *Beyond Counselling and Therapy*, New York: Holt, Rinehart and Winston.

Dilts, R. (1996). *Visionary Leadership*. Capitola: Meta Publications.

Genser-Medlitsch, M. and Schütz, P. (1997). Does Neuro-Linguistic psychotherapy have effect? New Results shown in the extramural section. Vienna: Martina Genser-Medlitsch and Peter Schütz, ÖTZ-NLP.

Gottman, J. M. (1999). *The Marriage Clinic*. New York: W.W. Norton.

Hall, L. M., Bodenhamer, B. G., Bolstad, R., and Hamblett, M. (2000). *The Structure of Personality*. Carmarthen, UK: Crown House Publishing.

Miller, S. D., Hubble, M. A., and Duncan, B. L. (1996). *Handbook of Solution Focused Brief Therapy*. San Francisco: Jossey-Bass.

Miller, W. (1985) Motivation for treatment: a review with special emphasis on alcoholism. *Psychological Bulletin* 98(1): 84–107.

Prochaska, J. O., Norcross, J. C., and Diclemente, C. C. (1994). *Changing For Good*. New York: William Morrow & Co.

Rizzolatti, G. and Craighero, L. (2004). The mirror-neuron system. *Annual review of Neuroscience* 27: 169–192.

Wiseman, R. (2009). *59 Seconds: Think A Little, Change A Lot*. London: Macmillan.

Please visit www.transformations.net.nz for a series of online articles which explore the use of the RESOLVE Model in other contexts and give more detail about its use with specific client issues.

**John McWhirter**

John has over thirty years' experience of working with children, adults, families, communities and organizations. He has explored and developed models for thirty-five years creating Developmental Behavioural Modelling as a field committed to the exploration and development of all things related to models and modelling. He was personally certified by Richard Bandler in 1990 as a Master Trainer of NLP. He is the designer and main trainer in a DBM Masters degree at the University of Valencia, Spain. He is based in Glasgow, Scotland where he is Director of Sensory Systems Training and coordinates research, development, and training and a private practice as a therapist and consultant.

# 6 Behavioral Remodeling
## Advancing NLP's Linguistic Model

*John McWhirter*

The world is a wonderful place where we can deepen our sense of wonder the more we explore and experience it. One of the saddest subjects to contemplate is how humans create such pain and trouble for each other with wars, oppression, and intolerance. In contrast we can joyfully witness countless examples of loving, caring, charity, and self-sacrifice. Underlying all of these are specific understandings of how the world works and how the world should be worked. At the core of this we can identify specific models of the world and the different modeling that created the models.

If we can understand more about models and modeling we can greatly increase our range of resources for helping a world in challenging times. The more we can develop tools for increasing our understanding and tolerance for different cultural and individual models of the world, reduce the imposing of models from one group of people onto another, and resolve conflicts and promote healthy development, the more potential we will have for making positive changes, reducing the trouble in the world, and promoting happiness and fulfillment for all.

## My Development of Modeling and Re-Modeling

While completing my degree in the late 1970s I worked the summers in a residential children's home that was used for the reception, assessment, and treatment of children taken into care. Later I worked with gangs in a community treatment program where I researched solvent addiction. I realized that academic psychology offered me little for day-to-day care and therapy for their varied problems. Searching for more useful tools, I read books and attended various training courses in gestalt therapy, family therapy, and Ericksonian hypnosis. I heard about Bandler and Grinder and later about NLP. What excited me was the description of modeling—identifying what actually worked for the various therapeutic wizards who were inspiring me at that time: Fritz Perls, Virginia Satir, and Milton H. Erickson. Modeling seemed to be the ideal tool to help me integrate and further develop my knowledge and skills. At that time there was little written about how *exactly* Bandler and Grinder modeled so I began to create my own version.

In 1985 I began formal training in NLP. I was certified as a Trainer and then Master Trainer in 1990 by Richard Bandler while assisting and training for him. I found the products of modeling—the distinctions, models, and techniques—very useful but they did not cover all the difficulties and problems experienced by my clients. If I could model the things not yet covered by NLP it could help many more people. In the training I did not find the modeling methodology that created these great products. While working for Richard I had the privilege of seeing him in action and though he did not teach how he modeled at that time, he did offer hints and encouragement to develop my own modeling.

At that time NLP had centered on two main types of modeling, *replication modeling* and *product modeling*. Replication modeling is most often exemplified through the aim of "replicating excellence" and is the core of traditional NLP. This naturally leads to product modeling, which aims to develop a simple version of what is created through replication modeling—a model that will be easier for others to learn and apply. Bandler's ability to replicate some of the therapy approaches of Erickson, Satir, and Perls was simplified into easy-to-follow techniques. The value of product modeling is in its effectiveness for achieving specific changes without the years of experience and depth of skills of the exemplars. The limitation is the lack of depth of understanding the exemplars use to produce the excellence.

As my interest in modeling extended beyond the replication of successful therapy, I aspired to develop a universal modeling methodology—one that could potentially describe *all* that humans do, describe the world as it is, however it is. If successful it could model all of the NLP models, the models of individual clients, and all theories including psychology, physics, and chemistry.

Formal and natural models can be utilized at different levels. They can be applied as simple procedures and techniques, which is the aim of most product modeling. They can also be applied with a deeper knowledge of how things work and understanding of the processes involved. A chef learns cooking processes, the *fundamentals of how things work*; the beginner and amateur cook learns recipes and *specific procedures* (techniques), without the deeper understanding. Understanding the deeper processes enables the cook to adapt to variations in ingredients. My interest in modeling moved from producing techniques to teaching the deeper processes involved.[1] This was necessary for creating a universal modeling methodology in contrast to a modeling method, such as Strategy Elicitation.

## Extending the Core Modeling Question

In the *Structure of Magic*, Bandler and Grinder state:

> The Question for us is: How is it possible for different human beings faced with the same world to have such different experiences? Our understanding is that this difference follows primarily from differences in the richness of their models. Thus the question becomes: How is it possible for human beings to maintain an impoverished model which causes them pain in the face of a multi-valued, rich, and complex world?[2]

From working with a range of clients I realized that for many people re-modeling the current content of their model, or their use of their model, was not enough to prevent them from continuing to model their world in limiting ways. Therefore for me the difference that Bandler and Grinder identify is only one important difference; there are additional equally concerning differences including the *modeling that creates the impoverished model* and will continue to do so no matter what changes are made in the existing model, and *how clients use their model poorly, even when it is a rich and accurate model.*

I now had three areas, two of them new to NLP:

1. How do we all build our models?
2. How do we maintain them?
3. How do we use them?

When clients continually model the world as dangerous, threatening, and depressing, then the only relief possible through changing the current content is temporary. The new opportunity of helping clients to create and use their model more usefully opened up many new therapeutic possibilities. I was inspired in my pursuit of this by the transcript of Richard Bandler in *Magic in Action* (1984) and the work of Milton Erickson. I began to teach this as a process of "Live Re-Modeling" to Master Practitioners in 1993 as Systemic Therapy and Consultancy.

All models can potentially be improved by re-modeling to develop their individual accuracy and especially to integrate them as a whole. In re-modeling the aim is to improve the model in as many ways as possible to make it fit more accurately and to work more effectively, both internally and externally.

One of the key elements in modeling and re-modeling is questioning. Questions direct what we attend to, what we investigate and prioritize. The questioning tools we have set limits on what we can intentionally investigate. NLP was created using the key questioning tool of the meta-model.

## Re-Modeling the "Core" Model In NLP: The Meta-Model

I was very impressed by the meta-model, which Richard Bandler always described as the core of NLP. From my reading of *The Structure of Magic* (1975) I was aware that it was not a complete model for all applications and I was very curious about the potential for further enhancements for other applications:

> The parts of the transformational model relevant for our purposes have been presented.
>
> Thus, we have adapted the model, selecting only the portions relevant for our purposes and arranging them in a system appropriate for our objectives in therapy.[3]

Further language patterns from Transformational Grammar and other language models were not included in Bandler and Grinder's "well-formed in therapy model."[4] There are also other application areas into which NLP has expanded, such as education, personal development, organizational management, that were not included. I began to explore some of these Transformational Grammar distinctions and language models to check out their potential application in these areas.

The distinctions of deletion, generalization, and distortion are presented at first as "general mechanisms,"[5] becoming "major processes,"[6] and then without any supporting argument, description, or source becoming "three universal processes of human modeling."[7] For me they were not modeling distinctions but simply three different transformations from the deep structure in the model to a surface structure. While this is very useful it presupposes the prior existence of a model and offers no explanation of *how* the model came to be there in the first place. As a modeler I needed tools for building models and describing how they are built. In 1986 I created the modeling distinctions to do this.

All models include specific *details*. These details are *scoped*—numbered, sized, bounded, and qualified—in specific ways. Within this scoping the details are *connected* in very specific ways. These are also three integrated distinctions. This met one of my main criteria for modeling, that it should be holistic. Others were that it should be systemic, developmental, and recursive (it should be capable of being applied to itself).

Detail, scope, and connection could also describe the meta-model transformations as taking away detail, scoping or connecting (deletion), increasing scope (generalization), and changing details, scoping, or connections (distortion).

Through this modeling I was able to create a holistic integrated language model, firstly of sixteen meta-model distinctions and the Milton Model distinctions. This was the Integrated Language Model. I realized that the detail, scope, and connection distinctions could be further distinguished using detail, scope, and connection. This created a fractal structure for the model, so I called it the Basic Fractal Language Model. This model had eighteen integrated distinctions. Continuing with the fractal modeling to the next level greatly extended the language model to eighty-one integrated distinctions. This language model has been invaluable for precision modeling.[8]

## Modeling and Re-Modeling Knowing and Doing

We need to understand the world well enough to meet our needs. We need to have accurate knowledge and skills if we are to effectively respond to challenges in life. As we are born with none of this knowledge and skill we need to build it with our own modeling and from modeling external sources such as parents, friends, teachers, books, television, and the Internet.

Understanding this modeling of what we "know" and what we "do" became the next important step in modeling how we build, maintain, and use our models of the world.

Three different distinctions emerged as very important when I modeled how we understand the world: knowledge, belief/doubt, and conviction. First is knowledge itself—what we know. We know our name and where we are right now. Knowledge is a digital distinction—we know things or we don't know them. We have evidence for what we know. When we know we do not doubt. Knowledge is our strongest understanding distinction. It is also very resilient to change.

Until we know things we have a second tool, one where there is some evidence but also some doubt. This tool is an analog or continuum of doubt to belief. The more we doubt the less we believe; the more we believe the less we doubt. This is why we can have strong or weak beliefs and never strong or weak knowledge.

The third tool, useful when we have no evidence and where no evidence is possible but it would be very useful to "know" something, is conviction. Convictions are often our first guess at things and ideally develop into the belief/doubt structure. Convictions operate like knowledge but because they do not require evidence they are potentially the most "dangerous" of the three distinctions. Inaccurate knowledge and beliefs are modified by counter examples and other evidence; convictions are not. Convictions are one of the distinctions at the heart of many of the problems in the world. Political, religious, cultural, and individual convictions are not easy to change. By understanding their structure and function we can identify them and increase the potential for changing them.

Ideally we would make provisional models of what could be (conviction/hypothesis), then test the model (changing the level of belief/doubt), and through this consolidate credible evidence-based knowledge. We need to know how the world works and how to effectively work the world to meet our needs. This is a very useful process to use in therapy to assist clients to create accurate models, and is central to modeling how we build, maintain and apply our models of the world.

### *Modeling and Re-Modeling "Knowing"*

To enrich the client's model it is helpful to quickly and easily get to the key elements of the model. The following process is useful for this task, rapidly getting to the thinking that created knowledge and to the understanding of how the world works. It is very effective for "owning" knowledge from external sources. It is also used to identify the type of knowledge (conviction, belief/doubt, knowledge) and as a basis for re-modeling poorly formed or inaccurate knowledge.

As with any application of a model the following sequence can be used as a technique and as a process. It was designed to be used as a process and when used as such there are many additional possibilities in each stage for further enriching the client's model of the world. It is a useful contribution to the therapy process, but is not the whole therapy process. A number of other NLP elements integrate well with them (e.g., counter-example strategy, changing personal position, the As–If frame).

The aim is not to "fix" a problem, but to enrich the model and modeling of the client.

In both these modeling sequences we begin with a surface detail, increase the scope, and then explore how things are connected. This is a general modeling sequence very much like building a jigsaw: start sorting out the bits (detail), gather the similar bits and get the border (scoping), and then start connecting them up.

When we investigate the client's knowledge there are three possible responses at each step:

1. Continue deeper into the modeling of the knowledge.
2. Identify a source of the knowledge.
3. Identify the limit of the knowledge.

**Figure 1:** *Knowledge Tree: Investigating Knowledge*

## Step 1:

Select knowledge statement (often in the form of a judgment). This can be reactive, in response to a statement made by the subject, or proactive, through asking what they know about a specific topic.

## Step 2: Identify evidence for the knowledge

How do you know?

If the response is "don't know" or an external source then proceed to Step 4.

How else?

How sure are you that this is correct?
Do you have any doubts about it?

## Step 3: Identify thinking process
When did you first decide this?
How did you think it through?
If the response is "don't know" or an external source then proceed to Step 4.

## Step 4: Enriching the model of the world
a) New modeling: For convictions or very inaccurate models then creating a new model is the most useful approach.

b) Re-modeling: For partially inaccurate models and for belief/doubt structures re-modeling the existing model is the most useful approach.

c) Develop model: For accurate models adding additional things to further develop the model, such as future checking and updating, is the most useful approach.

d) After modeling: consolidate:

> "How would you think it through now?"
> "How would you test it?"
> "How would you keep it up to date in the future?"

The following short examples highlight the different stages used in response to conviction, belief/doubt, and knowledge.

*Example 1 (Young Man)*

**Client:** My boss hates me.

**Therapist:** How do you know?

**C:** He is always criticizing me. (Evidence)

**T:** Anything else?

**C:** He gives me more work than everybody else. (Evidence)

**T:** How sure are you that this is correct?

**C:** Totally!

**T:** Do you have any doubts about it?

**C:** No. (Operating as knowledge)

**T:** When did you first decide this?

**C:** I remember sitting in a meeting and he was friendly with everybody else and it became clear he didn't like me.

**T:** How exactly did you make your mind up?

**C:** Well, the way he looked, together with all the other things he had done before that. If he did like me he would be nice to me. He's not. So it's obvious he doesn't like me.

(Intervention option: re-modeling and develop model)

**T:** Well, that may well be the case, but it would be good to be really sure that you were correct. You have not been in the job long and your boss is used to dealing with the other people. I don't know how much he knows you and how much he may be reacting to how you are in the meeting and elsewhere. If you were in his position what would you think about what you are doing? What do you think about it now?

**C:** You are right. I have not really checked it out thoroughly. I think that he just doesn't notice me and won't if I keep sitting there quietly not contributing to the meetings.

**T:** How could you check things in the future?

**C:** Notice how I am with my boss and not just how he is with me.

**T:** What else would be useful?

**C:** Notice how I am feeling and check what the feeling is about.

**T:** Good.

*Example 2 (Young Woman)*

**Client:** I don't have enough confidence.

**Therapist:** How do you know that you don't have enough confidence?

**C:** My mother told me. (Source)

**T:** Anything else?

**C:** I feel nervous when I do new things. (Evidence)

**T:** How sure are you that this is correct?

**C:** Pretty certain.

**T:** Do you have any doubts about it?

**C:** Well, sometimes I feel OK doing new things. (Operating as belief/doubt)

**T:** When did you first decide that you didn't have enough confidence?

**C:** I didn't. My mother told me that was what was wrong with me and it seemed to fit really well. (Source: Proceed to Step 4: re-modeling and developing the model option)

**T:** When anyone is going into new situations there are things they don't yet know and can't yet do. It can be very useful to appreciate that so you can work out what they are and what you need to do. Sometimes being excited and a little nervous helps to direct our attention more than when we are relaxed and calm. Too much though can get in the way. A funny thing about new things is that you can only really be appropriately confident about them after you are doing them well. Confidence comes from competence and you often need to practice to build the competence. Often people would like the confidence before doing things, when in fact they need to begin doing them to build the confidence. You can be generally confident beforehand—about how to approach them and about your ability to learn new things—but not about the things you can't yet do. So it can be useful to be appropriately concerned going into new things. Now I don't know what level of concern you would be comfortable feeling and using to help you when you are dealing with new things. What do you think?

**C:** Mmmm. I hadn't thought about it that way before. I think that most of the time I should be feeling concerned in the way that I have been and that it is a good thing. A few times though I did get caught up in the feeling and I realize now that that distracted me from paying attention to what was happening and that wasn't helpful.

**T:** And about your level of confidence?

**C:** It's clear to me now that it's not really about confidence but about how I deal with new things generally, how I think about them and how I manage myself to make learning them easier.

**T:** What can you do to help yourself do this?

**C:** I will remember what you were saying and when I am going to do new things I will pay attention to how I am preparing and what I am feeling and check that it is not too much and not too little either.

## Example 3 (Young Boy)

**Client:** Poor people are lazy.

**Therapist:** How do you know that poor people are lazy? (Identify evidence)

**C:** They just are! (Conviction and limit of knowledge so proceed to new modeling)

**T:** In your street there are a lot of different people; all of them are poor, aren't they?

**C:** Yes.

**T:** Some of them might be lazier than others. Some of them work when they can get jobs and some of them work very hard at the jobs they have got; getting up early, getting home late. Some of them would love to work, but can't get jobs. Your father, for example, I know that he works hard and he is poor. I know that your mother works a lot at home and she is poor. So maybe some people are lazy. Maybe some rich people work hard and maybe some rich people are lazy. How would you really know which were which? What do you think? (Check the new model)

**C:** Well, now I think that some people are lazy whether or not they are poor, it's just that poor people can't get work sometimes and that makes them seem lazy.

**T:** How could you tell the people that were lazy?

**C:** I would need to know more about them, what they did and stuff like that.

**T:** OK.

### Modeling and Re-Modeling "Doing"

Our knowledge of how the world works is the basis for what we do to meet our needs. Modeling and re-modeling the planned working of the world can greatly improve the effectiveness of all that we do. In our own model of the world, and often in communication, only the surface detail is given for rules, guidance, and directives, and not how exactly these will work. They are often not sufficient on their own and using them effectively is greatly enhanced with a deeper knowledge of how they are intended to work.

**Figure 2:** *Knowledge Tree: Investigating "Doing"*

## Step 1:

Select a "To Do" example (can be in the form of a Statement "I am going to do X", a Directive "You need to do X", or a question "Should I do X?"). The selection can be reactive, in response to a statement made by the subject, or proactive, through asking what they plan to do.

## Step 2: Intended benefit

"I am going to do X." "What will you get if you do X?"
"You need to do X." "What will happen if I do X?"
"Should I do X?" "What will happen if you do X?"

If the response is "don't know" or an external source then proceed to Step 4.

## Step 3: How it will work

How will that work?
Is that all that is required?
Could it result in anything else?

If the response is "don't know" or an external source then proceed to Step 4.

## Step 4: Enriching the model

a) New modeling: If the previous response has been "don't know" or an external source then new modeling is necessary.

b) Re-modeling: For partially inaccurate and incomplete models re-modeling the existing model is the most useful approach.

c) Develop model: For accurate models adding additional things to further develop the model, such as future checking and updating, is the most useful approach.

d) After modeling: consolidate:

> "What do you plan to do now?"

*Example:*

> **Client:** I need to exercise more.
>
> **Therapist:** What will you get if you exercise more?
>
> **C:** I will be healthier.

**T:** How will exercising make you healthy?

**C:** It will make me fitter.

**T:** Is that all that you need to do?

**C:** No, I need to eat better as well.

**T:** Are there any potential dangers in exercising more?

**C:** Well, if I do too much I might strain myself.

**T:** What would you plan to do now?

**C:** I need to do more than just exercise and I need to be careful how I exercise.

## Summary with links to detail, scope, and connection

| | Knowledge of: how the world works | Knowledge of: how to work the world |
|---|---|---|
| Detail | Knowledge | What to do |
| Scope | Evidence | What it will get |
| Connection | The thinking that created the model | How it will work |

From 1993, when I completed my re-modeling of NLP,[9] I continued modeling beyond traditional NLP into areas that had not yet been explored such as the structures of ideas, knowledge, and convictions, the formation and development of emotions, how hypnosis actually works, the structure of bonding and relationships, how we form models, the different "forms" that models take, the formation and difference between the thinking processes of generalization, abstraction, conceptualization, and how change and all types of learning function holistically.

I was greatly influenced by the work of Gregory Bateson[10] and realized that universal modeling methodology, in addition to NLP and other technology, required an integrated methodology, epistemology, and ontology, so that is what I created. For this expanding field of modeling I continued to use the name that I had created for my embryonic modeling in 1995, Developmental Behavioural Modelling (DBM).[11]

DBM aims to model all of the processes of natural modeling and to develop tools and processes to improve therapy, education, managing, and the quality of life experience. DBM has also developed many new tools for modeling and re-modeling formal models and theories. The major innovation for modeling though has been the modeling of modeling, which has created a new meta-field of modeling.

## Potential Challenges, Limitations, and Concerns

My development of modeling as a complete methodology for change created new challenges in training and application. One of the benefits of the techniques approach is that a therapist knows the techniques and what he/she will be doing ahead of time. This creates a feeling of security. The modeling methodology is the opposite; it starts with not knowing and requires the building of an understanding of the client before knowing what will be useful to re-model. This may make one feel more insecure, but an appropriate discomfort lets the modeler know that they don't yet know. The comfort provided by the knowledge of the techniques is a potentially misleading good feeling. The therapist does not necessarily know about the client, only their knowledge of their techniques. This is also the case in the increasing emphasis in a variety of brief therapies on "getting rid" of bad feelings as a rule rather than understanding the useful function of this discomfort. Metaphorically it is the same as switching off a fire alarm because the noise upsets you.

The modeling methodology helps students to appreciate that not all changes are useful for clients and that discomfort can be very useful information from the unconscious which should be used and not "got rid of."

A formal modeling methodology cannot by itself be good or bad; only in its application by individual people. The ethical application of modeling however is in the hands of individuals.

One potential limitation in learning and applying the modeling methodology is the increased commitment required from the practitioner to learn the detailed distinctions, models, and processes. With many more distinctions and models there is a lot to learn and apply (at the time of writing there are over 400 formal models in DBM). The modeling methodology does not offer a simple technique that can be used for a quick fix. The accurate "not knowing" when beginning with a client is appropriately uncomfortable. It takes time to develop comfort with this natural discomfort, but it is important to do this as it alerts the practitioner that they do not yet know about the unique individual they are working with. This goes against our Western education, that knowing is good and a sign of intelligence, and that not knowing means you are stupid! Simple classification systems and techniques are popular, in part, because the user begins with "knowing" the system and is only waiting to fit the client into one of the techniques.

A modeling methodology starts from zero content. It offers a methodology similar to what Milton Erickson used—"a new theory for every client." Indeed Erickson is a major inspiration for the development of the modeling methodology. Another concern is equally applicable to the Ericksonian field; the copying of specific outputs from the modeling and not how they were created. It is easy to superficially repeat what Erickson said, to create similar tasks, just as it is easy to apply some of the DBM models superficially rather than create a unique model for each client. Careful training and supervision goes some way to reducing this risk.

There is also the danger of reverting to using modeling as a technique or to impose ready-made models onto the client. This is avoided when using the DBM modeling methodology but it is easy for anyone to take bits of it and use them without the checks and balances of the full methodology.

## Conclusion

A major step toward a happier and more fulfilling world for all can be made by increasing our sensitivity and understanding of the modeling process, developing our skills in using models more effectively, identifying inaccurate, incomplete, and inconsistent models, and promoting the mutual understanding and development of all people and peoples. Trouble will continue throughout the world as long as people create inaccurate models, dogmatically abuse formal models, encourage intolerance of difference, and use violence to impose changes.

By modeling all things related to modeling we can potentially improve our natural modeling—how each of us creates our understanding of reality. By modeling and remodeling formal models we can improve the theories that are used as the basis for change in all areas of life. For this NLP can lead the way by role modeling effective modeling and use of models, promoting positive self-criticism, and committing to constant learning and development.

## Notes

1. For examples of some of my techniques, as well as perspective patterns and cognitive pre-qualifiers, see Andreas (2002, 2006b).

2. Bandler and Grinder (1975a), p. 14.

3. Bandler and Grinder (1975a), pp. 35 and 40.

4. Grinder and Elgin (1973).

5. Bandler and Grinder (1975a), p. 14.

6. Bandler and Grinder (1975a), p. 25.

7. Bandler and Grinder (1975a), p. 179.

8. McWhirter (1999a).

9. Outlined in my *Rapport* articles on re-modeling NLP (see McWhirter, 1998, 1999a, 1999b) and McNorton (2004).

10. Bateson (1979, 1991).

11. DBM and the DBM logo are trademarks belonging to John McWhirter and Sensory Systems Training.

## References

Andreas, S. (1999). Modeling with NLP. *Rapport* 46: 7. Available at http://www.steveandreas.com/Articles/modeling_NLP.html (accessed August 15, 2011).

Andreas, S. (2001). Perspective patterns. *Anchor Point* 15(4): 5–18. Available at www.steveandreas.com/Articles/perspatt.html (accessed August 15, 2011).

Andreas, S. (2002). *Transform Your Self: Becoming Who You Want to Be*. Moab, UT: Real People Press.

Andreas, S. (2003). Breakthroughs and meltthroughs. Available at http://www.steveandreas.com/Articles/breakthroughs.html (accessed August 15, 2011).

Andreas, S. (2006a) Imaginal disc NLP Group. Draft proposal. Available at www.nlpiash.org/Conference2006/Site/Presentations/ImaginalDisc.htm (accessed August 15, 2011).

Andreas, S. (2006b). *Six Blind Elephants: Understanding Ourselves and Each Other*. Moab, UT: Real People Press.

Bandler, R. (1984). *Magic in Action,* Cupertino, CA: Meta Publications.

Bandler, R. and Grinder, J. (1975a). *The Structure of Magic*. Vol. 1: *A Book about Language and Therapy*. Palo Alto, CA: Science and Behavior Books.

Bandler, R. and Grinder, J. (1975b). *Patterns of the Hypnotic Techniques of Milton H. Erickson, M.D., Vol. 1*. Cupertino, CA: Meta Publications.

Bateson, G. (1979). *Mind and Nature: A Necessary Unity*. New York: Dutton.

Bateson, G. (1991). *Sacred Unity: Further Steps to an Ecology of Mind*. New York: HarperCollins.

Grinder, J. and Elgin, S. H. (1973). *Guide to Transformational Grammar: History, Theory, Practice*. New York: Holt, Rinehart and Winston.

McNorton, D. (2004). *Counselling Fundamentals in the Workplace: A Comprehensive Counselling Methodology*. Kemble, UK: Management Books 2000 Ltd.

McWhirter, J. (1998). Re-modelling NLP, Pt 1: Models and modelling. *Rapport* 43.

McWhirter, J. (1999a). Re-modelling NLP, Pt 2: Re-modelling language. *Rapport* 44.

McWhirter, J. (1999b). Re-modelling NLP, Pt 3: Feeling, conflict and integration. *Rapport* 45.

For more information on DBM applications see my "Re-Modelling NLP" articles from *Rapport* magazine, Parts 4 to 13, and other related material at www.sensorysystems.co.uk. Also Steve Andreas's blog at http://realpeoplepress. com/blog/.

# Part II
# Innovative Applications

From Models emerge patterns. In NLP a "pattern" is any process that enables a person to achieve a particular outcome. As such it is a step-by-step process that offers a procedure for how to do something. This endows patterns with a specificity of focus and purpose as well as a specificity regarding the how-to knowledge that is required to pull it off. For any and every pattern, you will want to know several things:

- **Context:** When and where is this pattern useful and effective? When and where is it not useful?

- **Elicitation question:** What should I ask in order to invite or elicit this pattern? How does it begin?

- **Trouble-shooting:** Where in the pattern could it go off and if that happens, what are my options for handling that?

- **Completing:** How does that pattern end? What is an effective way to bring closure to the process?

While a fully-fledged Model has numerous prerequisites, patterns do not have as many, yet there are some. So what is the criteria of a pattern?

- There is a *step-by-step process*. A pattern will have steps, usually between four and ten and sometimes even more. What are the steps of the pattern that you are working with?

- There are *distinctions* that a person needs to know that make the pattern effective. Every pattern comes from a Model and works because there are one or more distinctions that it incorporates and activates. What are the conceptual distinctions that are inherent in this pattern?

- There are *questions* that drive the pattern. Since patterns are processes that facilitate a client or coachee to experience something, there are typically questions that can be asked that activate or evoke something within the person experiencing the pattern. What are the questions that drive this pattern?

- There is *trouble-shooting information*. The problem with simply asking the questions and leading a person through the step-by-step process is that they may respond in a way not anticipated by the pattern and have to be brought back. Given this, where might this occur in the pattern and what would the person using the pattern (trainer, coach, consultant, etc.) do or say at that point?

- There needs to be an *ecology check* somewhere in the pattern. For the pattern to be ecological—respectful to all of the systems that the person is experiencing— there needs to be a check somewhere in the pattern. Typically this occurs at the end, yet it can occur at the beginning or at various places along the way. Ecology checks could be tests for congruency, value alignment, meaningfulness, fitting-ness, or appropriateness.

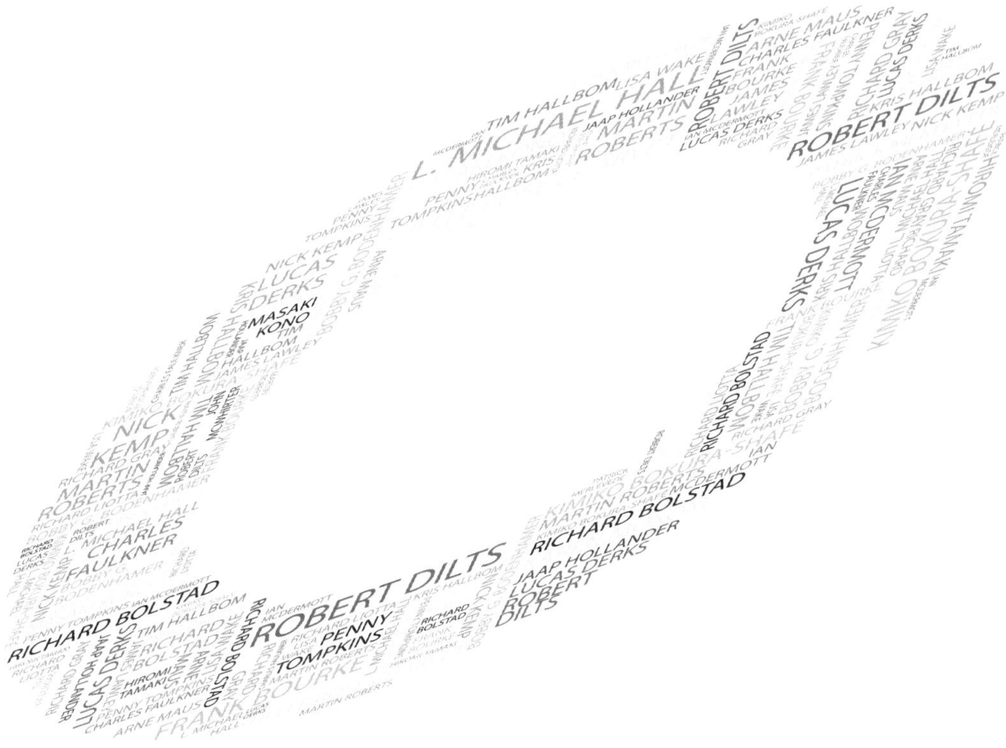

**Ian McDermott**

A thought leader in the field of leadership coaching, the author of fifteen books on NLP, coaching and systems thinking, Ian McDermott has a global perspective from working with international companies such as Shell, BP, GSK, FQML and EY. As a Master Trainer he knows what it takes to run a long-term successful NLP Coaching business having founded International Teaching Seminars (ITS) in 1988.

Ian is both External Faculty at Henley Business School and an Honorary Fellow of Exeter University where his focus is on entrepreneurship and innovation. He is also on the Association for Coaching's Global Advisory Panel.

He continues to work with global teams and individual clients.

web: www.itsnlp.com

# 7 NLP Coaching
## How to Develop a Coaching Mindset

*Ian McDermott*

## Why NLP Coaching?

Innovation frequently happens at the interface between disciplines. NLP coaching is a case in point. Over the last fifteen years I have been at the confluence where NLP practitioners have come to appreciate how coaching as an approach can enhance their way of working, but equally where coaches have come to understand how learning NLP can make them better coaches.

At its best NLP is a demystifying and profoundly democratic approach. By revealing the structure of excellence it can lay bare what previously seemed extraordinary, even unattainable. By generating replicable procedures and ways of working—often in the form of techniques—it can make what has been the province of the few available to many. In this way it has the potential to be a powerful engine of knowledge transfer and cultural liberation.

As with any human endeavor though, the virtue is potentially the vice. The process of modeling has created a trail of dazzlingly effective techniques. Over time these have come to be associated with NLP to the point where for many they *are* NLP. The danger is that practitioners are too eager to default to a technique rather than to engage *this* person, *this* team, *this* organization in *their* model of the world.

In 1974 Tim Gallwey offered a radical re-evaluation of what really worked in coaching with his book, *The Inner Game of Tennis*.[1] As a tennis coach he found that detailed procedural instructions and general exhortations were far less effective than helping clients attend to their own internal mental processes. Essentially he developed ways of working which helped clients get out of their own way. In the process he developed a methodology for promoting a more self-reflexive awareness. Clients could become aware of how they got in their own way and then let go of self-defeating internal and external behaviors.[2]

The demonstrable performance improvements he achieved resulted in many of his clients inviting him into their boardrooms to work with senior personnel. Favorable television exposure soon meant Inner Game coaches were spending more time working in corporations than on the tennis court.

In the years that followed many other key developers made their own distinctive contributions to this new form of coaching. One of the striking things about so many of them is that they were used to focusing and being assessed on results: Thomas Leonard, founder of Coach U, came from a background of financial planning; Laura Whitworth, co-founder of the Coaches Training Institute arrived via accounting; and Fernando Flores, whose work spawned numerous schools of ontological coaching, spent years refining computerized workflow management.

NLP, from its inception, has been a synthesis of what works. Excellence is found in so many different places, people, practices, and disciplines, and coaching is no exception. It seemed to me that:

1. If you put the coaching mode of inquiry together with NLP you could combine a self-reflexive methodology with the most developed practical applications of neuroscience and modeling available.
2. This could deliver a lot for individuals, teams, organizations, and even cultures.

## What is NLP Coaching?

NLP coaching combines neuro-linguistic insight about how experience is structured with coaching self-reflexivity and additional core coaching competencies.

What this actually means is that NLP coaching integrates the study of the structure of subjective experience and excellence with a focused way of engaging with oneself, which produces extraordinary results for both individuals and teams in their lives, careers, businesses, and organizations. Through this process individuals and teams deepen their learning, improve their performance, and enhance the quality of their lives.

NLP coaching is not a single technique but a synthesis of two allied disciplines. Both coaching and NLP are solution focused and committed to demonstrable results, and so are evidence based. Practitioners of both disciplines are used to rapid intervention and short sessions (fifteen minutes to an hour). However, while NLP could be a one-off session or meeting, coaching has often been characterized as regular, consistent, and ongoing.

So what is NLP coaching and what makes it different? Where and how you focus your attention is going to make all the difference. Some NLP practitioners have approached coaching like this: "Give me the skills, help me practice them, and I'll be a coach." But there's more to it than that. Coaching is not just something done *to* others. The best coaching habituates a person—be they coach or coachee—to paying attention to their own experience. It requires you to know how to engage with yourself and so fosters a self-reflexive awareness. Coaching is the Zen of NLP.

At its best NLP coaching operates at the highest logical level of self-awareness while at the same time delivering a practical result at the appropriate level in keeping with the client's needs and wishes. Every single NLP intervention potentially is usable. However, the frame is different. More often than not the coaching focus is on clients learning rather than coaches teaching. Those techniques and interventions will be in the service of client-generated solutions and strategies. Ultimately credit goes to the client not the coach; the magic of NLP is still there but the danger of the narcissistic magician is avoided.

I would say that if you're human, creating a space where you can regularly check in with yourself, refocus on what really matters, and then have that as the focus of action is invaluable. Good coaching does this. Good NLP coaching enables you do this even more effectively because of the additional distinctions it makes available about subjective experience and how to modify it. These can provide a different way of engaging with ourselves.

NLP coaching integrates working with the structure of subjective experience—and all the attendant tools and interventions that have been developed—with a self-reflexive awareness grounded in the presuppositions of coaching. These presuppositions have been variously coded. One widely used coding speaks of these in terms of core competencies. The International Coach Federation (ICF) posits eleven such competencies.[3] Here I have chosen one of the eleven core competencies—establishing the coaching agreement—to highlight how NLP coaching combines and supplements the best of both disciplines.

One might think it is obvious that being clear from the outset about the nature and terms of engagement of one's work with another would be a good idea. However this is by no means the norm in human relations, nor is there a universally agreed way of doing this. People are forever being surprised about what another party understands the arrangement between them to be and what that entails. This applies in both personal and professional life. Such ambiguity throws up all sorts of questions:

- What kind of relationship do we have?
- Who decides and how?
- Can terms be renegotiated?
- If so, when and how?

This is where the concept of the *designed alliance* comes in. Coach and client are in an alliance which they design together. They come as *equals*. If coaching is ongoing, this relationship will evolve over time. Consequently this alliance will need to be reviewed and renegotiated periodically. This fundamental part of the coaching concept is so important that the term is also used as an imperative in the field—design the alliance![4]

This is also a skill and it needs to be learnt and practiced. Designing an alliance with the coach is for most people a unique experience. One of the pay-offs is that clients learn how to actively design other relationships in their lives. Learning how to co-create such a working relationship is an excellent skill-set for any NLP practitioner.

Designing this alliance is part of what will happen in the first coaching session. For many coaches and NLP coaches this may be the longest session they ever have with a client. A number of pre-session tools may be used. I remember my coach emailing me a packet of documents to fill in ahead of time which we then walked through in my first session which lasted ninety minutes. These helped me clarify what I wanted to be my primary focus in the coaching, my values, and the relative balance of different activities in my life at the time. Whether or not there is such preparatory material designing the alliance requires some framing. Here's how I began a session recently:

**Ian:** I want to say a few things about coaching which I think will give you some choices about how to get the most out of our time together. Would that be useful?

**Client:** Yes it would 'cos I've never done this before.

> **Ian:** In coaching, you and I can actually *design* how we're going to work together. It's an alliance really. Instead of me just telling you, we will actually design the way we're going to work together. I work in very different ways with people because *people* are very different. So I'd like to ask you some questions so I can know what would suit you best. OK?
>
> **Client:** Fire away.

What follows is a conversation not a Q&A session. It has the natural ebb and flow you'd expect. The sequence varies considerably but these are the questions I would usually cover:

- When you think about having the chance to check in regularly with yourself what seems most important to you to focus on?

- What would you say are your top ten values?

- How do you imagine getting the most out of these coaching sessions?

- How do you imagine using me as a coach?

- Do you want me to hold you accountable to take action?

- Would it be useful to have assignments between sessions?

- Being able to review and revise is part of a healthy ongoing alliance, so will you undertake to let me know if this seems like a good thing to do at any time?

All these questions presuppose a working relationship that the client can shape. I will also explore length, frequency, and duration of coaching sessions. This is often the first place where I can begin to introduce the client to their own inner sense of what is most appropriate for them. So begins the journey into greater self-reflexive awareness. Here are a couple of samples of how this promotes the process:

> **Ian:** When you think about these coaching sessions going forward I want to get a sense from you about what feels like the right length of time for a session. Let me give you some options and see which feels most comfortable. Also let me know if any of them seem really out of whack. That'll be just as informative. If you imagine the next session being thirty minutes how is that? ... How about two hours? ... An hour?

**Client:** Two hours feels enormous and thirty minutes feels too short.

**Ian:** So would you like to start with an hour and then see how that is?

**Client:** Yes, that feels good.

**Ian:** And if you want we can always adjust as we go along.

The same elicitative approach applies to frequency and number of sessions:

**Ian:** Everyone has their own rhythm. If we set up a weekly time how does that feel? Suppose instead it was once every three months? What's that like?

Again the client is engaged in self-calibration which then drives our working relationship. What becomes clear from the outset is that they actually do have a sense of what will be right for them. This is often a surprise to the person—especially when they had begun by thinking of me as the "expert." The demystification of experience and expertise has begun. With it comes democratization and owning by the client of their own wisdom.

From an NLP point of view of course there will be a wealth of information provided throughout this conversation: if face to face, physiology and accessing cues for instance; if on the phone, breathing, state, tempo, and tonality changes. And, of course, in both cases linguistic markers will provide invaluable insight into how this person's model of the world works.

When supervising NLP coaches I'll often ask them:

- What deletions, generalizations, and distortions do you need to address?
- What is the appropriate chunk size for you to be working with this client at?
- What particular meta-programs need to be taken into account?

The NLP coach will factor in all these considerations to enrich the alliance and both parties' understanding of it. The same could be said for all the core competencies.

NLP coaching counterbalances any tendency on the part of NLP practitioners to default to technique rather than modeling experience. However, coaches can also fall prey to poor practice. The most obvious example is what I call "junko coaching" which is peculiarly content driven. Here clients emerge with task-focused to-do lists (as if most of us don't have enough of these already!). Underlying this can be a mistaken and fearful belief on the part of the coach that if the client does all these things this will demonstrate that the coach is adding value. My experience of teaching NLP to pre-trained coaches is that they leave this kind of performance anxiety behind. It enables them to work at a more profound structural level and frees them from getting hooked on their clients' content.

## How Does It Work?

At the heart of NLP and also NLP coaching is rapport: the ability to establish and maintain rapport with others, which is critical for successful living. Rapport is like charity—it begins at home—so establishing rapport with oneself is one of the most important things to do. Trust is critical to rapport. It's hard to imagine being in rapport with yourself if you can't trust yourself. To a degree trust is contextual. You may, for instance, know that you can do a good job professionally but that doesn't mean you necessarily trust or know yourself in other ways.

Fundamental to effective coaching is the ability to ask good questions because these can have a profound impact when they assist the listener to engage in their own *quest*. NLP coaching enables us to pursue a process of internal investigation that generates questions which can help us build trust in ourselves.

Also consider physical symptoms. Some people do their best to ignore them if they're unpleasant. From an NLP point of view it is more useful to engage with them. To illustrate how this comes into play in NLP coaching, here is a short excerpt from a recent coaching conversation. My client was a senior executive who was considering making a major investment in a new business. When she arrived for her appointment she had a bad headache. She wanted it to go away "so that I can think straight." She'd already taken medication but to no effect. I think she was sufficiently desperate to try something different, so we began.

**Ian:** Where exactly is this headache?

**Client:** Just here (touches the right side of her head and closes her eyes).

**Ian:** Yes, just stay with this and notice what's going on.

**Client:** It's really intense—right here.

**Ian:** So that's where it's most intense. Notice where it's less intense.

**Client:** Oh yeah.

**Ian:** Now notice where the boundaries of this headache are ... What is most striking to you about this headache?

**Client:** That's odd—it's green and throbbing ... and now it's starting to get lighter.

**Ian:** Just continue to give this experience your attention and let me know what's happening.

**Client:** It's not quite as bad.

**Ian:** That's interesting. What do you make of that?

**Client:** I don't know. I've never done this before.

**Ian:** So just continue to allow this experience to be the way it is.

What I made of this was that she was beginning to develop a self-reflexive awareness—she was becoming aware of her experience. She was beginning to find that her experience was potentially malleable and that how she engaged with it could affect it.

**Client:** Wow! I never knew this was possible. The headache really is getting less.

**Ian:** How come, do you think?

**Client:** I don't know but the more I stay with it the better I feel. And I don't feel so tense now.

**Ian:** So let me see if I've got this right, by paying attention to your headache you seem to have changed what was going on. Is that right?

**Client:** Yes, I think it is.

From here it was a natural next step to inquire what the headache might be signaling. This was a new idea for her. Whether to go into a new partnership or not was troubling her. When I asked her to imagine saying yes and to monitor her physical responses the headache became "just terrible." This seemed to be a very clear communication to her *from herself*. She rapidly became clear that she would be saying no. Then the headache abated. A few moments later there was no headache.

So before we were even halfway through the session she'd got the clarity she came for. The speed of this process really impressed her. The business decision was made. This was very useful. But her way of reaching this decision was even more so. She had learned to engage with her experience through paying attention to her body, and she had a new respect for such physical symptoms. Seeing them as feedback was a powerful reframe. She left with a new skill and respect for herself. She experienced being able to engage with herself and it gave her a new confidence. As she left she summed things up by saying, "I've learnt to trust myself in a new way."

She came to explore a business decision. She also came with a bad headache. My job was to enable her to build rapport with herself and I did this through NLP which provided a way of listening to the *entire* client. In this sense it is holistic, dynamic, systemic, *and* provides the tools to facilitate profound change.

Rapport, trust, feedback, and communication—each of these is crucial to our ability to function effectively. It's not necessary to have a blinding headache before you start your own quest. Take your time and feel your way. You might like to explore for yourself using these questions:

- How in rapport with yourself would you say you are?

- Does it vary over time? In different circumstances?

- Do you feel you can trust yourself?

- Are there some contexts where this is more or less true?

- How do you pay attention to yourself?

- What might you learn from paying attention to yourself in a more somatic way?

- What aren't you noticing? Is there anything you're trying not to notice?

- So, what happens when you begin paying attention right now?

Continue to be curious and open rather than presupposing you know the answer because of what's happened before.

# Evolution of the Approach: From NLP Coaching to the NLP Coaching Mindset

## *Phase 1: NLP Coaching*

Developing a comprehensive NLP coach training that is recognized in both the NLP and the coaching world took some time. The result was a twenty-day training course which recently celebrated its tenth anniversary and can reasonably be said to have trained a generation of NLP coaches.[5]

However, it became clear that the majority of people taking the training were not intending to become full-time NLP coaches. Many simply wanted to master NLP coaching as an *approach* so they could learn a more elicitative way of engaging people and their potential—be they colleagues or their own children.

## *Phase 2: NLP Coaching Mindset*

This stimulated my thinking and gave rise to ways of working which I have pioneered in various organizations. I see this as where things are going in the future. Combining NLP precision with a coaching mindset has proved particularly fruitful.

Too often in corporate life people want to give a presentation rather than engage in a real conversation. At the extreme this means "Death by PowerPoint." One multinational organization I worked with had a monthly meeting where all the country heads would fly in and spend a marathon day together subjecting each other to PowerPoint presentations, then complain that there was no time to discuss things.

Clear strategic thinking doesn't just happen. It requires enough time and space to have the conversations which give rise to it. So often creating this time and space where people can actually *think* is the difference which will make all the difference. This is at the heart of the NLP Coaching Mindset. Invariably it involves entering into a conversation with another, or others, or yourself. Out of this comes clarity and perspective and a felt sense of what is appropriate. Instead of getting lost in the drama of the day there is an opportunity to step back and see the bigger picture and then to take action—essential if you're being a team leader or a parent.

One of the challenges of talking about an approach rather than a specific technique is that there aren't necessarily six steps to be outlined. However, it certainly is possible to flag the key elements and the benefits. Below is what I've shared with my corporate clients.

*How to Create an NLP Coaching Mindset*

- Be present.
- Be curious.
- Stop telling, start listening.
- Pay attention in every representational system and at every logical level.
- Help people to attend to their own internal experience and how it is put together.
- Start asking good questions.
- Presuppose they've got the answers.
- Create time and space for a real conversation.

*Benefits of an NLP Coaching Mindset*

- Gives you tools to find out what's really important to others.
- Frees you from the tyranny of thinking your authority resides in you knowing the answer.
- Empowers people.
- Promotes accountability and responsibility.
- Encourages greater self-reliance in subordinates.
- Can move individual and team thinking from short-term fixes to long-term generative solutions.
- Promotes curiosity and a useful questioning culture.
- Develops people's questioning and thinking skills.
- Stimulates more seeking out of what's important to clients.
- Unleashes the power of incremental change.

## Caveats

NLP is a good servant but a bad master. It needs to be in service of something bigger than itself. The same is true of NLP coaching. I think there are three questions for any practitioner to consider. Would-be clients may want to ask these of practitioners too.

1. *Why are you doing this and where are you coming from?*
   There is a sacred trust between practitioners and their clients which is essential for the best work to be done. What is your mission and how is NLP coaching helping you achieve it? Are you utilizing NLP coaching in service of your client?

2. *Have you actually mastered the approach?*
   Many people jump on the coaching bandwagon and appropriate the "coach" label with little understanding of the elicitative co-creative approach at the heart of coaching. Some NLP practitioners and schools have simply taken the view that as coaching is now the flavor of the month, it's a smart move to co-opt the label and incorporate it into what they claim to be offering. Here "NLP coaching" is really just a marketing ploy. So it's useful to inquire about a person's training and what standing it has.

3. *Are you using the product yourself?*
   If you're not using NLP coaching yourself why would I want what you don't use?

## How Did You Create the Model?

I remember in the mid-1990s being astonished when I realized that the worlds of NLP and coaching had grown up in the same part of the world (California) during the same time frame (mid-1970s), shared assumptions about the importance of effective elicitation and practical procedures for promoting desired change, yet were largely unknown to each other. It seemed to me that each could benefit from what the other had to offer. That's the short version of how I came to be dubbed "the man who brought NLP and coaching together."

Then there was the challenge my students regularly presented to me. Often they would quiz me on what else it was I was doing when I was working with people beyond the NLP techniques I was demonstrating. The truth is that I bring everything I know to bear when I am working with people, but the most important thing I bring is a trust in the person I am working with and the process that is unfolding. This is an existential state of being really where I do not know what is going to happen but I know that I will be sufficient to engage with it.

For me coaching became a way of giving my students a learnable experience of this—and in a format that could provide them with a recognizable skill qualification. The challenge then was to format this being present, self-reflexive approach into a teaching program which could integrate the core elements of coaching with NLP. Together Jan Elfline and I fashioned a program which benchmarked against the eleven core coaching competencies and gave NLP practitioners a way of integrating these into their way of working.

I wanted to subject this synthesis to the scrutiny of a credible coaching credentialing body so we went with the International Coach Federation. This proved to be an exhaustive and indeed exhausting process. But in this way I felt we had truly bridged two disciplines.

One final piece was essential to the development of NLP coaching and that was my own work with a bona fide coach. It seemed obvious to me that I would need to have this experience to know coaching from the inside out. For three years I worked with Laura Whitworth, starting as a client, then becoming a colleague and exchanging coaching sessions with her until her untimely death.

Bringing two different fields together and fostering mutual appreciation is an ongoing commitment. It requires collaboration which has been very patchy in NLP. This is a shame because collaboration is frequently the engine of innovation. Developing an approach is one thing; ensuring it takes root and flourishes is quite another. This fact has caused me to commit to a number of initiatives. I'll finish by signposting two.

In recent years I have been working with Henley Business School which is part of the University of Reading. Our first venture has been to create a masters degree in coaching which is academically rigorous but avoids the dangers of dissociated academic learning. All alumni are required to take the International Teaching Seminars NLP Practitioner training as part of their first year on the course. The full title of the program makes clear why: it is an MSc in *Coaching and Behavioural Change*. The NLP gives them the tools to deliver on behavioral change and has been very positively received. So NLP and coaching become intertwined in the thinking and experience of an important section of the business community. Is it "pure" NLP coaching? To me this is the wrong question. Innovation frequently generates hybrids—and that's good.

Over the past fifteen years I have made a point of talking to the NLP world about coaching and to the coaching world about NLP. I have done this partly by speaking at both groups' conferences but also by writing three books on the subject, starting with *The NLP Coach*. These I have deliberately co-authored, again partly to model collaboration. Having contributed the chapter "NLP Coaching" to the Association for Coaching's industry guide *Excellence in Coaching* (2006), I feel as though I have now completed the circle by contributing this chapter to *Innovations in NLP*.

## Notes

1. Gallwey (1974).

2. Having stood on a tennis court with Tim and experienced him redirect my attention away from trying to improve my strokes, the thing I always remember is not the consequent improvement in my tennis (though that occurred) but the heightened sensory experience. One example was the extraordinary blueness of the sky for me on that day in that moment. I saw the sky in a way I had never seen it before which I shall never forget.

3. The eleven core coaching competencies are:

   **A. Setting the foundation**
   1. Meeting ethical guidelines and professional standards
   2. Establishing the coaching agreement

   **B. Co-creating the relationship**
   3. Establishing trust and intimacy with the client
   4. Coaching presence

   **C. Communicating effectively**
   5. Active listening
   6. Powerful questioning
   7. Direct communication

   **D. Facilitating learning and results**
   8. Creating awareness
   9. Designing actions
   10. Planning and goalsetting
   11. Managing progress and accountability

   Each competency is extensively annotated on the ICF website: www.coachfederation. org/icfcredentials/core-competencies/.

4.  Nor is it the only one. In the NLP coaching program we have twenty key coaching concepts. Each involves attendant skills to be mastered.

5.  The International Teaching Seminars (ITS) NLP Coaching Certification Program.

## References

Gallwey, W. T. (1974). *The Inner Game of Tennis* (1st edn). New York: Random House.

McDermott, I. (2006). NLP coaching. In J. Passmore (ed.), *Excellence in Coaching: The Industry Guide*. London: Kogan Page, pp. 106–118.

McDermott, I. and Jago, W. (2001). *The NLP Coach*. London: Piatkus.

McDermott, I. and Jago, W. (2003). *Your Inner Coach*. London: Piatkus.

McDermott, I. and Jago, W. (2005). *The Coaching Bible*. London: Piatkus.

O'Connor, J. and McDermott, I. (1996). *Principles of NLP*. London: Thorsons. (Reissued as *Way of NLP*, 2001.)

O'Connor, J. and McDermott, I. (1997). *The Art of Systems Thinking*. London: Thorsons.

 **Robert Dilts** has a global reputation as a leading developer, author, coach, trainer and consultant in the field of Neuro-Linguistic Programing (NLP). Robert worked closely with NLP co-founders John Grinder and Richard Bandler at the time of its creation and also studied personally with Milton H. Erickson, M.D., and Gregory Bateson. Robert pioneered the applications of NLP to education, creativity, health, leadership, belief systems and the development of what has become known as "Third Generation NLP."

Robert is the principal author of *Neuro-Linguistic Programming Vol. I,* which serves as the standard reference text for the field, and has authored or co-authored numerous other books on NLP including *Changing Belief Systems with NLP, Beliefs: Pathways to Health and Well-Being, Tools of the Spirit, From Coach to Awakener* and *NLP II: The Next Generation.*

Robert's recent book *The Hero's Journey: A Voyage of Self Discovery* (with Stephen Gilligan) is about how to embark on the path of learning and transformation that will reconnect you with your deepest calling, transform limiting beliefs and habits, heal emotional wounds and physical symptoms, deepen intimacy, and improve self-image.

# 8 Success Factor Modeling™
## The Secrets of Entrepreneurial Leadership

*Robert Dilts*

## Why This Model?

While earlier generations of NLP grew out of a focus on psychotherapy and personal development, more and more NLP practitioners today are working in the areas of business and organizations as consultants, coaches, and trainers. A vast number of NLP practitioners are also entrepreneurs, working to start up or grow their own businesses or coaching and training practices. These developments require NLP practitioners to increasingly integrate personal development with supporting effective communication, leadership development, team building, and other aspects of organizational change management.

Social, industrial, and economic developments in recent years have brought about both revolution and crisis in the world and the way people and businesses must operate. Accelerating changes in technology and the explosion in the use of the Internet have led to the establishment of an evolving economy, characterized by e-commerce, virtual teams, and a global marketplace. Technological progress is continually "pushing the edge of the envelope," creating both opportunities and challenges for new ventures and forcing traditional companies to adapt.

Recurring economic fluctuations have created additional challenges for businesses attempting to cope with change, requiring them to accomplish more with fewer resources. Companies are relying more and more on strategic alliances and outsourcing to conduct key aspects of their business. As a result, the boundaries between synergistic companies have become more flexible, leading to the notion of the "extended organization." This has led to an increased emphasis on relationship building and alliances; which calls for the ability to create effective win-win partnerships.

Such rapid technical, social, and economic changes have placed an increased demand on individuals and companies to respond quickly and innovatively in order to keep pace with fresh developments, manage resources more efficiently, and stay ahead of competition. If individuals and companies try to operate in the same ways that were successful twenty years ago, they will not be successful today. This raises key questions, such as "How do we keep up in a rapidly changing world?" and "How do we find the formulas for success in today's evolving economy?"

People and organizations must learn to embrace diversity and foster innovation in order to survive and succeed in the rapidly changing global economy. It is in response to the needs imposed by an increasingly complex and rapidly changing environment that Success Factor Modeling was developed.

## What is Success Factor Modeling?

Success Factor Modeling (SFM) is a modeling process developed by myself and my late brother John Dilts, as a method to identify and transfer the critical success factors necessary to promote the growth and impact of individuals, teams, and organizations, and to help them be maximally prepared to create, recognize, and take advantage of opportunities when they arise.

Success Factor Modeling asks the question, "What is the difference that makes the difference between successful individuals, teams, and organizations, and those that fail or only reach an average level of performance?"

Success Factor Modeling is founded upon a set of principles, procedures, and distinctions which are uniquely suited to analyze and identify crucial patterns of *business practices* and *behavioral skills* to identify the critical success factors employed by successful entrepreneurs, teams, and business leaders, and then to define specific models, tools, and skills that can be used by others to greatly increase their chances of producing impact and achieving success.

One of the strengths of the SFM process is its integration of effective business practices with important behavioral skills. Benoit Sarazin, author and consultant on Breakthrough Innovation and former marketing manager for the Communications Solutions Services Division at Agilent Technologies, points out: "Many methodologies exist to help people with effective business practices. If you go to a library or bookstore, you can find all types of resources for making business plans, forming marketing strategies, protecting intellectual property, etc. But there are no methodologies for the behavioral skills. This is what makes Success Factor Modeling totally unique."

Success Factor Modeling takes into account multiple levels of behavioral factors related to success:

- **Environmental factors** determine the external opportunities or constraints to which start-ups must recognize and react. They involve considering *where* and *when* success occurs.

- **Behavioral factors** are the specific action steps taken in order to reach success. They involve *what*, specifically, must be done or accomplished in order to succeed.

- **Capabilities** relate to the mental maps, plans, or strategies that lead to success. They direct *how* actions are selected and monitored.

- **Beliefs and values** provide the reinforcement that supports or inhibits particular capabilities and actions. They relate to *why* a particular path is taken and the deeper motivations which drive people to act or persevere.

- **Identity factors** relate to people's sense of their role or mission. These factors are a function of *who* a person or group perceives themselves to be.

- **Vision and purpose** relate to people's view of the larger system of which they are a part. These factors involve for whom or for what a particular action step or path has been taken (the purpose). In a business, this usually relates to the customers, the shareholders, and the team.

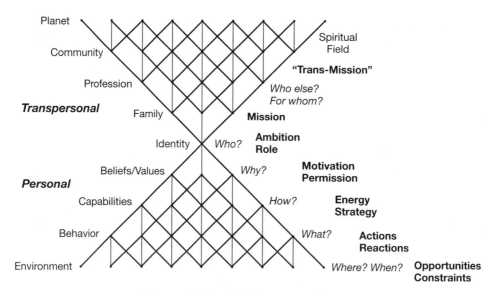

**Figure 1:** *Levels of key success factors*

## How Does SFM work? Critical Success Factors Questionnaire

Before continuing, take a few moments and explore the significance of each of these factors for yourself. Identify a project or initiative that you were personally involved with that has already been successfully achieved. To bring the critical success factors out more clearly, it is useful to have a contrast. In this regard it can be useful to identify a project or initiative that you were personally involved with that was not so successful or maybe even failed. What were some of the differences that made a difference?

Model some of the critical success factors by considering the following SFM questions:

1.  What role did *vision* play in reaching success?

    How important to the success was having and communicating a vision?

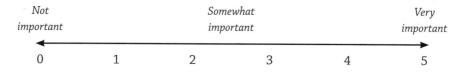

    What was the vision?

2. What *identity* factors were involved in the successful project?

How important to your success was having and communicating a clear sense of brand or identity?

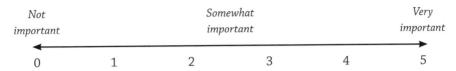

*Not*
*important*

*Somewhat*
*important*

*Very*
*important*

0          1          2          3          4          5

How would you describe your identity and mission? What would be a good symbol or metaphor for your identity and mission?

3. What *values and beliefs* supported achieving the success?

a) How important to your success was having and communicating core values?

*Not*
*important*

*Somewhat*
*important*

*Very*
*important*

0          1          2          3          4          5

What were those values?

b) How important to your success was believing in what you were doing?

*Not*
*important*

*Somewhat*
*important*

*Very*
*important*

0          1          2          3          4          5

What beliefs supported or motivated people to follow through and succeed?

4. What competencies and *capabilities* contributed to the success?

How important to your success was having specific skills and capabilities?

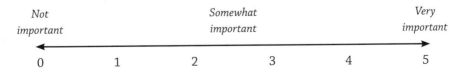

*Not*
*important*

*Somewhat*
*important*

*Very*
*important*

0          1          2          3          4          5

Which skills and capabilities were most significant?

5. What specific *behavioral* steps and actions were most responsible for the success?

How important to your success was having a specific behavioral plan?

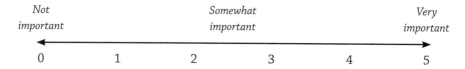

Which actions were most important? Where was it important to be flexible in your plan?

6. What *environmental* opportunities and influences were part of the success?

How important to your success was reacting to the environment (opportunities and constraints)?

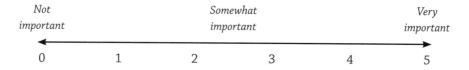

Which environmental factors were most significant?

7. Review what you learned from making this reflection:

Which level(s) of factors seemed most critical for the success of your project or initiative?

Were there any combinations of factors that seemed particularly important?

How can you use what you've learned in order to be more likely to succeed in future projects and initiatives?

Over the past decade and a half, my brother John and I explored these critical success factor questions with countless leaders and entrepreneurs. We have built an entire coaching and consulting practice from the results that we have discovered. The critical success factors we have discovered are far too numerous to cover here and are the subject of a forthcoming book on Success Factor Modeling. For this chapter I will focus on a few of the most significant factors.

## Creative Vision

While all of the levels of success factors are important, we have discovered that vision is one of the most significant; specifically, a *vision* that our lives or our world could be enriched or improved in some way. Such visions of the future often provide guidance and direction for our lives and our work, furnishing the motivation and impetus for change on many levels.

Vision, in this sense, has to do with the ability to imagine longer-term possibilities, at different levels of activity and experience. The most powerful visions stem from the sense of being a part of something bigger than oneself. They relate to our sense of purpose, mission, and calling. Such visions relate to the questions *for whom* and *for what* do we exist and act in the world? A person may have a vision for himself or herself, for his or her family, organization, community, planet, or universe.

This type of vision is different to a specific image, picture, or objective. A vision captures an overall sense of direction rather than a particular objective. It is a reflection of our deepest motivation and values. It involves the ability to see beyond the confines of the here-and-now and imagine future scenarios. It also involves the capacity to set and stay focused on longer-term goals and clearly define one's ambitions, adopting long-term plans and a holistic view.

In the words of Silicon Valley entrepreneur Steve Artim (CEO of DoOnGo.com):

> I believe vision is absolutely critical to a young start-up. You have to take a stake and drive it into the ground in the future, and do everything in your power as a leader of a company to drive your engineers, your sales and marketing people, and your financial people to go make that happen. Without that there is no differentiation between you and other large companies that can go out and do the same thing—and frankly they probably can—but you are wholly focused as a team and as an entity on going out and making it happen.

Artim's comments on the importance of vision are echoed in the words of Apple CEO and founder Steve Jobs who says, "It's like when I walk into a room and I want to talk about a product that hasn't been invented yet. I can see the product as if it's sitting there right in the center of the table. It's like what I've got to do is materialize it and bring it to life." According to Jobs, a key success factor for entrepreneurs is their ability to clearly communicate their vision and get others to be as excited about it as they are. He points out: "Innovation has nothing to do with how many R&D dollars you have. When Apple came up with the Mac, IBM was spending at least 100 times more on R&D. It's not about money. It's about the people you have, how you're led, and how much you get it."

Steve Jobs's comments and Steve Artim's description of a stake in the ground in the future imply that there is a clear quality of focus in entrepreneurial vision. Their observations indicate that the entrepreneur's vision of the future becomes the focal point for all of the activity of the entrepreneur and his or her team. As Steve Artim explains:

> For a start-up it takes a lot of partnerships to move yourself forward. It takes a lot of ability to get in there and solve a couple of problems very, very well for your lead customer. And picking your customer is critical for driving your company forward into the mainstream.

In addition to forward focus, there is also a lateral dimension of entrepreneurial vision; a type of *peripheral vision* that operates like a radar sensor to pick up ongoing influences in the current environment. As Steve Artim describes it:

> You have to be completely customer focused. You have to be outward facing at all times. You have to completely understand everything that is happening. There are large players in the market that are moving things, but there are also a lot of small players that are below the radar screen, that are just coming up on the radar screen. You have to understand what they're doing, how they are funded, and what their strategic backgrounds are to really understand and to make the right fit for your company.

Both of these dimensions of vision—distance vision and peripheral vision—are necessary for entrepreneurs to effectively manage uncertainty and change and stay on a successful course of action.

Another dimension of vision has to do with where it is focused. The visions of successful entrepreneurs frequently arise as a result of having first developed a strong understanding of customer needs through what we call "second position" with potential customers (the ability to put yourself into their shoes and understand their felt and latent needs). Successful entrepreneur Mark Fitzpatrick (founder of Tidalwave Technologies) claims:

> Our vision was centered on what our customer needs were, and we knew there was a need for a certain product. We then applied our vision to that need, and we used a lot of customer feedback to constantly adjust the vision, because we knew that without a captive audience, the product would be worthless and we would be wasting our time.
>
> I am sure that there are people brilliant enough to see beyond what the customer thinks that they need, but we certainly weren't that. We felt that working with the customer we could come up the best possible solution for them. They had problems today that they needed solved today, and we weren't really looking beyond today. We saw a need, the customer had a need, and we were just going to do our best job to fill that.

Typically, strong technology alone will not make a company successful for the long term. The development of a solid understanding of the future challenges facing a start-up will more likely determine the success of a new company. Thus, multiple forms of vision are essential in order to be able to navigate to accommodate a global marketplace, satisfy customer needs, foresee changes and make adjustments, and to anticipate competition.

In summary:

- The vision sets the course to be followed in the long term. What you are aiming at, in the longer term, for yourself and your customers or stakeholders?

- The vision involves solving challenges that turn into competitive advantages.

- The vision defines clearly the end goal but inspires creativity as to how to reach it.

- The vision generates an inconsistency between current resources and future ambitions.

- The vision brings the future into the present.

## Forming a Vision

Many entrepreneurs have begun their quest to create a new product or service because they see a problem that they want to solve or they dream of a better way of doing something. This is sort of a *calling* to create something new and different. Their success at fulfilling this calling will consume them mentally, physically, emotionally, and financially. The calling becomes a very personal endeavor that is extremely close to the core of their identity. It is what drives them far beyond what they ever dreamed possible and causes them to grow their confidence and their skills to new heights.

An example is Steig Westerberg, who was the CEO of Stream Theory, a California-based software company that enables software to be streamed for real-time use over broadband networks. Westerberg developed the idea for this product while working as a computer consultant for a law firm. A large part of his job was to make sure that all of the computers in the law firm had current software loaded on their hard drives.

Westerberg began to dream that there had to be a better way of distributing current software titles to the computers in large organizations. He began to create his plan for streaming software over the Internet from a central server where only the software on the server would need to be updated. The software would then be streamed to individual computers throughout an organization.

Westerberg's calling was to solve a problem he faced in his everyday tasks. He began to pursue his dream of streaming software and widened the scope of his technology to include streaming any kind of software over any broadband network to any computer anywhere in the world. In the process of pursuing his dream, he would sell his house to finance his company, he would reach the brink of bankruptcy, and he would face employee revolts over not being paid. But Westerberg persisted and stayed true to his dream. He ultimately struck a US$10 million deal with Japan's Softbank, the most advanced broadband network in the world. The technology now enables software to be streamed to millions of people, and it all started with Westerberg's personal commitment to his vision.

Not all entrepreneurs have a happy ending in creating a new product or service for a variety of reasons. One common reason is that they are not personally aligned with their vision. This brings up the issue of truth and passion for what you do. There is a common saying that you should strive to make your hobby or passion your profession. This saying easily describes what should be the goal of every entrepreneur: to find what it is that you care deeply about and for which you have talent and pursue it with all of your heart.

A major success factor among effective entrepreneurs is that they have a very solid understanding of who they are and what they want in creating a new company and the product or service it provides. Asserting the combination of passion and truth can have explosive results and serves as the genesis for the long-term success of most thriving companies.

An entrepreneur's passion can be highly infectious. The reason for this is that the entrepreneur's primary activity is to inspire others to join him or her in pursuing the vision. It is a unique gift that the successful entrepreneur has acquired and mastered. It involves opening up his or her heart to share this passion, then backing up the vision and plan for going forward with the rationale behind the firm belief inside the entrepreneur that his or her vision is possible.

As a result of our Success Factor Modeling work, John Dilts established Maverick Angels in 2006. Maverick Angels is a special angel investor network that brings together visionary entrepreneurs with great ideas and early stage investors. Entrepreneurs, who are carefully screened and coached, present their vision and plan for their business to a group of qualified investors. Time and time again, we have seen the power and importance of the entrepreneur's ability to communicate his or her vision in a way that encourages others to be as inspired and excited about it as the entrepreneur. Investors rarely choose to invest in an idea, product, or plan alone. They invest in the entrepreneur and his or her vision, ambition, passion, and commitment to make things happen.

The more closely aligned your personal truth and passion for your vision, the more likely you are to persevere, continue to innovate, improvise, and stare down failure against all the odds.

Another critical success factor involves giving yourself permission; permission to take a risk, permission to succeed, and permission to fail.

Once you have made the personal commitment to pursue your truth in a passionate manner, there is still the challenge of what that will mean to you and those around you who rely on your ability to provide for them. More than any other challenge facing an entrepreneur, the obstacles involved in obtaining permission from yourself, from your spouse or family, is the most formidable.

At the end of the day, a solid and grounded understanding of one's self, knowledge of one's core identity and personal mission, coupled with a passionate desire to transform one's vision into reality is the most important success factor.

In the words of Apple co-founder and CEO Steve Jobs:

> Your time is limited, so don't waste it living someone else's life. Don't be trapped by dogma—which is living with the results of other people's thinking. Don't let the noise of others' opinions drown out your own inner voice. And most important, have the courage to follow your heart and intuition. They somehow already know what you truly want to become. Everything else is secondary ...

> You've got to find what you love ...The only way to be truly satisfied is to do what you believe is great work. And the only way to do great work is to love what you do. If you haven't found it yet, keep looking. Don't settle. As with all matters of the heart, you'll know when you find it. And, like any great relationship, it just gets better and better as the years roll on. So keep looking until you find it.

## Visioneering Exercise

The creative vision of successful leaders and entrepreneurs has to do with the ability to imagine and project themselves into longer-term possibilities. The following exercise is an example of what we call *visioneering* that we use in our coaching sessions with leaders and entrepreneurs. It is intended to be a practice; something that you do on a continuous basis.

1. First, put yourself into a relaxed state. Sit comfortably and check that your breathing is regular and from the stomach. (Short, rapid breathing from the

chest would indicate that you are in a stressed mode.) Put your attention into the soles of your feet. Then begin to be aware of your body, starting with your feet and moving up through your legs, pelvis, and hips. Become aware of your belly center and say to yourself, "I am here." Continuing to stay aware of your lower body, move your awareness up through your spine and chest. Focus on your heart center and say to yourself, "I am open." Then expand your attention to move up through your shoulders, arms and hands, and up through your neck, face, and skull. Bring your awareness to the center in your head, behind your eyes, and say to yourself, "I am awake, alert and clear."

2. Raise your head and look into an imaginary horizon. Begin to picture your ideal day in the future. Turn it into a world to which you and others would wish to belong. As an individual, you should be working to visualize something you're passionate about (your ambition), but that also projects itself and serves a bigger purpose beyond just yourself.

3. Imagine a film of the future and where the vision will take you. Start acting in that film of what the ideal day would look like and feel the objectives becoming a vision. What can you see, hear, and feel? What are you doing? How are you acting? The vision has to become alive and real in you, not only as if you were watching it from the outside but living it from the inside.

## More Of/Less Of

A useful tool for helping explore your vision is the "more of/less of" chart. This chart asks you to describe the future condition, listing what you expect to see *more of* and *less of* in your future environment as compared to the current reality. You will want to describe the future condition in behavioral terms.

1. Begin by reflecting upon the future environment, taking into consideration both potential opportunities and constraints.

2. With this snapshot of the future in mind, list what you expect to see more of and what you expect to see less of in the future environment. In some cases, the two aspects may be correlated ("more time for creative exploration" and "less time spent on busy work"). In other cases, you can simply complete one side of the chart first and the other side of the chart later.

```
Vision _____

                    BEHAVIORS

        MORE OF                        LESS OF

     _____              _____

     _____              _____

     _____              _____

     _____              _____
```

Another way to use this chart consists in identifying "what will change" and "what will not change." In this case, you describe the future as a combination of "old patterns" and "new patterns," attempting to clarify the true nature of the change. For example, one could put that the "number of hours worked" will change to become fewer, but the "quality of result" will not alter. Another example might be that the "working tools and environment" will change, but the "individuals in the team" will not change.

## Moving From Vision to Action

Successful leaders and entrepreneurs must have the behavioral skills to define and express a clear vision, identify the people and the path through which that vision can be put into action, and constantly seek and respond to feedback. These multiple roles of an entrepreneur are probably best reflected in the comment made about Walt Disney (a quintessential entrepreneur in his own right) by one of his co-workers, that "there were actually three different Walts: the dreamer, the realist, and the spoiler." Reaching success involves the coordination of these three perspectives: dreamer, realist, and critic. The dreamer is necessary to form new ideas and goals. The realist is necessary to transform ideas into concrete expressions. The critic is necessary as a filter and as a stimulus for refinement.

According to David Guo, former CEO of Display Research Laboratories and an avowed "serial entrepreneur," "A successful entrepreneur needs to be able to communicate his or her vision and ideas, and to understand people and their motivation."

Guo goes on to add, "An entrepreneur has to be an eternal optimist, but also a pragmatist. The optimist says, 'I can always do this,' but the pragmatist says, 'If I don't do this by a certain time, I'll miss the window, so I'd better move on.'" The entrepreneur must also heed the critic, and welcome feedback. Respecting the critic also means to "learn from the mistakes of others, not just yourself."

Most people have strengths in one area: dreamer, realist, or critic. The tools and methods of Success Factor Modeling can be applied to develop all three abilities and ensure they are used in a balanced way, and to incorporate all of the perspectives relevant to success as an entrepreneur.

While it is not possible to guarantee success in any entrepreneurial endeavor, there are critical success factors that can ensure that entrepreneurs will be prepared to take the best advantage of the opportunities that arise for them. The Success Factor Modeling process provides a significant edge for people and companies to reach their highest potential.

## Mapping Your Path from Vision to Action

As a concluding exercise take a moment and consolidate what you have learned in this chapter by answering the following questions that take you through the various levels of success factors for bringing your vision into action.

1. What is your vision? How are you "pushing the edge of the envelope"?

    What will your project allow people to do?

    more of _____

    more quickly _____

    better _____

    more economically _____

2. What is your mission?

    Who else and what else will benefit from your success?

    Clients/customers will benefit because _____

Investors/contributors will benefit because _____

Partners will benefit because _____

Team members will benefit because _____

What is a good metaphor for your mission?

3. What are the key values represented by your vision and mission?

4. What beliefs drive the vision and mission?

5. What core competencies (i.e., dreamer, realist, critic) do you need to improve to reach your vision and mission?

6. What are your next concrete steps and when will you take them?

## Conclusion: Cultivating "Luck"

It has been said that, "Luck is the meeting of preparation and opportunity." Thomas Jefferson, for instance, claimed that he had been "a very lucky man"; but also noted how remarkable it was that the harder he worked, the "luckier" he got. The implication of Jefferson's comment is that you cannot make yourself be lucky but you can put yourself in positions where you are more likely to find opportunities. New pathways open up when you stay in action. Opportunities arise when you are in communication with other people. Many entrepreneurs relate how one day they'll have a terrible meeting and feel like giving up. The next day they'll run into someone on the street who knows someone else who is exactly the person they needed in order to make all of their plans come together.

As Mark Fitzpatrick points out, "You cannot make things follow a certain path, but if you stay active, you can do things to increase your chances of success. Your vision focuses you to be aware of opportunities and not filter them out. To succeed, you've got to take steps to improve yourself and keep looking for opportunities."

In the words of Steig Westerberg:

> The dream is something that can never die. The dream quite literally is part of me. It is something that I think about all the time. It is something that permeates everything that I do.

On the other hand, the realist aspect comes in equally strongly. You end up with a multiple personality. It's weird. So by having the realist, and also the critic, you are sitting there analyzing what you are doing—you're analyzing the directions that the company is taking at all times—realizing perhaps that even as you start to execute, you can see that that's not the appropriate one, based on other things that can happen in the marketplace and the forces that come in and interact with the company. And then what do you do? You make a change and you keep on going as rapidly as you can.

So all three (dreamer, realist, and critic) play equally important roles. However, if you lose the overall dream and you allow the everyday realities and the problems that you face to become too overwhelming or too strong, then you are in trouble.

## References

Calonius, E. (2011). *Ten Steps Ahead: What Separates Business Visionaries From the Rest of Us*. Portfolio Penguin.

Deering, A., Dilts, R., and Russell, J. (2002). *Alpha Leadership: Tools for Leaders Who Want More from Life*. London: John Wiley.

Dilts, R. (1993). *Skills for the Future*. Capitola, CA: Meta Publications.

Dilts, R. (1996). *Visionary Leadership Skills*. Capitola, CA: Meta Publications.

Dilts, R. (1998). *Modeling with NLP*. Capitola, CA: Meta Publications.

Dilts, R. (2003). *From Coach to Awakener*. Capitola, CA: Meta Publications.

Dilts, R. and DeLozier, J. (2000). *Encyclopedia of Systemic Neuro-Linguistic Programming and NLP New Coding*. Santa Cruz, CA: NLP University Press.

Dilts, R. B., Epstein, T., and Dilts, R. W. (1991). *Tools for Dreamers*. Capitola, CA: Meta Publications.

Jobs, S. (1998). *Fortune*, November 9.

Jobs, S (2005). Stanford University commencement address.

 **Nick Kemp** has been involved in the field of personal change for thirty years, having studied many forms of communication and personal development, including Hypnosis, Provocative Therapy and NLP, before creating his own Provocative Change Works™ approach that he uses in his private practice. In 2004 Nick Kemp met Frank Farrelly, (creator of Provocative Therapy and influence on the creators of NLP) and began an intensive training with him to become an approved Provocative Therapy Trainer. Nick and Frank have become firm friends, co-presenting at the UK PT events as well as spending far too many hours watching classic movies at Nick's home cinema in Leeds West Yorkshire.

Nick set up The Association for Provocative Therapy (or AFPT) and released the "Provocative Change Works for Phobias" which was the first of a number of DVD sets with commentary from Frank Farrelly himself. In 2006 Nick Kemp was a guest for twenty-six consecutive weeks on BBC Radio working with clients live on the air.

For Nick Kemp's official site see: www.nickkemp.com
For Nick Kemp's trainings see: www.nickkemptraining.com
email: info@nickkemp.com

# 9 Provocative Change Works™
## Improvisation and Humor in Therapy and Coaching

*Nick Kemp*

Bill Cosby once commented:

> Through humor, you can soften some of the worst blows that life delivers. And once you find laughter, no matter how painful your situation might be, you can survive it.

Throughout some of the most turbulent times in history, humor has been invaluable in ensuring that people do not become too full of their own self-importance. The court jester could speak to the king of things others would be beheaded for, and in so doing assist the king in his decision-making. Satire and humor in plays, poems, writings, and, in modern times, various forms of media, allow the ordinary man or woman to make sense of the conflicts of life.

Humor is central to the Provocative Change Works (PCW) process, which is an accelerated approach used to help individuals and groups move from "problem states" to greater freedom, choice, and opportunity.

## Why This Model?

I created Provocative Change Works because of my interest in producing effective, useful, accelerated change for clients. This is achieved by working in a conversational manner, so the client can immediately relate to it and does not need any special training simply in order to attend. This process was inspired by my extensive contact and training with Frank Farrelly, the creator of Provocative Therapy, and from my three decades of exploring numerous forms of personal development including the work of Milton Erickson.

By working in this conversational, improvised, and spontaneous way, without the need for jargon terms and extensive analysis (both of which in my view impede good client results), it is possible for the client and therapist to work together. The client then benefits from having an "honest person" with whom to discuss matters, who accepts the issue, no matter how much it is perceived by the client as, for example, problematic, shocking, sad, revolting, or difficult, and together new insights can be made.

In NLP there is a great deal of discussion about the need for creating rapport in communication. Sometimes it is suggested that this means both parties need to be in agreement for this to occur, but the reality is that in PCW discussions both parties can be wholly engaged in the conversation, and in rapport, while at the same time maintaining wholly different views!

Many of the insights that produced this approach came from spending over twenty-six consecutive weeks on BBC Radio live on the air solving client phobias. In each instance I had an hour to produce substantial and measurable change before revealing the outcome of each session to 50,000 listeners. Each week the BBC would advertise for members of the public wanting help to phone in to request help. I would conduct a brief telephone interview with prospective candidates and then the producer and I would select a member of the public for each show. I would first meet each client at the radio station, when we would appear live on air during which the client would describe how the phobia had affected them to date. I would then work with the client off air and an hour later we would return to feed back the results to the live audience.

In most instances we would be able to test the change in client response in the studio, for example with spider, snake, or balloon phobias. In the case of bird phobias and other problems that couldn't be tested in the studio, we would find a place outside to record the results to then present on air. One of the most talked about client sessions was with Mary Craven who'd had a phobia of birds for over fifty years and which was solved in a very short period of time. This news generated a host of other members of the public all seeking help with this exact same issue!

The key benefits of PCW are the immense flexibility in being able to deal with such a wide range of client conditions and the ability for a practitioner to work in a very time effective manner. The practitioner uses a number of techniques, but crucially does not rely solely upon them for client change. This more improvised approach means that the practitioner can adopt a huge range of different stances to assist the client. These stances are designed to deliberately provoke responses from the client to create new ways of thinking and feeling. This is done "as if talking to an old friend" with great warmth and humor. These stances include interrupting the client, blaming the client, blaming everything else for the problem, and insisting the client makes a choice between two presented options amongst other stances.

## What Is Provocative Change Works?

PCW combines three key elements that are used to shift clients from "a stuck state" to a more fluid state, allowing greater freedom and choice:

1.  Provoking or stimulating client responses by verbal and non-verbal interactions.

2.  Using non-specific or indirect hypnosis and metaphor explorations—to create "fluid states" for the client.

3.  Time framing—promoting new ways of moving through time and space.

The practitioner deliberately provokes (calls forth responses from) the client by adopting different discrete stances, which stimulate the client into new ways of thinking and feeling. The practitioner seeks resistances in the client and approaches most what the client seeks to avoid in the discussion, identifying the client's "blind spots" and improvising with a great deal of humor. This means "running suggestions up the flagpole" and seeing if the client responds. The practitioner creates the momentum for the session and can be talking for large sections of the interaction which is very different to many other talk therapy approaches. Flowing both after and sometimes through this element of the session, hypnotic and practical exercises are used to enable the client to integrate insights made and discover new strategies, and responses for the future. I have included an example of incorporating this hypnotic aspect in the client session at the end of this chapter. There are of course many exercises I use with clients including the voice tempo exercise that works really well for anxiety-related issues and was published in Steve Andreas's book *Help with Negative Self Talk*.

Below are some examples of the stances (a full list can be found at www.provocativechangeworks.com):

## PCW Stances

### *Interrupting the Client*

Interrupting the client can be done in lots of different ways. By interrupting client responses the practitioner has the ability to move the client away from their previously established way of thinking to new possibilities. These interruptions can also be useful as tools to deliberately confuse to provoke a new way of thinking.

### *Blame vs. Don't Blame: It's Not Your Fault (Blame Everything and Everyone Else For the Problem)*

This stance allows the practitioner to blame everything else for the client's predicament. This is often done in the most extreme manner. Here are some examples of blame and not blaming that can be used.

> "It's not your fault; it's just that you were born in the wrong place."
> "It's not your fault, it's because you wear brown shoes."
> "Not only is this your fault, but here's a whole bunch of other things that are your fault as well!"
> "Well of course it's you, nobody else was there!"

### *Speak Louder or Speak Quieter*

Changing the volume of how you speak can be hugely impactful in client sessions. Speaking in hushed tones and speaking louder can produce all manner of responses that provoke new ways of thinking and feeling.

### *Go Into More Detail or To Greater Universal Descriptions*

The stances of asking for more detail or a more universal view provoke a wide range of useful responses. Here are some examples of adopting these stances.

> "What was the color of that car?"
> "How many times did you think that?"
> "What astrological sign are you?"
> "That's just how things line up from a cosmological perspective."

### Suggest the Client Does More of the Same

Here the practitioner suggests the client continue to do more of the same problem behavior. In NLP this could be described as "reframing." Here is an example of the more of the same stance.

**Client:** I have a phobia of public speaking.

**Practitioner:** That's great; it allows more opportunities for the rest of us to speak in public.

### Tell a Story

Milton Erickson used storytelling to great effect. By adopting this stance it's possible to provoke a wide range of client reactions. Here are some examples of how this can be done:

"That reminds me of a story ..."
"I heard that ..."
"I read that ..."

### Digital Choice

Here the practitioner insists that the client has only two choices and demands that they choose A or B.

## Client Session Adopting Provocative Stances to Provoke Useful Change

The session is recorded so the client is able to subsequently listen to the session from a third position. This feedback process creates an ongoing stimulation for new ideas. As a practitioner I ensure that the many suggestions and new possibilities discussed during the session are phrased so the client hears both my suggestions and their own responses in the "here and now." Often when I use hypnosis in client sessions I will frame the suggestions in the following manner: "As you are listening to this *now*, you have already noticed what's useful ..."

The CD recording of the session given to the client produces a feedback loop for the client and repeated listening ensures ongoing change.

Here are some parts of a verbatim transcript from a client session. This illustrates adopting some of the provocative stances used in this approach. The client is a highly successful manager who feels extremely anxious when talking to what he describes as "people in authority."

**NK:** So Mighty Greg, what's the problem?

**Greg:** When I am talking to, or dealing with, senior execs in the company, I lose ...

(Nick interrupts—example of adopting the "interrupt the client" stance)

**NK:** Smart people?

**G:** Not necessarily.

**NK:** OK. Stupid people?

(Here I am also adopting the "digital choice" stance to provoke the client)

**G:** Not necessarily. We have all of the above. (Greg responds in a defensive and animated manner)

**NK:** OK. So they're intermittently smart. On a good day they might make some good decisions and on a bad day they're like the village idiots.

**G:** True.

**NK:** Alright. Yeah.

(I deliberately now pause and look at him for a response—this is an example of adopting the "pause" stance)

**NK:** In Egyptian times you had the pharaoh, who might say "I want that pyramid moving a little bit to the right, go to it boys."

**G:** Yep.

**NK:** Then you had the guy who's in charge of doing the work. Then you have the workers and then you have people who assist. They're not going to be the pharaoh anytime soon.

(In this exchange I am presenting the image of a hierarchy and then proceed to place Greg in the lower parts of the hierarchy to provoke a response)

**G:** But if one has the potential to become the pharaoh …

**NK:** Well, that's just such a nice romantic idea. Yeah. The Universe just decides, you know. Some people are just mud people, while the very few are pharaohs.

**G:** I'm one of the pharaohs. I don't mind about the mud people.

**NK:** Isn't that a nice idea? (Said in an unbelieving tone of voice)

**G:** That's reality.

**NK:** Of course it is. (Again said in an unbelieving tone of voice) So what's the problem?

(This is done to check if he still thinks about the issue in the same way or if I have done enough to change his perception about this)

**G:** When I'm one-on-one with people I perceive to be more senior pharaohs …

**NK:** There aren't any more senior pharaohs. That's the first rookie error! In the Olympic Games there are gold, silver, and bronze medals. You heard that? You say "I want a golder than gold medal." It doesn't exist!

(Greg laughs)

This initial session is about how Greg sees himself in relation to others "in authority" to date. I deliberately choose a strong stereotypical image of the pharaoh to provoke a series of responses from him which in turn will change his perception about this issue. Greg is of course already highly successful in management and also highly competitive, running an international team.

I deliberately frustrate his ability to provide me with answers by interrupting him as well as challenging his intelligence. By constantly suggesting that he is not as smart as others, he is then provoked into fighting his corner and insisting that this is not the case. By using the digital choice stance I also suggest that everything is black and white with no shades of gray and the Egyptian metaphor is constantly used to emphasize the idea of a pecking order. The Olympic metaphor is also used to reinforce the idea of status and winners and losers, again to provoke him into placing himself in a hierarchy of skills and ability.

## *Follow-Up After He Has Listened To the Initial Session on CD*

**G:** I noticed two things. Frustration from some of the discussions …

**NK:** Hey, good. That's a good thing.

**G:** And determination.

**NK:** Determination?

**G:** To be successful.

**NK:** Alright. Well a guy can dream …

(The devil's advocate stance)

**NK:** Alright. Close your eyes. Take a deep breath in. Are you right or left handed?

**G:** Right. (Greg follows instructions for this relaxation exercise)

**NK:** OK. Take your right arm and hold it straight out in front of you. Just like that, not like a Nazi soldier. We really don't want that on the camera. Are you of German descent?

(Even though I am introducing a relaxation exercise I continue to use humor to provoke responses from him)

**G:** No.

**NK:** OK. That's what the Nazis would say. Now if this is a five in terms of relaxation, if I put my finger there, relax your arm down to a four, and down to a three, and down to a two, up to a three, down to a two, and down to a one, and let your arm go down. Take a deep breath in and as you feel your feet flat on the floor, notice which foot is the most relaxed foot and notice which hand is the most relaxed hand. Relax the corners of your eyes and relax the corners of your mouth. And as you listen back to this now on CD, you can begin to notice what's worth keeping in mind and what's worth letting go. What's worth keeping seriously in mind and what's worth just letting go. And begin to notice those changes which are useful for you to now begin to bring to mind in this way. And as you think about it in this way, keeping your eyes closed, what's the whole thing like?

(A hypnotic induction, while also maintaining the provocative approach and exploring the client's metaphorical map relating to the problem)

**G:** I'm not sure.

**NK:** OK. If you think about the question you came with before, what's the whole thing like?

**G:** I think much smaller than I thought it was before. (Greg looks very relaxed and focused when giving this response)

**NK:** Take another deep breath in. Just relax back into your chair. As you let whatever comes to mind in terms of thinking about the single, smallest step that would make the biggest difference for you to start to move in a new direction, notice what comes to mind.

**G:** I think it's just to talk to them as any other normal person.

(This is a key shift and shows he is now thinking in a new way)

**NK:** OK. So what else are you noticing from our little discussion?

**G:** That it's actually just a very simple thing.

**NK:** OK.

**G:** Talking to them as I would talk to anyone else.

**NK:** OK.

**G:** Erm. That I can go into it, not with trepidation.

**NK:** Trepidation?

(Nick starts humming the *Jaws* theme tune—and continues through Greg's talking, adopting the "ignore the client" stance)

**G:** So I think … traditionally I can go into some key execs thinking I've got to make sure I say the right thing. Whereas now it's just go in and have a conversation, a happy conversation, and come out with a positive outcome.

**NK:** Alright. So what's different when you think about it in that way?

**G:** I think it's the manner in which I view them.

**NK:** In what way?

**G:** So I'm not putting them on a pedestal.

**NK:** Pedestal?

**G:** Yeah.

**NK:** OK.

**G:** I'm just talking to them as I would talk to anyone else.

**NK:** What's that like when you talk to them like anyone else, when you think about it in this way?

**G:** They're just a normal person.

**NK:** Alright. Did you think they were abnormal previously?

**G:** Some of them, yes.

**NK:** OK. Close your eyes. Check for anything else that's different if you think about it now. As you listen back to this on CD, notice what you've noticed so far and continue to notice only those things which are useful for you, to begin to notice more about how this is different when you think about it in this way. Then in your own time, open your eyes and come on back out. Anything else?

**G:** I think the key thing is I feel more relaxed going into it, so I don't feel in a pre-agitated state.

### Follow-Up After He Has Listened to the Second Session on CD

**G:** The second session I had to listen to twice because I kind of came out of it the first time and I was like "wow"—I kind of felt like we were going round in a lot of circles, but I think the key part of it was simply like making me challenge my own status. Then when we got into the final session, it's kind of like … I think it's like releasing the thing that's most blatantly obvious.

**NK:** Really?

**G:** I know.

**NK:** Really?

(Feigning surprise)

**G:** You pay good money to learn the obvious. That's an amazing thing.

**NK:** What was the thing that was the most blatantly obvious?

**G:** I think the blatantly obvious thing is that it doesn't matter who you are, they're people just like you or I, and we should treat them as such.

## *What Happened Next*

Within six months of this session Greg was headhunted by a major competitor in his field and now works at a far more senior level than previously. He is now responsible for a number of managers who would have been his counterparts in his old managerial role. He was always a highly competitive skilled manager. These short sessions helped him become more assertive with his bosses and more confident about his own skill level. In total I spent less than an hour with Greg, as these short demos were part of a London PCW event.

In private practice this approach has worked successfully with a wide range of client conditions including obsessive-compulsive disorder (OCD), phobias, anxiety problems, public speaking, social phobia, anger issues, food related problems, jealousy issues, and many other problems.

The main advantage in using this approach is that both the client and therapist are working strictly in the "here and now," in a dynamic manner, which produces a different kind of creative thinking. The approach provokes and stimulates in a conversational manner. This creates the sense that "anything could happen" during the client session. Such a dynamic teaches us more about what is possible, beyond logical digital sequential thinking, and of course, the session is conducted with great warmth, kindness, and humor, resulting in greater self-awareness, improved strategic thinking, and problem-solving skills.

My view is that in some instances the field of NLP has become too focused on techniques and jargon. I first studied NLP in the 1990s and ran certificated courses for many years before focusing on my own work. NLP contains some excellent skills, but often courses don't promote the idea of working in a conversational manner, which is engaging and invaluable for the client. If a therapist cannot communicate easily enough to speak normally to their client, how exquisite is their communication?

I find PCW inspiring as a catalyst for creative thinking so that a practitioner explores realms of communication far beyond traditional talk therapy and NLP approaches. Having conducted thousands of client sessions using this approach I am excited by how quickly client issues can be resolved with lasting effects. This works especially well with many of the tougher client issues that NLP can sometimes struggle to address, including longstanding drug and alcohol addictions and different kinds of compulsions.

## Caveats

One of the key considerations in using this model is to ensure that the interactions with the client are framed "as if talking to an old friend." Provocative does not mean "aggressive" and the practitioner needs to ensure that they create what Steve Andreas describes as a state of "rollicking flexibility" for the client.

The PCW approach works for client responses to problems where they can be provoked into discovering new and more useful responses. The model will not work with issues such as spelling problems, bereavement, and similar scenarios, but it can help with the client's responses to such issues.

The practitioner needs to adopt a playful attitude and focus on working only with client responses in the "here and now." This means that the practitioner needs to be fully at ease in working in an improvised manner and as Frank Farrelly once commented: "Take your imagined professional dignity and throw it out the window in the service of the client."

The usefulness of the session will depend greatly on how flexible the practitioner is with their responses and ensuring that at all times they respond "as if talking to an old friend." The practitioner also needs to be comfortable in adopting the provocative stances and be at ease in simply interacting with the client without fear or hesitation.

## Final Thoughts

This chapter outlines key elements of the Provocative Change Works approach, but is really only an overview. There are many different stances and routes a practitioner can adopt to provoke changes in client behavior. My view is that the combination of provocation, hypnosis, time framing, and exploring metaphors provides a set of tools that to date has worked extremely well with a wide range of client problems including OCD, addictions, anxiety issues, food problems, jealousy, anger issues, and phobias amongst other issues.

In these troubled times I am keen to pass on these skills to as many people as possible and have run events in the UK, USA, Europe, and India, with many more workshops and products planned in forthcoming years. My interest is in making these skills available to help as many people as possible.

## References

Andreas, S. (2009). *Help with Negative Self Talk*. Boulder, CO: Real People Press.

Farrelly, F. (1974). *Provocative Therapy*. Cupertino, CA: Meta Publications.

Kemp, N. (forthcoming). *Provocative Change Works*.

A number of DVDs have been released which explain the PCW approach and show me working with a variety of client conditions including needle phobia, claustrophobia, public speaking phobia, anticipatory anxiety, insomnia, bruxism, and social anxiety:

*Provocative Change Works for Anxiety*—4 DVD set dealing with client conditions and with some explanation of the Provocative Icon System.

*Provocative Change Works for Phobias*—2 DVD set with commentary by Frank Farrelly.

*Provocative Change Works in the USA*—6 DVD set of Boulder, Colorado workshop with explanation of the PCW approach and with numerous client session demonstrations.

These are available from the Anglo American Book Company (www.anglo-american.co.uk) and www.nickkemp.com.

 **Charles Faulkner** is a cognitive-behavioral modeler of the knowledge and performance of exceptional individuals and organizations. His projects range from executive decision-making to metaphoric sense-making to modeling market wizards—the latter featured in publications ranging from *The New Market Wizards* (1992) to *The Little Book of Trading* (2011). A prolific NLP innovator, Charles is the co-author of ten titles including the best-selling audios and book *NLP: The New Technology of Achievement* (1991, 1994), *Success Mastery with NLP* (1992), and the video *NLP in Action* (1993). His early research into how metaphors and life stories influence identities, values and actions is in programs ranging from *Metaphors of Identity* (1991) to *Creating Irresistible Influence* (2003). His scope and category research created the first NLP game: *Trimurti* (2001) as well as a new form of modeling, teaching and coaching. Charles is the senior researcher and consultant for Mental Edge Trading Associates, a principal in Influential Communications, Inc. and also involved in high tech ventures. He is a Visiting Senior Fellow at the University of Surrey School of Management on the NLP Research and Recognition Project. He was the Executive Director of NLP Comprehensive, and later their Director of Programs. He is a Diplomat of NLP (NLP International) for his numerous contributions to the field. These days, Charles is using Cognitive Linguistics to model the decision-making heuristics and biases of Behavioral Finance creating new tools and applications.

# 10 Modeling Market Wizards
## Revealing the Methods of Outstanding Traders and Investors

*Charles Faulkner*

## Why Is This Model Relevant?

Many people define themselves by the decisions they make in life, and how well they make them, yet few of us are given any real education in how to make good decisions. The NLP Strategies model—which includes representational systems, Test–Operate–Test–Exit (TOTE), meta-programs, and criteria[1]—set NLP apart and ahead of other approaches to decision-making at the time. So much so that the inclusion of emotions in decision-making was not widely accepted until Antonio Damasio's popular work in the mid-1990s.[2]

The essence of human decision-making is our tendency to "satisfice."[3] When faced with decisions, we tend to use simple rules and apply criteria sufficient to the moment in a way that involves the least possible effort. Consequences are not given much attention, and since they can occur long after the decision, are often difficult to backtrack. There are too many competing explanations and often causes as well. So, the satisficing process is simply repeated. When I began to model top futures traders, it became clear to me that the NLP Strategies Model worked well for sensory-based situations that are near in time, limited in information, and cause–effect in outcome. That is, where the outcomes can be specified and the strategy/technique has a particular and highly expected result, such as ordering off a menu.

This is why trading and investing—where complex and ambiguous information and events occur over extended periods of time with a probability of outcomes—needs a different kind of decision-making process. In fact, our world is so much more complex and interconnected than just a few years ago that many decisions that used to be causal are now probabilistic—technically known as "decision-making under uncertainty."[4] It is therefore becoming crucially important to know how to use these probabilistic decision-making skills, how they differ from our everyday ones, to know which one to use when, and how to improve each of them.

That successful trading and investing requires a different kind of decision-making explains why very few people learn how to do it well. And there is more. Few other fields are so fraught with misleading myths and deliberately enticing hyperbole. For example, amateurs at home with computers can beat professional fund managers with billions who themselves often fall short of passive market indexing strategies. Few topics bring up as much emotion as money—especially suddenly gaining and losing it.

And there is more. As the complexity and/or ambiguity of a decision increases, so does the amount of information. To keep our information processes from being overwhelmed, we resort to metaphors and analogies—templates—to simplify our decisions. We find an idea or image that reminds us of the current situation and use that idea/image's decision-making process—without examining what we think made the two decisions similar. Also, as the time frame of a decision increases, the amount of information increases as well, and we often resort to a simple story that reminds us of the current sequence of events—again, without examining how we picked that particular story or how well it really fits.[5]

At the same time, a few traders and fund managers, some quite famous—with very different portfolios and strategies—outperform the market year after year, sometimes by a large margin. The modeling of these exquisite probabilistic decision-makers—known in trading and investing as "market wizards"—is as much about managing mental representations as mastering financial mathematics. In this kind of advanced modeling, the various NLP models and distinctions are employed, albeit in a different way than the causal manner familiar to most NLPers.

## What Is the Model?

This model works by introducing a number of distinctions and practices that lift decision-makers out of their everyday satisficing decision frames and strategies to begin a process of thinking of trading and investing decisions in terms of their properties, principles, and functions instead of their content.

This is very unusual. We have not evolved to understand "chance"—where the outcomes of a decision are subject to significant degrees of "luck"—or its more technical expression, probabilities. Biologically we fend off chance with beliefs in hidden powers, grand designs, fate, or destiny. We say, "Everything happens for a reason." While these beliefs may relieve us—the decision-maker—of anxiety and fear, they also leave the decision process unexamined. Sometimes these decisions are "aided" with the "decision support" of magical predictive practices and/or empowering rituals. Retrospectively, successful decisions are often attributed to personal virtues and failures attributed to outside influences. The original investigators of these kinds of decisions were often professional gamblers, the original modelers of risk.

There are a number of interacting areas of expertise that make for a successful trader or investor regardless of the investment, time frame, or location of the activity. Moreover, a weakness in one will swamp the strengths in the others. So, *this is a system* rather than simply a strategy.

Initially, it is useful to think in terms of four properties of probabilistic decision-making:

1. Market indicators
2. Market mechanics (including trading strategy)
3. Money management
4. Mental models (including emotions).[6]

Conventional wisdom about trading and investing would appear to correspond with these, but this is misleading. The best traders and investors categorize these into more detail by function not by content, and they realize these are deeply interrelated.

The functions are:

1. Market indicators: to identify and monitor changes in opportunities.
2. Market mechanics: to find ways to profitably act on the opportunities.
3. Money management: to maximize profits with minimum risk.
4. Mental models: to have the appropriate metaphors, frames, and emotions for managing the previous three including matching the trading strategy time frame.

## How Does the Model Work?

Traders and investors most often start with *market indicators*, lavishing time, money, and attention on them. They do not realize they are seeking specific predictions of complex systems, and complex systems are unpredictable in the conventional sense of that term.[7] In contrast to this, market wizards seek to identify obvious market (system) opportunities.

Perhaps market wizards become who they are because they are among the first to recognize new and elusively obvious market opportunities. These opportunities are varied: from George Soros trading on world economic changes to Blair Hull profiting from infinitesimal mispricings; from John Bogle creating index funds to Jim Rogers and John Templeton opening emerging markets. A key to their success is separating the opportunity identification process from the market indicator used to monitor it. This greatly widens the possible opportunities.

### *Opportunity Identification Strategy*

- Separate the opportunity from what investments might be used to take advantage of it. What are the obvious trends or opportunities? For example, more people growing older, more mobile phone users, more emergent market consumers.

- Scope from micro-sensory based to macro-sensory based to identify obvious opportunities. As Warren Buffett put it, "two and a half billion males with hair growing while you sleep."

- Look in detail at various industries, businesses, and markets to see which are likely to express these opportunities. What are all the ways to take advantage of this opportunity? Create a wide-ranging list including connections with other industries and markets.

Market wizards often do their own research, or put together others' research in unique ways. They also expand the time frame and space of the obvious opportunity looking for equally obvious correlations. They get into specific details, often examining reams of reports and data, not looking for recommendations, but for large-scale number patterns.

Today a lot of research is available to traders and investors from brokerage firms, research firms, and charting companies. It's not the information that matters as much as thinking critically about it. Market wizards thoroughly apply the meta-model by questioning the reliability of the information sources ("According to whom?"), the accuracy of indicators ("How do you know that?"), and even the equations they use to ensure that they are indicating what they claim ("Where/when specifically?"). They counter-example their own assumptions and favored correlations and search for alternative ways to understand the opportunities until the most obvious ones emerge. They list these possible investment candidates.

This initial opportunity identification process is a major determinate of their financial success.[8] This process continues until they have found opportunities which are low risk as well. Commodities trader Jim Rogers: "Do *nothing* until you see money lying in the corner waiting for you to pick it up." Warren Buffett: "I don't try to jump over 7-foot bars. I look for 1-foot bars I can step over." Derivatives trader Blair Hull, once a serious blackjack player, saw the game not as risk-taking, but as "a clear financial opportunity that other people didn't see." This approach allows market wizards to often take less risk than other traders and investors, even other professionals.

*Market mechanics* describes how particular markets and investments function, and how to work those markets and investments. Market wizards assume there are many ways to implement an opportunity and that these investments have different risks, rewards, liquidity, volatility, costs, and fees which they want to work with their trading strategy and portfolio size.

For this next step, the trader/investor's experience grows so this knowledge becomes the criteria for vetting and ranking opportunities. Criteria include: contract costs/percentage of portfolio, transactions costs, entry/exit losses, liquidity, volatility, and access to information. A trader/investor will have a preferred, even optimal, mix of these. Choosing among the opportunities ultimately depends on which ones are most congruent with the trader/investor's trading strategy, disposition, and level of market sophistication.

*Money management* is the most overlooked area. Most investing approaches recommend some form of diversification—either asset allocation and/or a derivatives strategy—to reduce the risk of loss. Warren Buffett writes, "Diversification may preserve wealth, but concentration builds wealth." Many market wizards make most of their money on as few as 5% of their trades.

How does this square with opportunity identification? That is only the first step. Even with an eventual inevitability, the actual outcomes are all probabilistic, and one needs to preserve capital for future opportunities. Market wizards tend to do this more through controlling losses rather than diversification. When trend follower Ed Seykota was asked about the elements of good trading, he replied, "(1) cutting losses, (2) cutting losses, and (3) cutting losses. If you can follow these three rules, you may have a chance."[9] Few realize that Ed is talking about three different kinds of losses: loss of capital, transaction loss (overtrading), and advantageous position loss.

It's a market cliché that traders and investors should "Cut your losses, and let your profits run." It is the hardest thing to do because it goes against our biology, against psychological experience that has served our species well right up until recently. How those psychological experiences work and what to do about them are among the discoveries I made while modeling market wizards and subsequently trading my own accounts.[10]

It's the money in the mind that counts. For many traders and investors, as the amount of money in a trading or investment decision increases—either in absolute terms or as a percentage of their total portfolio—the size of their mental representation (or some aspect of it) increases as well. This creates increased urgency. You can hear this when an investor's voice unconsciously increases in volume when talking about larger and larger amounts of money. This mental distortion magnifies any existing glitches in their decision strategy—which include having no options, a divided mind, feeling forced, a lack of (stable) criteria, or a lack of evidence—paradoxically resulting in much poorer decisions when more is at stake.

For example, when buying a home, a strategy glitch may generate such intense anxiety that the decision becomes about relieving that feeling instead of getting a new home. It's no surprise that so-called "large" purchases are often distributed among a couple, family, or business partners. This allows them to compensate for each other's strategies and experience as well as distribute any anxiety. Many successful market wizards are or were in partnerships. Their different temperament, education, and experience make for better market coverage, more detailed examination of opportunities, and the possibility of contrary opinions. Traders and investors who know about NLP also have the option of resolving their decision strategy glitches[11] and their partners'.

Market wizards hold the mental size of their money more constant than the average trader, and at an optimal size for their trading—large enough to see and value, but not so large as to disturb their decision strategy. This can be mentally rehearsed so it becomes natural. Or, withdraw a relatively large sum of money and stack it in front of you, then you'll see how small it is.

While everyone who trades or invests thinks they do so to make money, it is only after a certain level of development that they realize that the preservation of current capital is more important than additional gains. That money lost or spent today is money that cannot be invested in future opportunities. It's not surprising that a number of famous investors are known for being a "Scrooge" with their money (an unanticipated side effect of holding the mental size of money constant—all amounts are equal).

Gerald Loeb, founder of E. F. Hutton wrote: "Accepting losses is the most important single investment device to insure safety of capital. It is also the action people know the least about and that they are least liable to execute …"[12]

Perhaps, because counter-intuitive, it is a matter of increasing the number of fine distinctions in one's Away From meta-program, becoming more aware of the pain of loss, so prompt action is taken to exit a trade at a specific predetermined level of loss. These strategies are usually learned though gaming experiences of chance and strategy: backgammon, blackjack, poker, and bridge. It's not surprising that many successful traders started as semi/professional gamblers.

Those familiar with the Strategies Model know that decision, motivation, and conviction are interrelated. The convincer strategy is a process that generalizes a number of experiences within a certain time frame into a positive or negative belief. Given our pattern-generating potentials, probabilistic decisions can quickly proliferate false positives and superstitious beliefs in (market) signs, seers, apparent authorities (gurus), and even ourselves, as exceptional. This works against better investment decision-making. After just a few profitable trades in a row, a trader can become convinced of the value of his choice of market, the infallibility of his market indicator, trading strategy, his own genius, or all four. No one is immune to this. These convictions are rarely revisited without a number of intense counter-examples, for example, extreme losses.

On the other hand, after losing several trades in a row, which is typical in the proba-bilistic world of investments, a trader can become convinced that there is no oppor-tunity for profits in what he has chosen to trade, or in using that market indicator or his trading strategy. Depending on the degree of identification the trader has with his occupation, this can lead him to believe that he lacks innate skill or even self-worth.

Having an appropriate *mental model* is essential. My work on metaphors of identity[13] and life stories[14] was sufficiently well developed that I knew how to model the men-tal models of market wizards. I asked, "How does this person know what to want?"

What a decision means, what it is made for, is largely unconscious, yet makes a huge difference in the kind and quality of one's decisions. For example, do you envision yourself as struggling to survive, in a pitched battle, playing a game, or on a journey? A market wizard's metaphor of identity shapes the strategy selection and decision criteria as well as which emotions are available and which market perceptions are important. Metaphors of identity operate within fairly distinct time frames cor-responding to ordinary language metaphors used to talk about and act out their trading: from the short-term immediacy of "taking a hit" (markets as combat) to "winning a round" (markets as games) to "figuring it out" (markets as puzzles).

Many traders and investors start out with the metaphor of identity of a game or a sport. These have the positive qualities of winning and losing (money), using strate-gies, and improving oneself through deliberate study and practice. The time frame of games is typically understood to mean a few minutes to hours, though not usually days. This means the natural rhythm of trading for someone with this metaphor would be minutes to hours.

When professional gamblers play games, losses and loss control are essential to win-ning. Similarly, professional traders and investors use this metaphor to put loss in perspective. This perspective pattern[15] comes more into play the longer the time frame. Some market wizards speak of "waging a campaign" in a currency or commod-ity. That is, the individual trades and their respective gains or losses are small moves in a much larger and grander plan—a natural and effective use of sub-modalities and multiple embedded representations to affect perspective and reduce the feelings of loss.

It is also well known that as the capital and experience of a trader/investor increase, there is a tendency to increase the time frame in which he trades—also increasing perspective.

The social role of a trader/investor is also a kind of metaphor of identity. Whether self-ascribed or assigned by another or an institution, it can compel actions that are not favorable to successful trading or investing. The sense of identity of a trader/investor means going to work to trade/invest. This need for activity is often envisioned in a manner and at a pace that differs from the activities and time frame rhythms a trader or investor would find most profitable. So the successful trader/investor needs to shift his attention from the conventional representations of trading/investing to the activities that support effective trading/investing behavior.

In probabilistic decision-making, the significant activities are the ones that improve the overall trading/investing process—from information gathering through calculation to efficient transactions, recordkeeping, and "after action reviews." These traders/investors need to reward themselves for doing these activities regardless of the particular outcomes/results so that the improving process leads to better results over time.

Despite the financial industry's blue reputation, and all these metaphors, market wizards are careful with how they use language. The best are aware of how language influences them and avoid speculation that clouds thinking. For example, on being asked why a particular market was increasing in price, rather than get carried away with self-generated stories, Ed Seykota simply said, "This market has the property of going up."

Market wizards acknowledge conventional wisdom and challenge its assumptions to find an opportunity edge. They do this in every aspect of their trading/investing. The conventional wisdom says that the trading/investing system is the computer and the trading strategy. Outstanding traders/investors expand this to include all of their sources of information, environmental influences (including others), brokerage behavior and trade execution, money management (including risk control and position sizing), and finally themselves.

Famous market wizards have often been among the first to exploit an aspect of trading others had not realized could be an edge. The now obvious ones include computerization, better information, new conceptualizations of the trades, a deeper understanding of investments, and/or risk and self-knowledge. With self-knowledge, this same challenging of assumptions continues as they examine their perceptions, strategies, emotions, and beliefs. The most successful ones put themselves in situations that challenge their thinking (by traveling, learning new methodologies, reading widely, or seeking out experiences that stretch them).

The choice of trading strategy depends in part on how the trader/investor understands the markets. Are they efficient or not? Or are they expressions of human emotions? And as important as these are, the key factor is the trader/investor's scope of time—the rhythm of events. The generally recognized trading and investing strategies are largely a function of their time frames. For example, Warren Buffett's is buy and hold: "My favorite time frame for holding a stock is forever."

My modeling of market wizards across the range of possible time frames shows that traders are most likely to succeed with the time frames most familiar to them. Ask, "How long am I likely to own this?" or "How long does this decision last?" If the trader/investor does not know the typical time frame for a desired trade, s/he might stick with a simpler strategy like index funds. Some traders and investors want to copy a market wizard on the assumption that this person knows how to make money. But that idea doesn't mean the investor's natural time frame is the same as his hero's. Better to buy his hero's fund than ignore his own rhythm. The trading strategy in each time frame has trade-offs. For example, shorter time frames demand more attention and have higher transaction costs. Longer time frames allow for more diverse trades and have larger volatility moves.

Emotions are twistier in the world of trading and investing. The kinds of people attracted to short time-frame trading often have higher base excitation levels. Trading price changes in a short time frame satisfy this excitation level (as do action films, amusement park rides, and extreme sports). The thing is, as with any kind of work, as the skills are mastered, the level of activity normalizes reducing the excitement.

Among market wizards, so-called negative emotions are critical to their success. Feeling fear indicates a lack of sufficiently detailed risk control (and time to recheck); feeling loss indicates insufficient evaluation of importance in the initial trade consideration (and making better evaluations next time); feeling anger indicates a violation of physical or psychical boundaries (which can be changed and allow the trader/investor a "space" to think).[16]

Jim Rogers has a particularly effective strategy for deducing the human desire to have things not already owned. He asks of a possible investment, "Should I already own this?" which mentally makes him an owner—a different point of view for evaluation of an opportunity.

Finally, while it is a cliché in finance that people try to use money to change who they were, market wizards embrace their personal histories to become more of who they are. Examples include George Soros, who used his university study of philosophy in the creation of his trading strategies and later his philanthropy. Jim Rogers was a student of history before going to Wall Street. His opportunity identification process looks across centuries of time as well as continents, and now he participates in the unfolding of history. Blair Hull, one of the founders of derivatives trading, was a high school physics teacher before he went on to examine the "atoms and molecules" of finance. Ed Seykota, a graduate of MIT in systems dynamics and computer science, applies both to trading. Even music majors use their knowledge of composition to "note" price changes in the markets more effectively. And many serious amateur and professional gamblers apply their skills when they turn to the markets—most famously Edward O. Thorp, author of the blackjack system book *Beat the Dealer*.[17] The opportunities they found were congruent with the content of their lives—their time frame rhythm and their metaphors of identity.

The importance of certain kinds of reference experiences that successful traders have early on is hard to over-estimate. Many of them report the importance of their experience with serious gambling or some rigorous probability influenced activity. Learning the odds, practicing the craft of effective betting, being patient, and following their system in all kinds of emotionally challenging circumstances was a rehearsal for later in life.

Given this, I encourage neophyte traders/investors to take up small stakes games of chance to build these requisite reference experiences. In addition, I have suggested to specific individuals activities such as acting to learn to think/act like someone else to expand their sense of self; playing an exhilarating sport or activity to replace the exciting feelings of trading; taking up a martial art or meditative practice to improve senses, concentration, and for new analogies for trading; studying previous trading and investment strategies to understand time frames and perspectives; and reading trading and investing classics for ideas.

For those who use financial advisors, this model suggests investors pay more attention to these qualities and activities in their advisors than to well-appointed offices or expensive suits. Ask about your investor's life experiences and metaphors for the markets to get a better idea of his investment strategies. Keep in mind that you may not want someone who is like you, but someone whose make-up matches the markets they are trading for you.

## Caveats

This modeling of market wizards suggests that while these skills are not magical, they are quite unusual. To learn them requires dedication and particular kinds of reference experiences—especially with probabilistic decision-making. While all of us need to invest, most of us are not going to go through what it takes to become effective active investors. Many market wizards acknowledge this and recommend passive index investing as a safer and more reliable wealth-building strategy for those without the requisite skills. Keep in mind that index funds are typically investments in the future of a country's economy. These days, you can pick the countries you invest in.

For those who wish to master these skills, it is important to realize your natural inclinations are likely to be wrong—not only about what to invest in, or when, but also in how to go about learning it. To accelerate your learning, start with money management. As soon as you discover how losses and transaction fees rob you of wealth, you will have the motivation to pay off those credit cards and have a better understanding of what kinds of investments fit for you when you turn to market indicators and opportunity identification.

If something sounds too good to be true or promises certainty, it's probably not worth investing in. In investing there are risks of loss and loss means it's gone. So it's important to start small and respect position size rules. This keeps you solvent and it gives you the opportunity to learn the market mechanics, mental models, and emotions without getting overwhelmed.

Those using financial advisors are in a similar situation to investors. They have to make an investment decision of which financial advisor or firm to use. The same skills apply with the difference that now the advisors are the investments. Examine them as such, start small, diversify, and be willing to revisit those decisions as time or circumstances change.

The model of market wizards presented here is for the decisions with uncertain outcomes in work and life, but that is not where we are accustomed to living. I also suggest that you take time with family and friends, going to clubs, parties, and concerts, and enjoy making even little things happen—like your child smile. This causal world will always be the basis for our acts of imagination and creativity—even our financial abstractions. Spend time there too.

## Notes

1. Dilts et al. (1980).

2. Damasio (1994).

3. Herbert (1969).

4. Kahneman et al. (1982).

5. McCloskey (1990).

6. Faulkner (2005).

7. Schwager (1992).

8. Sperandeo (1991).

9. Schwager (1989).

10. Nusbaum (1993). This 1990 "demonstration of modeling" account traded to an 84% return with a maximum drawdown of 27.2%.

11. Andreas and Andreas (1983).

12. Loeb (1935).

13. Faulkner (1991).

14. Faulkner (1993).

15. McWhirter (2000).

16. Seykota (2005).

17. Thorp (1962).

## References

Andreas, C. and Andreas, S. (1983). Strategies. In *eidem, NLP Comprehensive NLP Practitioner Training Trainer Manual*. Indian Hills, CO: NLP Comprehensive.

Covel, M. W. (2011a). *The Little Book of Trading: Trend Following Strategy for Big Winning*. Hoboken, NJ: John Wiley and Sons.

Covel, M. W. (2011b). Trading systems. In *Trend Commandments: Trading for Exceptional Returns*. Upper Saddle River, NJ: Pearson Education, Inc., p. 70.

Damasio, A. R. (1994). *Descartes' Error: Emotion, Reason and the Human Brain*. New York: Grosset/Putnam.

Dilts, R., Grinder, J., Bandler, R., Bandler, L. C., and DeLozier, J. (1980). *Neuro-Linguistic Programming*. Vol. 1: *The Study of the Structure of Subjective Experience*. Cupertino, CA: Meta Publications.

Faulkner, C. (1991). *Metaphors of Identity: Operating Metaphors and Iconic Change*. Longmont, CO: Genesis II Publishing.

Faulkner, C. (1993). *The Mythic Wheel of Life: Finding Your Place in the World*. Longmont, CO: Genesis II Publishing.

Faulkner, C. (2005). Inside the counterintuitive world of trend followers: it's not what you think, it's what you know. *Stocks, Futures and Options*, April, pp. 1–3.

Herbert, S. (1969). *The Sciences of the Artificial*. Cambridge, MA: MIT Press.

Kahneman, D., Slovic, P., and Tversky, A. (1982). *Judgment under Uncertainty: Heuristics and Biases*. Cambridge: Cambridge University Press.

Koppel, R. (1996). The many faces of intuition: Charles Faulkner. In *idem, The Intuitive Trader: Developing Your Inner Trading Wisdom*. Hoboken, NJ: John Wiley and Sons, pp. 71–92.

Koppel, R. and Abell, H. (1994). Staying in control: Charles Faulkner. In *eidem, The Outer Game of Trading: Modeling the Trading Strategies of Today's Market Wizard.* Chicago, IL: Probus Publishing Co., pp. 112–137.

Loeb, G. (1935). *The Battle for Investment Survival.* Hoboken, NJ: John Wiley and Sons.

McCloskey, D. (1990). *If You're So Smart: The Narrative of Economic Expertise.* Chicago, IL: University of Chicago Press.

McWhirter, J. (2000). Re-modelling NLP. Pt 6: Understanding change. *Rapport* 48.

Nusbaum, D. (1993). Charles Faulkner: mind reader. *Futures*, November.

Schwager, J. D. (1989). Ed Seykota: everybody gets what they want. In *idem, Market Wizards: Interviews with Top Traders.* New York: New York Institute of Finance, pp. 151–174.

Schwager, J. D. (1992). Charles Faulkner: mind of an achiever. In *idem, The New Market Wizards: Conversations with America's Top Traders.* Hoboken, NJ: John Wiley and Sons, pp. 414–438.

Seykota, E. (2005). *The Trading Tribe.* Incline Village, NV: Trading Tribe.

Sperandeo, V. (1991). *Trader Vic: Methods of a Wall Street Master.* Hoboken, NJ: John Wiley and Sons.

Thorp, E. (1962). *Beat the Dealer: A Winning Strategy for the Game of Twenty-One.* New York: Vintage Press.

 **Richard M. Gray, Ph.D.** is Assistant Professor of Criminal Justice, Fairleigh Dickinson University, Teaneck, NJ. Before his move to academia, Dr. Gray served for more than twenty years in the US Probation Department, Brooklyn, NY. He is the creator of the Brooklyn Program, an NLP-based substance abuse program which operated for seven years in the Federal Probation System. In recognition of that work, he was co-recipient of the 2004 Neuro-linguistic Programming World Community Award. Dr. Gray is the author of *Archetypal Explorations* (Routledge, 1996), *Transforming Futures: The Brooklyn Program Facilitators Manual* (Lulu, 2003) and *About Addictions: Notes from Psychology, Neuroscience and NLP* (Lulu, 2008).

He is a regular presenter at national and international addictions conferences and a recognized expert in Neuro-Linguistic Programming. He received his BA in Psychology from Central College, Pella, IA; MA in Sociology from Fordham University, Bronx, NY; and Ph.D. in Psychology from the Union Institute, Cincinnati, OH. Dr. Gray is a Certified Master Practitioner of Neuro-Linguistic Programming and a Certified Ericksonian Hypnotist. Richard is a member of the Federal Probation Officers Association, the Canadian Association of NLP, the Institute for the Advanced Study of Health and the NLP Research and Recognition Project.

email: rmgray@fdu.edu
web: http://richardmgray.home.comcast.net

# 11 Overcoming Addiction
## A New Model for Working with Drug and Alcohol Abusers

*Richard M. Gray*

## Why the Brooklyn Program?

Drug abuse and dependence are serious problems that affect more than 26 million people in the United States annually. More than 40% of all arrestees in the USA have used alcohol or some illicit drug within twenty-four hours of their arrest. Most arrests are drug-related or for minor crimes, however, 15–30% of them are for violent crimes. Jails and prisons are overflowing with people with minor drug offences. Millions of otherwise law abiding citizens struggle with addictions. This is a real problem and the classical solutions have not worked.

In the mid-1990s, working as a United States probation officer in Brooklyn, New York, I was assigned to a drug treatment caseload. Although I had been a probation officer for more than fifteen years and had dealt with addicts and substance abusers, I knew relatively little about addictions. While I had always listened to the experts, they seemed stuck. In their world every user was an abuser and every abuser was an addict; there was no middle ground. So everyone sent for treatment, regardless of how large or how small their problem, was subjected to the same regimen: detox and inpatient treatment followed by intensive outpatient treatment and interminable twelve-step meetings. Sometimes the inpatient phase was put aside but the outpatient features remained the same.

Despairing of help from the field, I began a period of intensive study that showed conclusively that this treatment pattern was demonstrably ineffective. Addicts and abusers were often confused with one another, drug education groups were ineffective, many people discovered they could safely return to the social use of alcohol and other drugs without problems, and twelve-step meetings were largely ineffective.[1]

Substance abuse is characterized by a pattern of use that persists for longer than twelve months and that interferes with or damages work, school, or relationships. Substance abuse is not a proper diagnosis for anyone previously diagnosed as substance-dependent. Addiction is characterized by similar problems but includes obsessive preoccupation with getting, using, and/or obtaining the money to obtain the addictive substance.[2]

Jungian theory holds that when people awaken to a pattern of growth into their full potential that life-path tends to become irresistible. In my work I had seen that pattern many times in addicts who had awakened to a spiritual reality, gotten a personally meaningful job, found a deeply satisfying relationship or some other source of meaning, and had walked away from their addiction. Whenever someone discovered something more important to them, in a deeply meaningful and ongoing way, he or she could leave the addiction or drug problem behind.

The Stages of Change Model is one of the most well-researched and empirically supported models of change in use today. It holds that when people change, they pass through predictable stages and, in each stage, specific interventions are appropriate. Crucial to the process of change is understanding that most of the process can be predicted by one thing—wanting something that is more important than the problem behavior.[3]

This resonates with two principles from NLP: (1) the well-formedness conditions for outcomes and (2) an observation by Bandler and Grinder about addictions. For an outcome to be well-formed, it must meet several criteria; it must be stated in the positive, under personal control, sensory-specific, contextualized, given a time frame, and ecological. Applying this perspective allows us to recast substance use treatment as a well-formed enterprise; instead of *moving away* from something, treatment can be framed in terms of something *positively desired*. Bandler and Grinder's statement in *Reframing* (1982) was a major inspiration: if you create a state that is more pleasurable, more intuitive, and more accessible than an addictive drug, you can cure any addiction.

The Brooklyn Program was originally designed to work with drug addicts and abusers, alcoholics, and problem drinkers assigned to drug or alcohol treatment by the Federal Court. It was specifically designed for clients who did not want treatment or had failed at other kinds of treatment.

Since leaving the probation department, I have found that the program, even in a shortened version, provides powerful, life-changing experiences for people with or without substance use problems. Because it was designed to create powerfully motivating futures that align with an individual's deepest instincts, it can be applied in many contexts.

The benefits are many:

1.  Practicing your ability to access remembered resources establishes self-efficacy regarding internal states and internal resources.

2.  Enhancing meaningful positive experiences reinforces that sense of efficacy.

3.  Anchoring those resources makes them transportable and easily available. Knowing about resources is one thing; having an amplified state available on demand is another.

4.  Any emotional state that is amplified until it is free from the source memory and context gives access to trance, meditation, and spiritual experience.

5.  Those deep states awaken a grounded sense of self. From that state it is possible to design meaningful futures and outcomes that can change the meaning of life and how it is lived.

## What Is the Brooklyn Program and How Does It Work?

The program assumes that preferences, desires, and behaviors are organized in hierarchies established in the mid-brain dopamine system. This system includes the ventral tegmental area (VTA), the nucleus accumbens (NAcc), and the left orbitofrontal cortex (OFC). The VTA is the source of the dopamine neurons that energize the system. These neurons project to the NAcc. The OFC, part of the frontal lobes, is intimately involved with conscious experience and making decisions.

When a pleasurable, rewarding, or biologically important stimulus impacts the organism, the cells in the VTA send a rush of dopamine to the NAcc. Inputs representing various stimuli are compared in the NAcc to find out whether the expected reward has increased, decreased, or remained the same. Surprise rewards are always evaluated highly. All rewards or targets of behavior are ranked by this system in terms of their survival value and immediate relevance.

The results of this ranking are registered in the left OFC as hierarchies of positively desired rewards. Things we want more are stored in full multisensory representations, closer to the center of the brain. Less valuable representations are stored further from the center as more abstract representations. The hierarchy is dynamic with different rewards or desires becoming more important, desirable, or salient as context, internal state, and current experience shifts. One result of this ranking is that we want some things more than others. This is known as incentive salience.

Drugs and addictive behaviors move to the head of the hierarchy by affecting dopamine concentrations or by becoming the habitual go-to answers for life's problems. However, just as drugs and alcohol move other things from the head of the hierarchy, so other things can bump drugs from the head of the hierarchy. People often give up problem substances when they find a dependable means of achieving states that effectively compete with the drugged experience.

## Description of the Program

The Brooklyn Program is implemented over sixteen weeks for one two-hour sessions per week. It teaches specific behavioral and cognitive skills and, as noted, it never discusses drugs or problem behaviors, but works to build emotional and cognitive resources that will ultimately outframe them. While it is conceivable that the program could be implemented in a shorter time frame, the sixteen-week duration allows for over-learning of the target behaviors and ensures that it will be taken seriously by persons unused to the speed of NLP techniques.

In the first several sessions, participants are taught how to access and enhance a series of positive resource states using standard NLP sub-modality techniques. As any NLP practitioner knows, this sub-modality work begins with a striking enhancement of the remembered experience and so validates the first promise to clients that they will be taught memory enhancement techniques.

During the same several sessions, the participants are taught to focus more and more on the feelings associated with the experience so that they discover a series of deeply pleasurable transcendent states. These pseudo-meditative states are designed partly to provide feelings of self-efficacy, but also to offer powerful positive experiences that are strong enough to challenge the salience of the problem state.

The generation of the states follows a simple pattern of sub-modality enhancement. After the participants have chosen an appropriate resource, have them close their eyes and experience the memory. Let them note just how they get to the memory: What do they notice first—a picture, a smell, a feeling? What comes next and next and next?

Once the client has stepped into the experience, they can then begin to vary the sub-modality structure of the memory. Instruct them to make the changes in a way that makes the experience work best for them. Let them experiment with each dimension to find a level that feels best.

Go through the sub-modality changes, pausing after each one to allow for processing time. After each change, ask the participants to note the change in their felt experience. Each instruction should be designed to provide a felt change in the experience and practice in the manipulation of feeling by changing the sub-modality qualities of the experience. Remind the client to take note of the kinds of perceptual changes that make the most positive difference in the experience. When you have gone through this process invite them to come back for a moment, shake out the experience, and talk about what happened: "Did that feel good? Did you know you could do that? What worked best for you?"

After a few minutes of discussion invite them to just close their eyes and return to the place where they left off and continue as follows:

> Now, step all the way back to the point where you just left off. For some of you the memory has gone away and you were just out there floating, that's good, go back there.
>
> Go back to the state where you left off and notice how easy this is.
>
> Notice how you breathe in this experience. Notice how you hold your body—the patterns of tension and relaxation that enhance your experience. Adjust your posture so that it enhances the experience.
>
> Notice the expression on your face. Adjust your expression so that it enhances your experience. Rest all of the way down into the very best part. Explore that and discover new ways of feeling and being, just by gently turning your attention to the very best part. Enjoy that for a few minutes and then come all of the way back.

Overload short-term memory with impossible dimensions of feeling: location, texture, spread, depth, breadth, height, temperature, imagined color and sound. As the participants focus on more and more of these, the context and content will be crowded out of working memory and they will be left in a powerful, peaceful ecstasy that carries the flavor and physical tone of the original state. It is a generalized state of autonomic arousal that is framed by the original state.

> Now, return to the experience once more. As you do, notice that you can zoom right back to the point where you left off the last time; right to the very most intense part. Step all of the way in and rest down into it. Notice the rush of feelings and sensations.
>
> And as you turn your attention, ... just gently turn your attention, ... to the center of the feeling, you can begin to notice, ... really notice, ... its temperature, ... its color ... Notice whether it makes a sound ... or a hum. And you can notice, really notice, ... how the feeling moves ... Whether it is centered in your body, or beyond your body ... Whether it moves in a circle ... or a loop ... or a spiral ... whether it turns clockwise or counterclockwise ... and whether it turns like a wheel ... or like a turntable ... And as you notice the pattern of this movement ... you can reach out with imaginary hands ... and begin to trace this movement ... with those imaginary hands ... and if the movement of the feeling ... is not a complete movement ... you can take those imaginary hands ... and guide that feeling ... through its own pattern, ... back into its own center, ... so that it grows .... and increases ... and flows and multiplies ... And you can use those imaginary hands ... to take hold of the feeling ... and move it faster ... and faster ... through its own center so that it doubles ... and doubles again ... and grows stronger ... and stronger, ... and the pictures fade ... and the memories fade ... and you find yourself floating ... and resting, ... down, ... all ... the ... way ... down, ... into pleasant, ... safe and ... warm ... Resting ... into your own ability ... to feel ... good ... now.

Allow participants to remain in state for a while. They may safely be allowed to remain in this state for extended periods. Then, gently call the participants back to the present time and place.

After some discussion, have them return to the experience using this last segment of the script (beginning with the word "Now") and explore it by "gently turning" their attention to the best part. Do this several times to enhance their facility with the tools and their enjoyment of the state. Next, in sequence, the participants are taught to anchor several predefined states that they have accessed and enhanced during the preceding sessions. These include:

- The experience of focused attention.
- A single good decision made in a systematic fashion.
- A moment of skill consolidation or streamlining of a learned behavior (e.g., riding a bike, driving a manual transmission).
- An experience of pure fun or enjoyment.
- An experience of confidence or personal competence.

These resources are enhanced to ecstatic levels—to the point where there is virtually no shadow of the original content or context. Each state is anchored to a distinct hand gesture. The anchors serve three purposes:

1. They make the resource transportable and accessible in multiple contexts.
2. They create a relatively mechanical means for evoking and enhancing the anchored state.
3. They create an automated access for later integration of these preliminary anchors into a more complex state (stacking anchors).

The anchoring technique used in the Brooklyn Program departs from standard NLP use in that it adheres to a standard, Pavlovian conditioning paradigm. This guarantees that the responses are truly automatic and that they can be used in spite of the participant's current mood or attitude. The basic pattern is provided in Figure 1.

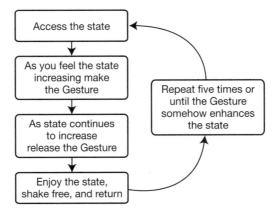

**Figure 1:** *The self-anchoring process*

Once the anchors have been practiced and enhanced several times, participants are encouraged to practice them in multiple situations so that they generalize into other life contexts. This ensures that the new behaviors—access to the resource states—generalize beyond the confines of the weekly session. A strong emphasis on homework and independent practice serves the same end. Participants are also encouraged to create several of their own anchors to make sure they understand that all of this is under their personal control and that the resource states are theirs alone. A crucial element here is an emphasis on the development of efficacy tools and beliefs about the participants' own feelings.[4]

At about the seventh week, the anchors are stacked into a single anchor which has been labeled "NOW" and which, according to my understanding, creates a basic felt experience (constellation) of Jung's Deep Self. Jung indicated that every person is being moved by unconscious processes toward the realization of a whole, integrated expression of all that they can be as psychological and spiritual beings. This inner potential serves as a life compass, in those able to use it, for personal development on all levels. The sense of this personal direction is evoked to provide an affective basis for creating a truly meaningful and compelling set of outcomes. This is done in the last sessions where we use the NLP well-formedness conditions to create a future that matches the function of the positive outcome in Prochaska's strong principle of change[5] and the observation that movement through the stages of change is propelled most significantly by the identification of a meaningful and compelling future.[6]

The process continues with the collection and anchoring of another series of resources from various time periods in the participant's life. These consist of times when the participants felt good about themselves—things that they did well, things that they learned easily, meaningful jobs and roles that they held, and things they wanted to be when they were kids. These are again anchored, enhanced, and integrated into the NOW anchor.

Finally, the felt state associated with NOW is used to create well-formed outcomes across several life domains: occupation, spiritual, relationships, intellectual, and health practices. Each outcome is created by accessing the NOW anchor and imagining life in each of these domains through the affective window of the felt state, NOW. This results in future outcomes that are consistent with a deep, felt sense of personal identity. Superficial outcomes—wealth, sex, possessions, and so on—are discarded in favor of behavioral outcomes that characterize the kinds of behaviors that give expression to the constellated sense of the Deep Self. The remaining exercises are devoted to enhancing the vision of the future and consolidating the learnings.

## A Few Observations

When used with individuals, these exercises will easily result in significantly decreased use of the problem substance or behavior or total abstinence. In the federal system, where the only measure of success is complete abstinence, the program garnered a healthy 29.6% abstinence rate for completers one year post-treatment. These were all federal offenders who, for the most part, had no interest in treatment. When you begin with a client who wants to change, things get a lot easier. These results have been reported in several peer reviewed journals.[7]

One of the important insights that came from running the program is that the skills, especially the state enhancement and anchors, must be practiced for their own sake. The program always works best when the client has first learned to enjoy the skills and states for themselves. *Let them understand the program as a precursor to treatment, as coping skills that they can use independent of drug treatment, or something that is just for them.*

We also never direct the clients in how to use the anchors, but allow them to discover their utility. The states should be practiced in session and at home, so that the behaviors are over-learned and become automatically available. After several weeks of practicing the anchors, after the clients have come to rely on them as tools in their own right, they can be used to counter urges and change behaviors. We prefer not to do this early in the program lest the states and anchors become devalued as *only* part of a drug treatment program.

## Precautions and Exclusion Criteria

There are no magic bullets and no panaceas. Not even this. It should be noted that some drugs, especially alcohol and benzodiazepines (drugs like Klonopin, Xanax, and Valium) can have life threatening withdrawal syndromes. Patients with severe or long lasting addictions to these substances will need medically assisted detoxification before they start the program. Other drugs have withdrawal syndromes associated with them but they are generally not life threatening. Use your best judgment.

These techniques have been used with an otherwise stable criminal population that was free of serious mental health problems (Axis I disorders). It is not recommended for persons who are heavily medicated or under psychiatric care. If the client is receiving treatment for other problems, you should coordinate care with the other providers.

Although the program was designed for use in a group context, it works well with individuals. For individuals, sometimes just creating and using the anchors expands their perceived options so that they can move toward better behavioral choices. In every case, however, I prefer to have the clients build personally relevant futures using the altered states and well-formed outcomes. Having a motivating future or set of futures can be the difference that makes a difference. Sobriety itself is not a sufficient reward.

An important part of the program is the capacity to test for compliance. No drug treatment program can be successful without monitoring. If you do not test urine, hair, sweat, breath, or blood regularly for the target substance you have no measure of your progress or the client's compliance.

This program provides clear success criteria at each stage. There are seven behavioral criteria. In a group context, provisions were made to assess progress with the skills and coach participants on anchoring during the first of two scheduled one-on-one sessions. If participants remained unable to meet the root criteria after the eighth session they were instructed to repeat the program or to seek another form of treatment. In a one-on-one or voluntary setting these may not be important considerations.

Here are the behavioral criteria (the exercises referenced indicate the phases of the program for which the criteria are relevant):

1. Name the five states and illustrate the appropriate hand gestures; do this in order (Exercises 2 and 3).

2. Describe your physiological responses as the state arises (Exercises 1–5 and throughout the program).

3. Physiological signs: changes in posture, facial expression, heart rate, breathing, and skin tone. Although they differ from person to person, state changes will be observable.

4. Response latency: persons who have entered the deep states required will either not respond to external stimuli (loud noises) or will respond with marked latencies (e.g., eye movements several seconds after the sound).

5. Perseveration: persons who access the states often take a few seconds to return to normal consciousness. Persons who immediately return to normal voice tone and reaction time are suspect.

6. Mood change: the state enhancement and anchoring exercises (1–5) and all of the subsequent exercises lead to strong positive feelings. People who begin the session in negative states quickly change to more positive affects. Persons who retain a negative mood are suspect.

7. States arise automatically in response to the anchors; there is no preparation time or conscious effort to access the state.

## Inspirations for the Program and from the Program

The program grew out of Jungian theory and my own experiences with drugs and redemption. One of the important things that happened after starting the program was a trip to a National Institutes on Drug Abuse (NIDA) presentation on the mid-brain dopamine system. At that time, the program was framed as a cognitive-behavioral approach with NLP elements added. After learning about the early research on incentive salience and how drugs actually worked, I realized that I did not have to teach or convince anyone about anything. *All I had to do was give them the opportunity to experience something that was available to everyone and important to them, and the experience itself would make the change.*

One of the more striking results of the program was the near universal and spontaneous use of anchors for anger management. Almost as soon as the participants found out that they had a reliable means to control their emotions, they began to use the anchors to create choice about anger. This is all the more striking in light of the commitment to never instruct participants on how or where to use the anchors.

One time, in the course of teaching the process of anchoring, two otherwise skeptical clients put their fingers together to evoke the state and were so surprised by the onset of the state that they literally jumped out of their seats. They were assured that they were completely in control of the process.

Another offender, who had violated several parole terms because of cocaine use, came into the session and called me aside and said that he had a problem. Encouraged to speak, he indicated that the previous night he had gone to the place where he usually bought his drugs and found himself confused. He did not know what to do. When asked what then happened, he indicated that he just left. He was congratulated for his decision. After graduating from the program the offender completed his parole without incident and as far as can be ascertained has not been rearrested.

During the regular weekly sessions, the anchors were used to provide access to ecstatic pseudo-meditative states. Outside of the treatment context, they often had the effect of bringing the subject out of depression or anger into a neutral state. One participant (who slipped past our attempts to screen out psychiatric problems) suffered from bipolar disease. In the course of a trip home, her mother died and, simultaneously, she began to experience her depressive phase. When she returned from the trip she reported her difficulties and was glad to say that she had not used any drugs (confirmed by urinalysis). She indicated, however, that she was disappointed in the anchors. She reported that when she found herself getting lost in depression, she fired off the anchors expecting a state of deep peace and meditative ecstasy. Instead, the anchors brought her to a relatively positive, neutral state that made the remainder of her visit quite bearable.

Toward the end of the program, after stacking the anchors to establish a deep sense of self, several clients were powerfully moved as they came to the realization that the program had allowed them to reconnect with their pre-addiction identities. In tears they thanked me for returning their pasts to them.

## Notes

1. Peele, Brodsky and Arnold (1991); Chiauzzi and Liljegren (1993).

2. American Psychiatric Association (1994); Schaffer Library of Drug Policy (2005).

3. Prochaska et al. (1994).

4. Bandura (1997).

5. Prochaska (1994).

6. Gray (1996).

7. Gray (2001, 2002, 2010).

## References

American Psychiatric Association (APA). (1994). *Diagnostic and Statistical Manual of Mental Disorders, Fourth Edition* (DSM-IV). Washington, DC: American Psychiatric Association.

Bandler, R. and Grinder, J. (1982). *Reframing: Neuro-Linguistic Programming and the Transformation of Meaning*. Moab, UT: Real People Press.

Bandura, A. (1997). *Self-Efficacy: The Exercise of Control*. New York: Freeman.

Chiauzzi, E. J. and Liljegren, S. (1993). Personal perspective. Taboo topics in addiction treatment: an empirical review of clinical folklore. *Journal of Substance Abuse Treatment* 10: 303–316.

Gray, R. (1996). *Archetypal Explorations*. London: Routledge.

Gray, R. M. (2001). Addictions and the self: a self-enhancement model for drug treatment in the criminal justice system. *Journal of Social Work Practice in the Addictions* 1(2): 75–91.

Gray, R. M. (2002). The Brooklyn Program: innovative approaches to substance abuse treatment. *Federal Probation Quarterly* 66(3): 9–16.

Gray, R. M. (2005). Thinking about drugs and addiction. *Anchor Point*. Available at: www.nlpco.com/library/therapy/addictions.html (accessed 09/02/11).

Gray, Richard M. (2008). *Transforming Futures: The Brooklyn Program Facilitators Manual*. Available as a free download at www.lulu.com/product/paperback/transforming-futures-the-brooklyn-program-facilitators-manual/3978079?

productTrackingContext=search_results/search_shelf/center/1 (accessed August 10, 2011).

Gray, R. M. (2010). The Brooklyn Program: applying NLP to addictions. *Current Research in NLP: Proceedings of 2008 Conference* 1(1): 88–98.

Peele, S., Brodsky, A., and Arnold M. (1991). *The Truth about Addiction and Recovery.* New York: Simon & Schuster.

Prochaska, J. O. (1994). Strong and weak principles for progressing from precontemplation to action on the basis of twelve problem behaviors. *Health Psychology* 13(1): 47–51.

Prochaska, J. O., Norcross, J. C., and DiClemente, C. C. (1994). *Changing for Good.* New York: William Morrow.

Schaffer Library of Drug Policy (2005). Addiction criteria. Available at www.druglibrary.org/Schaffer/library/addcrit.htm (accessed August 10, 2011).

Further articles, training audios, and audio tracks of the basic techniques and other materials can be accessed for free at: http://richardmgray.home.comcast.net.

L. MICHAEL HALL
ROBERT DILTS
RICHARD BOLSTAD
LUCAS DERKS
IAN MCDERMOTT
TIM HALLBOM
LISA WAKE
JAAP HOLLANDER
MARTIN ROBERTS
ARNE MAUS
CHARLES FAULKNER
FRANK BOURKE
JAMES LAWLEY
KRIS HALLBOM
NICK KEMP
RICHARD GRAY
PENNY TOMPKINS
HIROMI TAMAKI
KIMIKO BOKURA-SHAFE
BOBBY G. BODENHAMER
MASAKI KONO
RICHARD LIOTTA
JOHN MCWHIRTER

 **Kristine Hallbom** is an international trainer, author and coach. She is the co-founder of the NLP & Coaching Institute and WealthyMind International. She is also a contributing author to the best-selling book, *Alternative Medicine—The Definitive Guide,* and the co-developer of the Dynamic Spin Release approach. Recognized for her ability to translate complex ideas into practical skills, and for her warm, approachable style, Kris has trained and coached clients throughout Europe, Australia, Mexico, and the United States. She has been active in the fields of NLP and Psychology for over twenty-five years, and holds a degree in Psychology and Language. She is also a professionally trained Life Coach and Hypnotherapist, and maintains a private practice in the San Francisco Bay Area.

**Tim Hallbom** is the co-director of the NLP & Coaching Institute, and is one of the most experienced and successful international trainers, developers, and authors in the field of NLP. He is the co-author of *Beliefs: Pathways to Health and Well-Being, Coaching in the Workplace,* and *NLP: The New Technology of Achievement.* His areas of expertise include using NLP to enhance performance in business, health, and personal growth with an emphasis on working with beliefs and issues of identity. Tim has innovated and championed many of the most useful processes in the field for creating lasting change. He is a Coach Diplomat through the *Academy for Behavioral Medicine.* He, and his wife and partner Kris, were the keynote speakers at the European NLP Conference in 2009—and their keynote presentation was on Dynamic Spin Release.

web: http://www.nlpca.com/
email: (Kris Hallbom) krish@nlpca.com
        (Tim Hallbom): timh@nlpca.com

# 12 NLP and Money
## How to Create Empowering Beliefs about Money and Wealth

*Kris Hallbom and Tim Hallbom*

## Why Are Beliefs about Money and Wealth Important?

Many people have unconscious beliefs about money that keep them from having the wealth and prosperity they want and deserve. So they end up never being able to have the life they want—because at some level they *don't believe* they can.

At a conscious level, most people think they are doing everything possible to achieve their goals and dreams. However, there still might be some unconscious part of them (such as a hidden belief) that keeps them from having what they want. Think of all the people you know who read the "think and grow rich" books, attend financial seminars, say daily affirmations, but still have money problems. All of these activities are worthwhile to gain the knowledge to get ahead—yet they often don't get to the "core" of their issue, which usually involves an unconscious limiting belief.

Common limiting beliefs about money and finances include:

- You have to work hard to make money.
- I will never be rich.
- Having money isn't spiritual.
- Money is hard to manage.
- You need money to make money.
- It's too late in my life to think about getting wealthy.
- I don't have what it takes to be rich.
- I can't be successful because my parents weren't successful.
- Money is for other people; it isn't for me.
- I am not good enough to have what I want.

We call these limiting beliefs because they take away choices in behavior and prevent you from doing what you need to do to be successful. A very common belief is, "You have to work hard to make money." If you hold that belief, notice how it makes it difficult for you to make money and how you'll think you need to make important trade-offs in your life to make money—such as limiting your time with your family or enjoying recreational activities.

Another common belief is, "I'll never be rich." If you have this one, then you won't bother even trying to make money. Or, "Having money isn't spiritual." If you believe that, and spirituality is important to you, then you will keep yourself from being wealthy so you can be the kind of person you want to be.

These are just a few examples of how your limiting beliefs about money take away behavioral choices and can prevent you from being as successful as you would like to be. Once you identify and change your limiting beliefs, you'll be able to achieve a lot more of what you want in life.

## What Are the Money Beliefs and Imprints?

According to Bruce Lipton in *The Biology of Belief*, you have over four billion bits of information traveling into your nervous system every second.[1] However, only about two thousand bits can be processed consciously. Therefore, over 99% of your thoughts and emotions are unconscious. Your childhood memories, emotions, and beliefs move through your unconscious mind, and affect every aspect of your life.

You form your beliefs about money and wealth at an early age, and they are formed in several ways. The first is absorbing the ideas and beliefs that are being expressed in the family system and in the larger culture around you. For example, people with money issues may have had parents who lived in poverty, and they subsequently formed a "poverty mentality." An unconscious belief developed that they will always have to struggle financially because that's what their parents did. Or they might have had a parent tell them over and over again that they'll never be successful.

Beliefs are also formed through early reference experiences called imprints. Different kinds of imprints occur at different developmental stages of growing up. Some imprint experiences can lead to empowering beliefs and some to limiting ones.

Some of the beliefs that you may develop at an early age are not always useful, and are created as a result of a traumatic or confusing experience when you made a decision about yourself or the world. Moreover, how you unconsciously and consciously view the world in terms of money is generally based on such beliefs.[2]

For example, when I (Tim) was 4 years old, I had a little bank where I saved coins that I received from my family. One day I pried the coin holder off and took some money from the bank, and went on an adventure to a candy store several blocks away. When I returned with my little bag of candy, I was confronted by my upset mother. She asked if I had taken the money from my bank. I took what she said to mean that I shouldn't have taken the money—because she was clearly unhappy with me. As a result of this experience, I subsequently developed a limiting belief: "Money is for other people, but not for me."

Later, as an adult, when I connected the belief with the above imprint experience, I asked my mom about that specific event in my life and how she felt about it. Interestingly, she remembered my adventure to the candy store, but was not worried about me breaking the bank and taking the money. She was upset that I had traveled so far away from the house across a busy street without telling her.

## How Does the Belief Change Pattern Work?

### 1. Identify and Recognize Your Limiting Beliefs

Identifying your *limiting beliefs* is a critical first step. Once you've identified what some of those unconscious imprints/beliefs are, several different NLP belief change processes can enable you to quickly move through those obstacles allowing you to see and experience all of the financial opportunities available to you.[3]

Often, the first indication that you have a limiting belief is a feeling. Sometimes you may feel anxious or angry when faced with an issue or situation that you have a limiting belief about. Sometimes you may just feel overwhelmed, irritated, or depressed without knowing why.

We have had many clients in our private practices who wanted help because they were feeling anxious or angry about a recurring issue in their lives. They felt completely hopeless about the situation. More often than not there is a limiting belief or cluster of beliefs that are directly connected with whatever issue the client is presenting to us.

Sometimes, when a client is talking about a problem, the muscle tonus and the color in their face will change, or the speed and tonal quality of their voice will change. This tells us that they are accessing the deeper levels that are directly connected with their limiting beliefs. Then we will ask a series of powerful questions to help them identify the limiting belief(s) under the surface and directly connected with the physiological shifts that we observed while they were talking. We will be sharing those powerful questions later in this chapter.[4]

In general, there are four different types of limiting beliefs about wealth and prosperity to look out for. We have included several examples that we have discovered when working with our clients in private practice and with students at seminars. As you read through the following types of beliefs, you may begin to identify some of your own unconscious limiting beliefs about money and wealth.[5]

1. **Beliefs about cause:** This is where you presume there is a specific "cause" creating the belief. Often these kinds of beliefs have the word "because" or "cause" in them. Some examples of limiting beliefs about cause include:
   - I can't be successful because my parents weren't successful.
   - I don't deserve to have what I want because I am a woman.
   - Life is a struggle because I never get what I want.
   - We're not supposed to have money because we grew up poor.
   - Money causes pain.

2. **Beliefs about meaning:** As human beings we are always trying to find the meanings in things. What does it really mean to be rich or poor—what is the deeper meaning behind these things? The meanings that you give these beliefs will guide your behavior because they operate as filters for your belief systems. Some examples of these include:
   - Money doesn't buy happiness (having money doesn't mean you will be happy).
   - Money is the root of all evil (having money means evil will result).
   - Having money isn't spiritual (having money means I cannot be spiritual).
   - Money is unimportant (having money means I am trivial/superficial).

- Earning money would be boring (earning money means I am a boring person).
- You can't trust rich people (being rich means you are untrustworthy).

3. **Beliefs about possibility:** Beliefs can also be about possibility, and what is possible for us. There are two kinds of beliefs about possibilities:
   - The outcome is possible: If it is possible, then you have permission from your unconscious mind to go for the intended goal or outcome.
   - The outcome is impossible: If it is impossible, then you won't even bother with trying to get what you want. For example, if you believe that you can't get ahead because the economy is bad and you hold that belief firmly in your mind, then you won't do what it takes to be successful. You will give up ahead of time, and not do anything to create what you want.

   Some examples of limiting beliefs about possibility include:
   - Money is hard to manage; I will never be able to manage money.
   - I don't know how to make money.
   - Large sums of money are for other people.
   - I will never make a lot of money.
   - If I make money, I will mess it up and lose it all.
   - How to make money is a giant mystery.

4. **Beliefs about identity:** Beliefs that involve identity are about our worthiness and deservedness to attain wealth and success. Some examples of these kinds of limiting beliefs include:
   - I am not good enough to be successful.
   - I don't deserve to have what I want.
   - I am not smart enough to make money.
   - I don't have the right to live.
   - I am not worthy of success.
   - Nobody likes me; I'm just a loser.

The most common unconscious identity level belief issues about money and wealth tend to fall into the following three categories:

a) *Hopelessness*: Belief that the desired goal is not achievable, regardless of your capabilities. There is no hope that you will get what you want.

b) *Helplessness*: Belief that the desired goal is possible, but you are not capable of achieving it. You are helpless and incapable of getting what you want.

c) *Worthlessness*: Belief that you do not deserve the desired goal because of who you are, because of something you did, or because of something you haven't done.

Many of the belief issues that students identify at our WealthyMind trainings have to do with their own self-worth, and impact several areas of their life that go beyond their finances, such as their relationships, self-esteem, and overall health. Some examples of these identity level beliefs are:

- I'm not good enough to have what I want because … (I'm not smart enough, I'm not pretty enough, no one likes me, etc.)

- I'm not worthy of having what I want because … (I should have never been born, my parents didn't love me, I'm a bad person, etc.)

- I don't deserve to have what I want because … (No one loves me, I'm a bad person, I'm such a loser, etc.)

We all have limiting beliefs about what we do and do not deserve, and whether or not we are good enough or worthy enough to have what we want. At some level, these deeper core beliefs are directly connected to our self-worth and who we are in the world—and our sense of identity.

Limiting beliefs operate under the surface at an unconscious level and are not readily apparent. This is because they were typically formed when you were a small child and are outside of your conscious awareness, so they're more difficult to remember. For example, you could have an adult conscious belief, "Of course I deserve to have what I want," but somewhere in your unconscious mind there is a deeper hidden belief, "No, I don't deserve to have what I want." And that deeper core belief will end up acting as an internal saboteur that will keep you from getting what you want in life.

Beliefs about hopelessness, helplessness, or worthlessness can block you from having what you want because they are often in conflict with your more rational adult thinking.

*Seven Key Questions to Identify Limiting Beliefs about Money, Wealth, and Prosperity*

Take a moment to answer the following seven questions.[6] The more thoroughly you answer them, the more you will discover about yourself. Once you have answered the questions, you will then have a series of sentences that will point to your beliefs about money and wealth. Some of the beliefs that you discover from this exercise will be positive for you, and some of them will be limiting beliefs. The goal is to find as many limiting beliefs as possible so that you can change them.

1. What were the positive and negative events that shaped your relationship with money?

2. What was your parents' relationship with money like?

3. Finish the sentence: "I think that my Mom's/Dad's beliefs about money were ..."

4. What was the effect of their beliefs on you?

5. Finish the sentence: "I am (am not) in the exact money situation that I'd like to be in because ..."

6. What do you need to do or to have to make the money you want?

7. What stops you from having or making the money you want?

## 2. Identify Your Stem Beliefs, Belief Clusters, and Belief Systems

The next step will be to take the limiting beliefs discovered from the previous exercise and drill them down deeper into a *stem belief*. The goal in doing this is to identify your entire belief system around money and wealth because, more often than not, you will have several limiting beliefs around this topic.

A stem belief represents the underlying cluster of supporting beliefs that hold together a larger belief system. In a sense, your belief system is like a cluster of grapes on a vine. Each grape operates as a *supporting belief* and the grape stem represents the deeper *stem belief*, which holds together all of the supporting beliefs.[7]

The reason why it can be challenging to change a belief is because most people only work with the individual supporting beliefs which can be in conflict with each other, instead of the entire cluster of beliefs. *It can be difficult to truly change a belief without getting to the core of the belief.* This is why affirmations often don't work. They typically don't address the core stem belief—they only address one of the smaller, less charged beliefs within a cluster.

Changing a limiting stem belief is incredibly powerful because it allows you to let go of several limiting beliefs at once. In essence, many of the limiting beliefs that have held you back in your entire life will automatically fall off the cluster of limiting beliefs living inside your unconscious mind—and will no longer prevent you from having what you truly want and deserve in life.

The most common stem beliefs that we have come across are:

- I'm not good enough to have what I want.
- I don't deserve to have what I want.
- I don't exist; I don't have the right to be here.
- Others come before me.
- You have to work hard to make money.
- I'm not worthy of having what I want.

Usually a person will become emotional or even cry when they become conscious of their stem belief for the first time. It is often an intense experience to consciously realize they have been holding a limiting belief such as "I'm worthless" their entire life and to recognize how it has impacted every area of their life.

When this happens, invite the person to thank the unconscious part of themselves for being present and for expressing its long-held emotions. Reassure the person that they'll be changing their old limiting belief into a new empowering belief, and they only need to hang on to it for a few more minutes. Once they have acknowledged the stem belief and get past the emotional awareness of it, they can then begin the process of healing and transforming it.

The success rate for creating major personal change is very high when you focus on identifying and changing the stem belief—because the stem belief holds together the whole cluster of related beliefs.[8]

*How to Elicit a Stem Belief*

Most stem beliefs and belief clusters are formed when we are small children. They often sound childlike in nature and can be simply stated. They can also be difficult to find because they are so far outside of conscious awareness.

The first step is to help the person find a basic limiting belief by listening to their language patterns or by asking the seven questions above. Those questions are designed to help him or her find some of the more grapelike beliefs such as, "Money is hard to manage" or "You can't trust rich people."

The next step is to take their basic limiting belief and drill it down further by asking a series of questions to tease out the unconscious stem belief and belief clusters.

*Eight Key Questions to Identify Deeper Stem Beliefs and Larger Belief Clusters*

You can tease out the entire belief cluster quickly by asking the following eight questions[9] over and over:

1. "What must be true for you to say that belief statement?"
2. "What is presupposed in that belief statement?"
3. (Backtrack their belief statement) and say "because ..."
4. "What does it mean that ...?" (Repeat their sentence.)
5. "Why?" or "Why is that true for you that you hold that belief?"
6. "Tell me more about that" or "Say more about what you just said."
7. "How is that a problem?" (If you are unclear about their original belief statement.)
8. "What does that mean about you?"

## 3. How to Change Your Limiting Beliefs with Dynamic Spin Release

Dynamic Spin Release™ (DSR) is a practical approach consisting of several techniques and processes that can help you release your negative thought patterns and limiting beliefs around money in as little as ten minutes. Dynamic Spin Release combines tools from NLP and the psychology of metaphors, with the universal principle of "spin" to accelerate the process of change and transformation.

We began developing Dynamic Spin Release in March 2008 and since then have created several new DSR techniques to help our clients transform and release their unconscious conflicts, negative thought patterns, critical voices, limiting beliefs, physical pain, and much more.[10]

The Dynamic Spin Release technique is a process that we developed to help a person change their limiting beliefs and their deeper stem beliefs.[11]

*The Dynamic Spin Release Belief Change Process*

1. Think of your limiting belief. Say the belief out loud and notice the feelings you get from saying the belief.

2. Notice where you feel your feelings about the belief in your body. (Often when a person thinks about their limiting belief, they will get a strong emotional reaction and will be able to feel it in their head, chest, or stomach.)

3. Now pull this representation of the belief away from your body, and see it floating out in front of you in the form of a symbol or image.

4. Determine which way the symbol or image is spinning. Is it spinning clockwise or counterclockwise? If it appears motionless then ask, "If it was spinning, which direction would it be spinning in?"

5. Reverse the direction of the spin, and get it going faster and faster until it disappears, and a new healing image or symbol will suddenly appear. Identify the positive message the image offers. (This step involves getting the positive intention and all the positive healing resources from the gift. Please note that if for any reason you get a metaphorical gift that you don't understand or you don't like, then you can spin it again until another gift appears!)

6. Create a new belief that supports the positive message from the healing image or metaphorical gift.

7. Bring the new gift and belief into your heart space or wherever feels the best to you in your body—and as you do, be sure to say the new belief.

8. Write down the new belief on a piece of paper, so that you can remember it forever.

## The Power of Changing Your Beliefs

Mary attended our WealthyMind™ training program several years ago to work on her limiting beliefs about money and discovered she had a limiting belief which was, "It takes a lot of hard work to make money."

Mary let go of her old limiting belief and created a new belief, "I can make a lot of money, and the money comes quickly and easily to me." About a week later, she called to tell us she had already made US$100,000 since she had changed her belief. Apparently, she had gone real estate shopping with her fiancé for a new condominium when she got back from the training. She was living in Sydney, Australia and had finally found the condo she wanted overlooking the Sydney Harbor, where the famous landmark Opera House is. Even though, they could afford it, she hesitated on signing the papers because she thought she would have to work really hard to pay the monthly mortgage.

But then, her new belief suddenly popped into her head and she told herself, "I can make a lot of money, and I know the money will come quickly and easily to me. It will be a piece of cake to pay the monthly mortgage payment!" She went ahead and bought the condo and trusted that the money would come quickly and easily to her. Within twenty-four hours of signing the mortgage agreement, her real estate agent called and asked her if she wanted to sell the condo she had just bought. Evidently, it was the last unit in the building and another buyer really wanted it—and offered Mary US$100,000 beyond what she had originally paid.

Mary said that she was so glad she had changed her old limiting belief because, before changing her belief, she would have never bought the original condo. Because she changed her belief, she trusted that the money would come quickly and easily to her, and it did.

## When Does This Process Not Work?

This process will almost always work to make some kind of a positive difference for people. So far we haven't found any negative side effects. However, we wouldn't recommend using this process with someone who is having psychotic symptoms or some kind of serious thought disorder. If that's the case, then they should consult a qualified health practitioner such as a clinical social worker or psychologist.

**Notes**

1. Lipton (2008).

2. Hallbom and Hallbom (1993).

3. Dilts et al. (1990); Hallbom and Hallbom (2009a, 2009b).

4. Dilts (2000), pp. 866–868; Hallbom and Hallbom (2009b).

5. Dilts et al. (1990).

6. Hallbom and Hallbom (2000–2011).

7. Hallbom and Hallbom (2001–2011).

8. Hallbom and Hallbom (2001–2011).

9. Hallbom and Hallbom (2000–2011).
    Hallbom and Hallbom (2009–2011); Hallbom (2008).

10. Hallbom and Hallbom (2009–2011).

11. We later learned that Richard Bandler had been spinning sub-modalities for quite a while, and we were delighted to find this out because it confirmed our experience with "spin" and reversing it. You can find out more about how he uses spin in Bandler (2008).

**References**

Bandler, R. (2008). *Get the Life You Want: The Secrets to Quick and Lasting Life Change with NLP*. Dearfield Beach, FL: Health Communications.

Dilts, R. (2000). Neurological levels. *Encyclopedia of NLP*. Scotts Valley, CA: NLP University Press, pp. 866–868.

Dilts, R., Hallbom, T., and Smith, S. (1990). *Beliefs: Pathways to Health and Well-Being*. Portland, OR: Metamorphous Press.

Hallbom, K. (2008). Dynamic Spin Release and the energy of your mind. Available at www.nlpca.com/DCweb/Dynamic_Spin_Release.html (accessed August 10, 2011).

Hallbom, K. (2008). *Dynamic Spin Release: An Introduction to the DSR Process*. DVD. Burlingame, CA and Salt Lake City, UT: NLP and Coaching Institute.

Hallbom, T. and Hallbom, K. (2000–2011). *The WealthyMind Program Workbook*. Salt Lake City, UT: Bringforth Publishing.

Hallbom, K. and Hallbom, T. (2001–2011). *The WealthyMind Trainer's Training Manual*. Burlingame, CA and Salt Lake City, UT: NLP and Coaching Institute.

Hallbom, T. and Hallbom, K. (2009a). *Dynamic Spin Release: An Introduction to the DSR Process*. DVD. Salt Lake City, UT: Bringforth Publishing and London: Smartdreamers Productions.

Hallbom, T. and Hallbom, K. (2009b). *The Wealthy Mind Program*. DVD. Salt Lake City, UT: Bringforth Publishing and London: Smartdreamers Productions.

Hallbom, K. and Hallbom, T. (2009–2011). *Dynamic Spin Release Training Manual*. Burlingame, CA and Salt Lake City, UT: NLP and Coaching Institute.

Hallbom, T. and Johnson, K. (1993). Neuro-Linguistic Programming. In *Alternative Medicine: The Definitive Guide*. Beverly Hills, CA: The Holistic Book Project, pp. 376–384. Compiled by the Burton Goldman Group.

Lipton, B. (2008). *Biology of Belief*. Carlsbad, CA: Hay House Publishing.

To find out more about how Tim and Kris Hallbom created and developed Dynamic Spin Release, visit www.dynamicspinrelease.com.

### Kimiko Bokura-Shafé

*Director, NLP Medics Japan*

*MBA, CCHT, NLP Trainer*

Kimiko has been instrumental bridging east and west in the field of NLP. As the trainer/organizer, she brought numerous important Japanese trainers overseas, and foreign trainers to Japan, promoting the global development and advancement of NLP.

Born and raised in rural Japan, she pioneered early in her career as one of the first female executives in the multinational giants such as Proctor & Gamble and LVMH (Moët Hennessy Louis Vuitton). In parallel, she has been a devoted student of NLP, hypnotherapy, and positive psychology—all leading her to Santa Cruz, California where she resides.

Kimiko has been running a successful global practice in wellness coaching and communication seminars since 2000. She is the managing director for NLP Medics Japan, the highly reputable training organization for Japanese medical professionals, where she brings her business leadership and practical perspectives for the patients' empowerment reflecting her own experiences with a chronic illness.

### Dr. Masaki Kono

*Founder/Chairman, NLP Medics Japan*

*Pediatrician, Psychologist, NLP Trainer*

*Director, Wakaba-Ryoikuen Hospital (Hiroshima Prefectural Medical*

*Institution for Developmentally Challenged Children and Adults)*

Dr. Kono (aka Masa) is one of the most popular, influential NLP trainers in Japan while he runs a full-time medical practice as the director of a very successful medical institution. In 2002 Dr. Kono discovered NLP in his personal struggle to find better solution for PTSD of his patients. Subsequently, he has developed many practical medical NLP applications and founded NLP Medics Japan in 2006, which, by requests of fellow medical professionals, teaches NLP incorporating the specific needs of the clinical environment.

While Dr. Kono is highly respected as a prominent expert in developmental disorders, his childlike openness and pure dedication to NLP attracted many other medical doctors, nurses, and educators to the field of NLP. He has contributed to the credibility of NLP in the medical world as he and his team have presented research utilizing NLP at many medical conferences, some of which he chaired.

At 2010 IASH, Dr. Kono's work was presented to the global audience for the first time and received enthusiastic ovations. He is a leader in Medical NLP bringing about a paradigm shift in the health/illness model. He continues to pour his endless passion and energy into the healing of patients and the healing of healers themselves.

**Dr. Hiromi Tamaki**

*Trainer, NLP Medics Japan, NLP Institute Japan*
*Internist*
*Director, Matta Clinic, Osaka*

Dr. Tamaki (aka Hiro) encountered NLP in his spiritual pursuit of the meaning of life and death. As an expert in palliative care, he faced many deaths and became aware of many doctors and nurses living with a deep, suppressed sense of failure and survivors' guilt. As a beginner in NLP, Dr. Tamaki did a simple Second Position with one of his deceased patients, and it opened his eyes to a new paradigm of medicine: When there is understanding of meaning/message of illness for each individual patient, there is better care and healing, though it may not be physical healing in all.

Like Dr. Kono, Dr. Tamaki has a full-time medical practice as the director of a popular clinic, and he spends his weekends teaching, studying, and developing NLP. This brings a Win-Win-Win situation to the medical world, the field of NLP, and his patients. In his clinic, some of the medical staff are NLP Master Practitioners (influenced by the positive change in Dr. Tamaki), and they assist patients when Dr. Tamaki prescribes Anchoring, Position Change, Visualization, etc. just like he prescribes drugs.

Dr. Tamaki has been devoted to sharing NLP and to inviting many medical professionals, patients, and their families to this more empowering medical paradigm. With his warm, sincere personality and disarming humor, many medical professionals look up to Dr. Tamaki as a role model and leader in Medical NLP.

email: info@nlpmedics.com
web: http://nlpmedics.com

# 13 Medical Applications of NLP
## Using NLP in the Holistic Treatment of Cancer

*Kimiko Bokura-Shafé, Masaki Kono, and Hiromi Tamaki*

## Why Are Medical NLP Applications Important?

If we understand and accept health and illness in more resourceful ways, and if doctors and medical professionals are there for us as expert guides to bring out our resources, what impact does it have on our health and society? If doctors and nurses welcomed you with high rapport and calibration skills, how differently would you feel in dealing with your challenge?

NLP is developing a unique movement in Japan—medical NLP applications created, used, and taught by medical doctors for patients, their families, and medical professionals (doctors, nurses, therapists, pharmacists, etc.) fully adapted to the clinical environment. Dr. Masaki Kono (pediatrician, psychologist, and NLP Trainer) founded NLP Medics Japan in 2006 and has trained more than 300 medical professionals including over 150 doctors from across Japan in anchoring, mapping-across, reframing, and neurological levels in the treatment of patients, and each year the number of participants to the training courses has increased.

The impact of the NLP application has been observed both among patients and medical professionals. As shown in Dr. Kono's report (see Addendum), 96% of patients felt an improvement in their symptoms after NLP protocols, while 60% experienced a drastic improvement after only one or two sessions. Feedback from doctors includes improvement in their clinics' reputations, more success with patients, or they revamped their own energy and motivation after learning NLP from us.

As we seek and develop the effective medical application of NLP, we realize that it is essential to revisit the existing medical model itself—the meaning and purpose of medicine:

All people die. Medicine will always be defeated. Then, the question for us should be, what *kind* of death we can offer.

Dr. Shigeaki Hinohara[1]

What has been the meaning of death and illness in the long history of the human race? Often, illness and death cause human suffering and sorrow. That is why people try to avoid, quickly escape, and/or fight illnesses. The battle is becoming increasingly fierce as medicine progresses, and when an illness remains unalleviated, people consider it to be a defeat.

As patients, families, and medical professionals suffer through an illness, they ask the following questions consciously or unconsciously: "Whose fault is this?", "Why do I have to suffer so much?", and "Why is this happening to him/her, and not me?" Then they conclude, "I, he, or she must recover and return to how I, he, or she was."

Within this paradigm, they celebrate when a patient recovers from illness. On the other hand, when a patient fails to recover, they will blame themselves or others, or feel discontent or helplessness. Medical professionals may be driven to exert tremendous energy in fear of defeat or failure, potentially leading to the further snowballing of medical costs. Unfortunately, this phenomenon can happen in any country, not only in Japan.

To counter this situation, NLP Medics Japan offers a new alternative medical model which applies NLP protocols. By incorporating NLP, the model aims to raise a patient's negative condition up to a positive one, instead of simply reversing the negative condition back to the original status quo. The aim is to create medicine that brings wholeness—in other words, allowing one to meet one's wholeness through the experience of an illness.

We have also been presenting NLP as a viable tool at various medical conferences and in scientific papers, which has resulted in a medical community in Japan that is steadily embracing NLP and the power of human interaction. Showa University (a medical university in Tokyo) and the Department of Medicine at Hiroshima University teach NLP-applied communication classes delivered by medical doctors who are also experienced NLPers. Internationally, we presented our work at the NLP Institute of Advanced Study for Health (IASH) conference for the first time in 2010, in San Francisco, and received an enthusiastic response. NLP Medics Japan started as a small movement; however, there is growing interest across the world in our activities. This is a sign of new and exciting things to come in both fields of medicine and NLP.

Japan was hit by the horrific disasters of earthquake, tsunami, and radiation threat from a damaged nuclear power plant in March 2011. We promptly distributed information kits and a training DVD, and we conducted charity seminars to minimize stress and post-traumatic stress disorder (PTSD) in the impacted area. It is our sincere hope that our medical NLP applications will contribute to the resilience and recovery in face of this historic challenge.

## What Is A Medical NLP Application?

Where can we find a medical model that can open the door to wholeness? In *The Right of the Dying*, David Kessler writes:

> I met an elderly woman in the last year of her life. I say we "met" despite the fact that she was in a coma during the entire eleven months I "knew" her. When she died, I remember thinking that there had been no purpose to this lengthy coma. Some years after she passed away I ran into her daughter, who shared with me how she, her two sisters, and two brothers had led very individual lives, seeing one another only at the occasional Christmas or wedding celebration. "While I wish Mom had not been in that coma," she said, "we became a real family because of it. In that last year, we all pitched in to help and really supported each other. If it had not happened that way, we would have remained strangers who just happened to grow up together. I feel that there really was a purpose to that horrible year; it was Mom's last gift to us.[2]

This case has the structure we modeled. The death of the mother had initially appeared meaningless, but later on her family was able to receive it as her final gift as their mother. That is the difference we want to help everyone discover—the difference that makes a difference.

We found that patients and their families often have a behavioral level perspective (i.e., they pay attention to what patients and their families do). However, one of the key differences in our methodology is the aim that they also become aware of the values and beliefs behind behaviors as well as the shift in relations caused by such awareness, ultimately becoming aware of the shift at a spiritual level.[3]

Medical professionals can enable and empower their patients and their families to take similarly broad perspectives. At NLP Medics Japan, we promote NLP at three levels:

1. Teaching the fundamentals of NLP to bring out resources—respecting and utilizing the wholeness of patients and their families, not only at the environment and behavior levels, but also at the capability, belief, identity, and spirituality levels.

2. Developing and teaching medical NLP intervention protocols by applying and adjusting conventional NLP methods to the unique needs in medical and clinical settings.

3. Nurturing the community of medical professionals who share an interest in NLP and the wholeness of human beings.

We develop medical NLP applications—from how to use stethoscopes to how to deal with death—as an intervention tool for PTSD, panic disorders, cancers (tumors)/immunity disorders, allergies, depression, pervasive developmental disorders, unidentified complaints, and so on. We also teach NLP as a communication device used between patients and medical professionals, taking into consideration the unique day-to-day realities of medical settings. The results indicate a high level of effectiveness, and the support we have been receiving means that there is an opportunity for further NLP application in medicine.

We would like to share the NLP cancer care process we teach as part of our NLP Medics Intervention course, which is our advanced course to teach the medical NLP application for patient treatments.

### An Example of Cancer Care Protocols

Step 1 involves sharing the common, resourceful map of how cancer cells start and multiply, before moving on to coaching the visualization of healing images (Step 2), and finally checking beliefs and changing them if necessary (Step 3). This takes place alongside continual observation of the relationships between patient, family, and society, and advice on diet and lifestyle.

## Step 1: Take Time with a Patient to Create a Shared Map

Explain that cancer is not an external enemy, but is caused by a change in the immune balance:

- Cancer cells are cells that have transformed. They have lost their connection with other cells and thus keep multiplying.

- Everybody has cancer cells in their body but the number is controlled by immune cells such as lymphocytes.

- When the balance is disturbed due to changes in the environment (cells which surround cancerous cells, the nervous system, hormones, nutrition, etc.), these cells become the onset of cancer.

- Belief, diet, and lifestyle have a strong influence.

## Step 2: Visualize Cancer Cells Being Controlled By Immune Cells

- Following on from the explanation in Step 1, patients are led to imagine what is happening in their bodies in a metaphorical manner:

> Cows are grazing in the pasture. The grasses in the pasture are cancer cells, and the cows are immune cells. Grasses are growing rapidly, long, and wild. This is because there are not enough cows. Now imagine you are putting more cows onto the pasture so the grass does not become too long. When the number of cows reaches an adequate level, cows eat grass with gusto and excrete manure which nurtures the grass. Grass grows back, but it remains short and neat because a sufficient number of cows eat it all the time. These cows produce milk from delicious grass.

- Visualize this image repeatedly.[4] What sound or inner voice can you hear? What feelings do you have? (If the feelings are not comfortable, modify the image until it generates comfort.)

- Once you establish a good, congruent visualization, repeat it every day as many times as possible.

Please note that it is critical to create a visualization of ecological circulation and harmony, which are fundamental to Eastern philosophy; it should never lead to imageries of battles or altercations. Although the concept of a war has often been used in Western medicine, in our process it conflicts with the shared map (in Step 1) that the cancer cells naturally exist in our body as a part of a healthy system. The image of ecological circulation and harmony better suits and achieves the healthy coexistence and balance between normal cells and cancer cells. The circulation of water, air, and energy in nature is considered the source of life and constitutes the fundamental concept of health in Eastern medicine, while lack of it is believed to cause illnesses.

The image of a battle is also known to stimulate the adrenal gland and the stress response, which triggers the secretion of adrenocortical hormone and epinephrine (generally known as adrenaline), thus leading to a decline in the immune function. The visualization of ecological and harmonious circulation is expected to activate the immune function better as it helps a patient to sustain a more peaceful and calming state than the stress-triggering battle image.

### Step 3: Checking Beliefs and Changing Them If Necessary

This step is often completed by the patient as homework, then discussed in depth during a session.

- What are your beliefs about life? (As many as possible, e.g., Life should be thick and short. I don't want to live when I am a burden to others.)

- Since when have you had that belief?

- What kind of experience was that belief formed on? Who are the significant others in that event?

- How has that belief been useful to your life? (Positive intent)

- How has that belief been limiting your life? (Limiting belief)

- Does that belief serve your life and health now in every way?

- If not, think of as many alternative beliefs as possible.

- Find the one that fits you most.

- If and when you live on this new belief, how will your life change?

- What does this change mean to your life?

## Case Example: Lung Cancer Patient
## (Male, 76 years old, inoperable, Stage IIIB)

Dr. Tamaki applied the above cancer protocol to this patient. Figure 1 indicates the blood carcinoembryonic antigen (CEA) level (positive correlation with the growth of cancer cells) for eleven months. After chemotherapy, CEA typically drops temporarily, then returns to the previous level. However, as the nurse (a NLP Master Practitioner) continued with the above three steps under the supervision of Dr. Tamaki and Dr. Kono, the patient's CEA score remained low. The cancerous region shrunk and is currently unrecognizable. Today, four years later, the patient now lives healthfully with his wife.

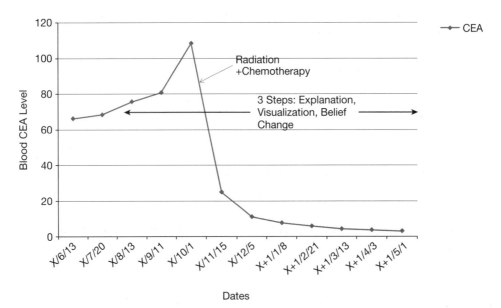

**Figure 1:** *Blood CEA level over 11 months*

While this is certainly a significant physical change, we believe that the psychological and sociological changes that followed could actually be equally important.

Previously, the patient believed: "If I fully pursue what I want to do, my family would fall apart." He had lived life holding himself back to take care of others with perseverance and reserve. He had demanded the same from his family. Through this intervention, he rewrote his belief into a new one: "When intuition kicks in, trust it, and run with it." He started to accept and express his feelings, which made it easier to accept his wife's feelings, and their relationship was further improved. It also made him realize how much joy he was receiving by making his customers happy in his small restaurant, despite believing previously that he did it only for the money.

He confided, "Well, I won't say that getting sick was a good thing, Doctor, but I am so much happier now that I can feel the kindness of other people," and "Every time I see people or beautiful scenery, I just can't help but be grateful." Through this experience, not only was he able to recover from cancer, but he was also able to revisit his life with a new perspective. He can now discover gifts from the past and new gifts to come in the future.

Based on this and other cases, we deduce that this intervention protocol is effective for cancer care. However, please note that we cannot yet substantiate the degree to which the NLP intervention contributed (or did not contribute) to this patient's recovery from cancer. One of our most important tasks now is to provide scientific evidence with many more clinical cases.

## How Does It Work?

We utilize a vast range of NLP models in our medical NLP protocols (see the Addendum). However, they almost always overtly and/or covertly involve the process of patients examining the meaning of the symptom and, if necessary, transferring it to a more resourceful one. Here, we repeatedly utilize concepts of modeling, neurological levels, and meaning (map).

We model our predecessors in medicine, our mentors, our personal experiences, as well as past contributions in NLP, especially those with amazing health benefits. We apply a holistic view of the neurological levels and share resourceful maps of health and illness. Our ultimate goal is to promote medicine that raises the negative condition to the positive—not medicine that simply reverses the negative back to the original status quo—in methods that *anyone* can apply. This is truly medicine which offers blessings and gifts and aims for wholeness.

Another significant uniqueness pertaining to the medical environment is the presence of patients' powerful emotions such as fear, anger, hope, joy, sorrow, and so on. As shown through the achievements of Dr. Milton Erickson,[5] states caused by such strong emotions are where the window opens to the subconscious mind. When medical professionals acknowledge and accept such strong emotions, it can bring out mutual opportunities for resonance and transformation between patients and medical professionals to walk the path to a brisk recovery together (see Figure 2).

**Figure 2:** *Characteristics of Effective Medical NLP Applications*

In such cases, patients' expectations and even their surrender to medical professionals could be utilized for pacing and deep rapport, leading to an effective execution of the intervention. This enables a drastic reduction in treatment time—a critical requirement in medical practice.

In addition to time constraints, medical NLP applications need to accommodate the following:

- Clear and simple protocols stated in specific scripts or step-by-step formats. This enables medical professionals to confidently use the protocol in their practice.

- Environmental flexibility by utilizing natural conversational patterns and pre-filled questionnaires. Especially in Japan, consultation rooms are typically small (thus there is little room for spatial sorting) and it is often hard to secure privacy due to the presence of nurses or paramedics; sometimes the patient's mobility can be limited.

The medical application of NLP may appear to be handicapped with inherent limitations such as length of time and the physical environment. However, it is quite possible to obtain good results from medical NLP protocols by pacing the patient's strong emotions and motivation, and the expectations of medical professionals.

Doctors Kono and Tamaki, both full-time directors in important medical facilities, fully understand the wishes and struggles of medical professionals; they are also well aware of the realities of medical practice. These considerations are reflected in our medical applications of NLP, which we teach only after confirming their safety, effectiveness, and efficiency through utilization in our own medical practices. This makes it easier for other doctors and medical professionals to accept and use our NLP applications.

## When Does It Not Work?

*Clashes with Existing Western Medicine Based on Mistrust*

As practicing doctors, Doctors Kono and Tamaki know about the wonders of modern (Western) medicine. They have often experienced new medications or treatments miraculously curing patients who were otherwise past remedy. At the same time, they have also witnessed the wonderful changes in patients when NLP is applied. When modern medicine and NLP clash due to mistrust, patients can become confused. NLP needs credibility at the level of modern medicine in order to establish a mutual and generative relationship. To promote mutual understanding, we must develop a common language between modern medicine and NLP through scientific testability and accumulating scientific evidence.

*Inconsistency in NLP Capability among Medical Professionals*

Our protocols are not as effective when a certain level of NLP capability cannot be maintained. Therefore, we need to make sure that a specific level of skill is maintained via self-effort, supervision, and intervision (synergistic exchange of visions from equal standpoint). We also need to establish a system to continuously improve capability, and we are in the process of developing one.

*Influence of Beliefs from People around the Patient*

When medical NLP is used, we can often bring out quick and significant changes. This surprises not only the patient but also their family and loved ones, some of whom may not accept the changes. "It is impossible to cure so easily," they may say. Such strong convictions from the people around the patient may neutralize improved conditions back to how it was before, just like inertia in physics. To solve this problem, we sometimes invite family members into the consulting room.

*When a Patient Is Unaware of the Improvement*

Patients can be unaware of the positive change, while those around them notice the difference. Alternatively, patients can be caught up by a minor remaining symptom. These situations require continuous follow-up.

# Personal Significance

### Dr. Tamaki's Case

A 27-year-old female patient came to me with a headache and abdominal pains. She was a professional caregiver in a nursing home, but the pain was making it difficult for her to continue this job. The clinics which she had been to previously concluded that she had tension headache and functional abdominal pain, thus she was prescribed pain medications. I could have prescribed more pain medication, but when I asked the positive intent behind her pain, the symptoms were immediately alleviated. She went home happily. However, every few weeks she came back complaining of the same headache and abdominal pain, and the pain was repeatedly alleviated every time she realized the positive intent of the pain. After a while, I noticed a pattern: her abdominal pain was a message telling her to rest and acknowledge her hard work, and her headache was pointing out to her that she was not doing what she really wanted to, and was telling her to focus on what she really wanted to do. So she followed these messages, started to take better care of herself, and engaged with what she really wanted to do.

What happened to her as a result of her choices was quite a surprise. She moved across the world to Spain and became a professional flamenco dancer who moves her audience to tears! Her headache and abdominal pain that had appeared to bring misery to her awareness had turned out to be wonderful guides.

## Dr. Kono's Case

A female patient in her sixties had a 30-year-old son who was institutionalized. He was born with severe cerebral palsy, with a combination of severe mental retardation and physical disability. One of her purposes in life was to visit her son at the institution, transfer him to a wheelchair, and take him out for a drive in her car. However, recently she had become unable to raise her arm, and she now had to ask for help from the institution staff to bring her son to the car. While the staff would happily assist, she was still ashamed of herself as a mother.

She had an egg-sized benign tumor beneath the edge of her shoulder blade. She consulted an orthopedist who refused to operate on her until the tumor became unbearably large, because her type of tumor was known to recur even after surgical removal and was impossible to cure completely. So she decided to come to me.

I coached her on visualization and changed her belief. Her previous belief of "My life purpose is to help my son" was updated to "I am here to receive help from my son." She visualized the image of cows grazing on grass every day and often fell asleep in her visualization. Every time she visited her son, she now asked him, "Please make the tumor smaller," and had him stroke it. Two months later, she came back for a visit. "Doctor, feel my back!" she said. When I did, I could no longer find the tumor.

As we explore the medical applications of NLP, what we find are not always the answers to "What/Who is at fault?" or "Why does this suffering exist?" What we do learn, however, is that it may be more important for that person to ask: "What do I realize from this illness or suffering?" or "What lies behind this illness or suffering?", and gain answers to these questions. Beyond simply reverting back to one's former self (while this in itself is an essential goal), with the above realizations the path of the disease may lead to the opening of new chapters in life. When one understands these possibilities, perhaps that is when one can truly accept illness and suffering as an integral part of that person.

## Notes

1. An observation by Dr. Shigeaki Hinohara (a prominent Japanese doctor actively practicing medicine at the age of 99) in Hinohara (1999).

2. Kessler (1997), pp. 13–14.

3. The concept of neurological levels is well explained in Dilts et al. (2010), pp. 63–74.

4. This visualization for health is described in Dilts et al. (1990), pp. 153–156.

5. Rosen (1991).

## References

Dilts, P. A. (1991). *My Pathway to Wholeness*. Santa Cruz, CA: NLP University Press.

Dilts, R., DeLozier, J., and Dilts, D. B. (2010). *NLP II: The Next Generation. Enriching the Study of the Structure of Subjective Experience*. Capitola, CA: Meta Publications.

Dilts, R., Hallbom, T., and Smith, S. (1990). *Beliefs: Pathways to Health and Well-Being*. Portland, OR: Metamorphous Press.

Duncan, B. L., Miller, S. D., and Sparks, J. A. (2004). *Heroic Client: A Revolutionary Way To Improve Effectiveness Through Client-Directed, Outcome-Informed Therapy*. San Francisco, CA: Jossey-Bass.

Hinohara, S. (1999). *Thought After Treating 640 Sarin Attack Patients. JOIN* 32 (June/July).

Kessler, D. (1997). *The Rights of the Dying*. New York: HarperCollins.

Rosen, S. (1991). *My Voice Will Go With You: The Teaching Tales of Milton H. Erickson*. New York: W. W. Norton.

Yanagida, K. (1986). *The Prelude to the Medicine of Death* (in Japanese). Tokyo: Sinchosha.

Yanagida, K. (1996). *The Diary for the Medicine of Death* (in Japanese). Tokyo: Sinchosha.

## Addendum: Patient Feedback after NLP Protocols

Presented by Masaki Kono, Hironori Suhama, Manabu Iwasaki, and Tomomi Mura-matsu at the 27th Congress of Japanese Society of Psychosomatic Pediatrics, June 2009.

- Subjects: 39 patients/47 sessions—12 males (13 sessions) and 27 females (34 sessions); 10 cases also had pharmacotherapy.

- Ages: 11–64 years old (average: 24.6 years old).

- Symptoms: phobia, truancy, PTSD/acute stress disorder, irritable bowel syndrome, anxiety, depression, self-mutilation, hyper-ventilation, emotional disorder, eating disorders, etc.

- NLP protocols used: anchoring, re-imprint, position change, sub-modality change, SCORE, visualization, positive intent, six-step reframing, phobia process, eye accessing, etc.

The result: 96% felt an improvement in their symptoms, 2% did not discern any changes, and 2% felt aggravation (see Figure 3).

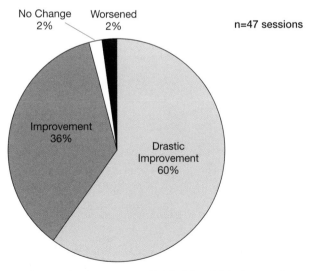

**Figure 3:** *Patient Feedback After NLP Protocols*

**Martin Roberts Ph.D.**

Businessman, speaker, author, academic and military historian. Martin originally trained as an engineer and subsequently, as a mature student, moved across into studying the realms of the mind, where he gained a Ph.D. in psychology. In the early 1980s he became interested in NLP and trained to trainer level.

He spent most of his working life in the business world either as a member of senior management or as an independent business consultant. Specialising in ICT and Change Management, a subject on which he has published a book and also written many articles. As a Research Fellow of Cranfield University he was in the 1980s and '90s a regular guest lecturer at the University. He is very widely traveled and this includes four years of his working life spent in the USA.

For the last ten years he has been chairman of Crown House Publishing and a non-executive director of a number of other companies. He was for some years a Branch Chairperson of the Institute of Directors in Wales and took a leading role in representing the business community at national level.

# 14 The Well-Formed Problem
## A New Model for Managing Change in Business

*Martin Roberts*

## Why is the Well-Formed Problem Model Important?

This pattern is one of the first created specifically for use in a business setting rather than derived from classical NLP techniques. Its application also differs; it deals with group and organizational problems rather than individuals. It is closely related to the Well-Formed Outcome Pattern and is an application of the meta-model. However, this pattern concentrates on producing a definitive problem often from a number of contending and sometimes conflicting possibilities. The description here involves models and tools of change management (CM) used in the business arena. The Well-Formed Problem enables organizations to identify which problem needs to be solved and gives a clear, usable definition of the problem to start the process of creating a solution that works.

NLP usually focuses on identifying outcomes rather than analyzing causes. This works well in business when there is only one possible outcome to one or more problems. However, often the issues involved are far more complex and multiple causes exist leading to a range of possible outcomes. In such situations a very strong case exists for examining which problems need to be solved, in what order, and by which method. Establishing a useful description of each competing problem is especially useful when large, complex systems are involved. Conversely, if instead a more direct outcome-orientated approach was used for each problem, the overall outcome would likely be similar to that of the London Stock Exchange (LSE) Taurus project mentioned below.

The pattern was originally developed between 1990 and 1993 by an eclectic group of five research fellows attached to the International Ecotechnology Research Centre (Ecotech) of Cranfield University, England. Each member of the group possessed a unique skill-set as well as having in-depth experience in the fields of information and communications technology (ICT) and CM. The author was the only person with a background in psychology and NLP. The group had come together to run a series of short public courses in CM while simultaneously researching the causes of failure in complex CM projects.

The most significant and widely publicized failure during that period was the LSE's Taurus project which was intended to be a new paperless share trading and settlement system. The development of this project had run into serious trouble in the late 1980s and collapsed dramatically in late 1992. Budgeted originally to cost £6 million and planned to take four years to build, at abandonment the total cost was estimated at £800 million and, although never delivered, was already eleven years late. Despite the magnitude of the failure, the precise cause was not identified. It was claimed that this was largely due to the complexity of the project but the true causes have never really been established. This was due to the unwillingness of key participants to contribute to an investigation into the failure, fearing that if they cooperated they could be held culpable for part or all of the failure.

The LSE system was not a unique example as many similar large ICT projects were running into difficulty. Some were considerably exceeding budget while others were running years late from the target delivery date. Like the Taurus project, others had to be abandoned altogether for a multitude of reasons, but mainly because they were not going to deliver what was expected. Total quality management has a failure rate as high as 80% and business process re-engineering nearly 30%. Yet little is really known about the true causes of failure. This is compounded by a management tendency to gloss over the facts to avoid the wrath of shareholders or stakeholders.

Little has changed in the intervening years, and failures in modern CM projects remain high. Today most of the significant failures are concerned with projects that have a high level of ICT content or are driven by packaged ICT solutions. Among these, enterprise resource planning (ERP), business intelligence (BI) planning, and customer relationship management (CRM) are often mentioned, but the causes of failure remain the same: failure to positively identify a Well-Formed Problem before selecting a solution.

To establish the principal causes of CM failures the initial task of the team at Cranfield was to accumulate and analyze the large amount of data concerning the failures. Next was to categorize the causes of the failures and rank them in order of importance (see Figure 1).

1. Not conclusively identifying the problem to be solved.

2. The organization adopting an inappropriate change mechanism.

3. The change agents not identifying and understanding the cultural implications of the change upon the subject of the change or those closely associated with it.

4. Understanding the time and effort required successfully to change beliefs and values closely associated with the change process.

5. Not developing a **genuine** "shared vision" by all those involved in the change process.

6. Not establishing the Critical Success Factors associated with the overall goal of the change program.

7. Not taking a holistic view of the organization and attempting to implement change in isolation from other parts of the business.

8. Not identifying the "human factors" implicit in the process of bringing about change.

**Figure 1:** *Causes of UK Change Management Failures*

Figure 1 shows that the first ranked item in the table is "Not conclusively identifying the problem to be solved." Definition of the problem is probably the most difficult phase of any investigation to get right. Most people involved in project management do not take adequate time to ensure they conclusively know the nature of the problem and its cause. This is seen as a major contributor to many failures among the projects. Conversely, when we compared projects deemed successful, no apparent difficulties had been encountered in obtaining a precise problem definition.

During the final stages of our analysis of the data obtained, a definition was created of the features that either caused or contributed to failure—Badly-Formed Problems. This gave rise to a list of characteristics, one or more of which are usually present in Badly-Formed Problems (see Figure 2).

1.  Being poorly defined and often described in generalizations.

2.  Having indistinct boundaries.

3.  Often having a long history.

4.  Frequently seen as having multiple causes.

5.  Containing an unaddressed "political" dimension.

6.  Having many symptoms but no/few identifiable causes.

7.  Lacking ownership.

**Figure 2:** *Features of Badly-Formed Problems*

With all this information available the task was then to construct a model to ensure that the features listed in Figure 2 would be identified and not be present in future projects. To achieve this, a better understanding of these causes was vital. The Well-Formed Problem was not intended to apportion blame, but rather to sort out exactly what needed to be solved.

## What is the Well-Formed Problem Model?

The first step in constructing a Well-Formed Problem is to effectively deal with the common causes of Badly-Formed Problems (Figure 2).

1.  **Problems poorly defined and/or described in generalizations**

    Often this is caused by communications failure at some level or across departments. Common examples are where a definition is stated as a given and assumptions are then made about how to solve the problem. Generalizations often occur because it is easier to generalize about a problem than to be precise.

2.  **Having indistinct boundaries**

    Lack of precision, if allowed to creep into a problem definition, can cause mayhem in a project. Then there are "messy problems" of different types and causes, chiefly defined by measurements of time, resources, expense, and so on, which have indistinct boundaries. If they are allowed to become incorporated into critical success factors (CSFs), they can be really damaging. To avoid boundary problems all projects should have an in-depth project specification detailing all aspects of the project and free of ambiguities.

## 3. A long history of not being solved

There are many causes for such problems, with most seen as insoluble. Those that have been around for a long time with no serious attempt made to solve them are perhaps the easiest to work with. Those with a history of failed attempts to solve them are harder, owing to the power of presupposition.

Those involved with the problem presume that further attempts to find a solution will end in failure. We now need a battle for hearts as well as minds and the first step is to give full recognition to past failures and what caused them. The next step is to see how these previous failures can be avoided. Finally a program is needed to get everyone involved to commit to success. A team leader who has a track record of getting things right and who continually informs people of progress and feedback can greatly increase the chances for success.

## 4. Seen as having multiple causes

Similar to "messy problems," many of the failures in the Cranfield study demonstrated some difficulty with positively identifying the real problem, often because of many different contributory causes. When the focus was on one cause, disregarding the rest, and the chosen "cure" was then applied, the problem remained or was only partially cured.

Cluster analysis is one of the simplest methods to solve this. The symptoms and suspected causes are listed and then connected by association. Clustering occurs around a common cause or symptom if the cause remains hidden. This technique is enhanced by the use of drawings or diagrams (Figure 3) which draw out information that cannot be obtained easily by any other method.

Figure 3 is a real-life situation where the management was about to embark upon a major change program intended to improve customer relations to increase sales and turnover. While this would have probably had some positive effect, it certainly would not have solved the underlying problems of overcapacity or the lack of quality management information. The diagram makes it easy to see the

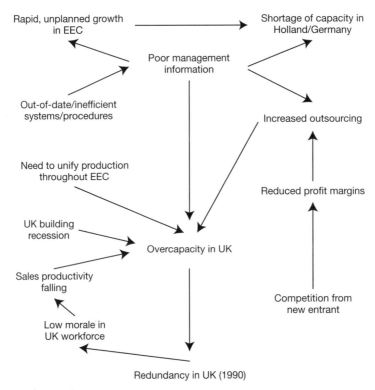

Rapid, unplanned growth in EEC

Shortage of capacity in Holland/Germany

Poor management information

Out-of-date/inefficient systems/procedures

Increased outsourcing

Need to unify production throughout EEC

Reduced profit margins

UK building recession

Overcapacity in UK

Sales productivity falling

Low morale in UK workforce

Competition from new entrant

Redundancy in UK (1990)

**Figure 3:** *Multiple Cause Diagram for the XYZ Company*

two clusters around "Overcapacity in UK" (arrows pointing toward it) and "Poor management information" (arrows pointing away).

Problems of this nature are more common than is often imagined and are particularly difficult to solve if a "wrong" solution has been chosen by a powerful advocate (e.g., a chairman or chief executive).

## 5. Unaddressed "political" dimension

Any significant CM project will attract the attention of most senior staff in an organization and some will see it as an opportunity to score points over rivals. While political maneuvering in business is part of the game for many senior managers, the practice is mostly covert, which causes problems. When identified as a potential cause of problems, the easiest way to progress is to bring it out into the open.

### 6. Having many symptoms but no/few identifiable causes

While this contributes to many failures, it is only the prime cause in a minority of cases. More commonly, symptoms are identified as causes. Sometimes the correct cause is identified, but too much emphasis is paid to symptoms. This leads to confusion as attention is diverted away from the solution.

Occasionally a number of symptoms are identified and management is persuaded that a particular packaged ICT solution will solve the problems but this tends not to fix the underlying cause.

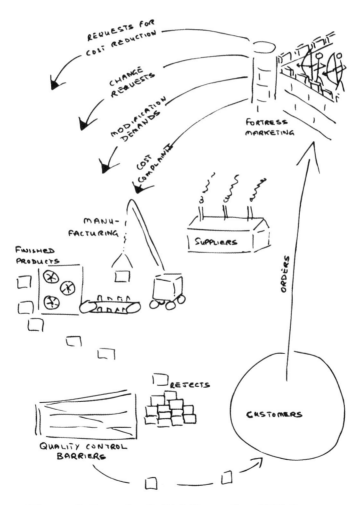

**Figure 4:** *Example of a Rich Picture from XYZ Company*

Many symptoms have parallels with Multiple Causes where there is a mass of problems with few obvious causes. A Multiple Cause diagram will not reveal something that has yet to be identified, but other diagrams such as Rich Pictures may. A splendid example is the London Underground map, a map rich in information but basic in form and designed with one purpose in mind—to enable a passenger to find their way with ease. Rich Pictures can be extremely helpful because a quick schematic diagram of a process may reveal one cause instantly.

The example in Figure 4 is taken from a real life situation and very ably demonstrates the high degree of angst present within the organization. Previously the consultants involved in planning a major CM project had not been aware of the hidden angst involved in this undertaking. In this case a picture really was worth a thousand words!

## 7. Lack of ownership

"Ownership" implies that the person who owns a problem has some responsibility for the solution. This is not about who caused the problem or apportioning blame. Failure often occurs where there is no clear "owner" of a problem or where the owner has relatively little power to effect change. We found this type of problem more prevalent in "flatter" organizations where there was "empowerment" yet nobody was empowered to "own" the problem.

Another version of this is "leave it up to the committee." While committees form a useful purpose in CM projects, it is unwise to leave the management of projects to committees.

Another ownership issue arises where problems map across and affect different constituent parts of a business. This includes situations where a problem is seen as being owned by one part of the business but the change work is imposed on another. This problem is similar to those with "boundary problems" and "politics." While these problems are often multi-faceted, the problem comes back to ownership and the need for strong leadership.

After establishing a methodology for dealing with Badly-Formed Problems at Cranfield, we made several attempts to identify the characteristics of a Well-Formed

Problem. We produced checklists to ensure that the root cause of a problem is discovered, yet these varied depending upon the type of CM project. However, over time and with testing, a set of eleven universal questions emerged (see Figure 5).

1. What's wrong?

2. How long have we had this problem?

3. What has caused and/or contributed to this problem?

4. How does having this problem limit us?

5. What will happen if the problem remains?

6. What was/is the worst example of this problem?

7. How have we tried to solve this problem previously?

8. Who else is affected by this problem?

9. Who are the problem owners?

10. Is the problem too large to solve as a whole?

11. Are we solving the right problem?

**Figure 5:** *Defining the Well-Formed Problem*

This list is not exclusive but represents the key questions to ask to form a Well-Formed Problem. Adding the meta-model challenges (who, what, where, when, how, etc.) and the magic words *how specifically* elicit "clean language" and remove ambiguities.

Obtaining a set of answers to these questions will not necessarily guarantee that one will always obtain a successful identification of the problem or problems. Answers come in many different forms. The key is quality. High quality answers come after due deliberation, with people who are prepared to stand by them. Low quality answers are those which are not properly thought through and which people may change later.

A major step toward success happens when there is acceptance of a common set of answers from all those involved in the project, although it is usual to expect conflicting answers. People have different ideas about solutions and may form their answers accordingly. Once you resolve these differences, you can start thinking about appropriate solutions.

## How Does It Work?

The most effective way to demonstrate the model is by working through an actual case. For consistency this example is based upon the Multiple Cause diagram (Figure 3).

Amazing Manufacturing Company (AMC—not actual name) is a well-established multinational manufacturing and marketing company with a wide base selling across Europe, North America, Australia, and South Africa. By international standards it is an efficient, modern, medium-sized business with aspirations to expand financially and geographically. It is a market leader in its field having won numerous awards for its products and designs.

AMC designs and manufactures a specialized range of construction products primarily used in shopping malls, large retail outlets, warehouses, and factories, manufactured in the United Kingdom, Germany, and Holland. All three factories produce the same products, with a large proportion of the output going to North America. Sales growth in Europe in the last decade has been a rapid 18% per year.

Until a few years ago the company largely dominated the European market and was able to charge a premium for its products. Four years ago a Spanish manufacturer entered the market. Although the products are considered to be slightly inferior, the prices are significantly lower. This has impacted the company's sales in mainland Europe. It responded by lowering its prices to compete. To safeguard margins a cost-saving program was implemented and the UK factory was updated with the latest computer-controlled machinery creating major changes in work practices. It also outsourced some production processes and reduced production costs considerably, increased efficiency, and reduced staff on the factory floor. The UK factory began running at less than 60% of its potential capacity, due to a downturn in UK sales caused by a recession in the building industry.

In Germany and Holland only a small amount of updating of equipment took place as both factories were equipped with modern machinery. Manufacturing across the company was inefficient as two factories were working overtime to keep up with demand while the UK one had insufficient work. Rationalization has been under review for a year, yet agreement on a way ahead has been hard to achieve.

The German market has been impacted by the new competition yet it has been delivering product on time as the factory has been operating at near capacity and also outsourcing. Similar problems beset the Dutch operation. The company has been reluctant to ship product from the UK because of the expense.

As each country runs its own ICT systems it has become difficult to obtain information about all aspects of performance, which is exacerbated by incompatible systems. Senior management has directed the ICT director to seek a replacement for the current out-of-date systems.

In pursuit of cost reduction the company's manufacturing director undertook a complete review and recommended that most of the company's German, Dutch, and some of the UK production be moved to either Poland or the Czech Republic where industrial land is cheap and labor costs are lower. He pushed hard for an integrated manufacturing ICT system capable of managing the production control processes across the company and to move towards a just-in-time (JIT) manufacturing system, believing product costs could be reduced by 30–50%.

The company's marketing director has complained for years about being unable to get adequate information from the ICT system while Sales and Marketing also view the old ICT system as a disaster. Sales are dependent upon the system to produce quotations yet these are not dependable and have to be reworked by hand. Order processing is highly suspect as are forecasting of delivery dates for products, invoicing, and receipts. While the marketing director has done a splendid job of boosting sales over the last few years, he has told the chief executive that he is now wasting his time sorting out the problems caused by the old ICT system and unless this is replaced, he will take his talents elsewhere.

The chief executive felt he could not afford to lose the marketing director and agreed to give a high priority to replacing the Sales and Marketing systems. As a first step, with external consultants, he looked at each of the problems closely to determine which are well-formed and which are symptoms of problems rather than causes.

In the Multiple Cause diagram (Figure 3) two clusters occurred around "poor management information" and "overcapacity in the UK," possibly indicating that one or the other is the prime source of most of the problems. It is sensible to test these two supposed causes first. "Overcapacity in the UK" has five arrows pointing toward it indicating that there are many contributory causes to this problem, while only one arrow points away from the problem to "redundancy in the UK."

*Seeking an answer*

Question 1: "What's wrong?" and defining a Well-Formed Problem, we get answers from the diagram: "poor management information," "increased outsourcing," "UK building recession," "need to unify production throughout EEC," and "sales productivity falling."

Question 2: "How long have we had this problem?" gives several answers: since we started outsourcing, or since the building recession, or since sales productivity fell off.

Question 3: "What has caused and/or contributed to this problem?" We get the same five answers as in Question 1. To these we can probably add the need to increase efficiency resulting from introducing new machinery and work practices.

Question 4: "How does having this problem limit us?" It reduces staff morale because there are fewer opportunities for them to earn bonuses and overtime. Not able to maximize the efficiency of the new machinery due to lack of work.

Question 5: "What will happen if this problem remains?" Possible loss of skilled staff and further reductions in staff morale. Bring back work that is currently outsourced.

Question 6: "What is the worst example of the problem?" Increase in staff disciplinary hearings. Production costs have increased as overheads have had to be spread across less output.

Question 7: "How have we tried to solve the problem previously?" Used spare time to train staff. Taken some production from Germany and Holland but transport costs eat into margins.

Question 8: "Who else is affected by this problem?" All parts of the business.

Question 9: "Who are the problem owners?" The senior management regarding the issues that are solvable inside the company.

Question 10: "Is the problem too large to solve as a whole?" Yes, there appear to be different requirements for each of the prime causes.

Question 11: "Are we solving the right problem?" No. Most of the in-house problems can be solved relatively quickly but management needs more accurate information to make a good decision. The cause "UK building recession" is a national problem and beyond the scope of the company to solve.

If we return to Figure 3 and the second cluster around "poor management information," we can see that this item has only one input arrow—"out-of-date/inefficient systems/procedures"—but four output arrows indicating it is the source of many problems: "overcapacity in the UK," "increased outsourcing," "rapid, unplanned growth in EEC," and "shortage of capacity in Holland and Germany." This is highly consistent with what has been said by the marketing and manufacturing directors and the auditors but needs to be tested to ensure that this is a Well-Formed Problem and not just a symptom of some other problem.

Question 1: Repeats: "overcapacity in the UK," "increased outsourcing," "rapid, unplanned growth in EEC," and "shortage of capacity in Holland and Germany" with an apparent cause of "out-of-date/inefficient systems/procedures."

Question 2: "How long have we had this problem?" Some time—many of the vital systems are long overdue for replacement and are no longer able to meet new requirements.

Question 3: "What has caused and/or contributed to this problem?" Recently exacerbated by introduction of new machinery into the manufacturing processes and the need to integrate information from multiple sources against a background of rapid sales growth in EEC. Major systems not compatible one with another and difficulty in exchanging information digitally across various parts of the business and outside agencies.

Question 4: "How does having this problem limit us?" The business as a whole is inefficient and cannot optimize its resources. There is a lack of quality information to run the business effectively. New manufacturing plant cannot be optimized due to lack of new hardware and software. Sales is similarly affected and is lacking vital marketing information which should be available from the company systems.

Question 5: "What will happen if this problem remains?" The company will have its accounts caveated by the auditors bringing public disgrace. This will have ramifications outside the business particularly with regulatory and taxation authorities.

Question 6: "What is the worst example of the problem?" The inability to produce accurate consolidated accounts across the whole company operation.

Question 7: "How have we tried to solve the problem previously?" Largely by patching up existing systems and procedures. However, the growth of the business is also creating strains as the current systems struggle to deal with increased workloads.

Question 8: "Who else is affected by this problem?" Suppliers to the company who wish to be paid digitally. Customers who don't always get accurate documentation.

Question 9: "Who are the problem owners?" Principally the board of directors and secondly the ICT director who will have to implement any solution.

Question 10: "Is the problem too large to solve as a whole?" Almost certainly, as replacing all the company's systems simultaneously would be too difficult to achieve. However, once a system is chosen it would be possible to roll it out across the company in phases.

Question 11: "Are we solving the right problem?" Yes, but only provided a fully integrated system covering all aspects of the business is installed and outside contractors employed.

These examples demonstrate the process for defining a Well-Formed Problem. The first set of answers attached to the problem of "overcapacity in the UK" suggests that there is no particular pressing problem to be dealt with. Instead it is seen largely as events/actions that occurred in the past that have an ongoing effect for which not much can now be done. However, there are remedial matters that should be dealt with if UK manufacturing is to get up to speed rapidly once the downturn in the construction industry comes to an end.

The questions from the second example suggest this is of much greater urgency to fix together with its associated problems. The general health of the business is being adversely affected and is likely to get worse if not addressed. However, the task is of such magnitude as to be beyond the capability of the company's internal resources, and specialist external experts should be brought in to assist.

With this real-life example, new ICT systems operating on an integrated database were installed and fully operational within two years after the board's approval. Simultaneously working practices were improved and updated. Slightly later a well-proven proprietary JIT manufacturing package compatible with other company systems was installed in the UK factory and then in Germany and Holland. This package alone produced significant cost savings in inventories and production costs. Without this evaluation exercise, it is likely the company would have chosen piece-meal solutions, starting with a new central accounting system, none of which would have helped solve the underlying problem of incompatible systems across the company, nor would it have solved the problem of poor management of information.

## Caveats

Generally the model can be used wherever it is appropriate to define a Well-Formed Problem. As with most things in life it can no doubt be misused but no knowledge currently exists of this happening.

## Summary

The Well-Formed Problem pattern was designed for use in business settings and particularly where multiple problems and causes exist which are competing for limited resources. The pattern provides a framework for evaluating the impact of a problem on a business or a function within a business and identifying the correct problems to solve. It is at its most successful when it is used in conjunction with other tools such as Multiple Cause diagrams, Rich Pictures, and so on, and ultimately with a process to produce a Well-Formed Outcome.

## References

Bandler, R. and Grinder, J. (1975). *The Structure of Magic I: A Book about Language and Therapy*. Palo Alto, CA: Science and Behavior Books.

Roberts, M. (1999). *Change Management Excellence*. Carmarthen, UK: Crown House Publishing.

L. MICHAEL HALL
ROBERT DILTS
RICHARD BOLSTAD
LUCAS DERKS
TIM HALLBOM
LISA WAKE
JAAP HOLLANDER
MARTIN ROBERTS
ARNE MAUS
CHARLES FAULKNER
FRANK BOURKE
JAMES LAWLEY
IAN MCDERMOTT
RICHARD GRAY
KRIS HALLBOM
NICK KEMP
PENNY TOMPKINS
HIROMI TAMAKI
MASAKI KONO
KIMIKO BOKURA-SHAFE
BOBBY G. BODENHAMER
RICHARD LIOTTA

**Bob G. Bodenhamer**

Bob Bodenhamer's undergraduate degree (BA) is from Appalachian State University in Boone, NC (1972). His major at Appalachian State University was Philosophy and Religion with a minor in Psychology. He received the Master of Divinity (1976) and the Doctor of Ministry Degree (1978) from Southeastern Baptist Theological Seminary in Wake Forest, NC. He is a certified Master Trainer of NLP.

With Michael Hall, Ph.D. he has co-authored nine NLP/Neuro-Semantic books. With John Burton, D.Ed. he co-authored the book *Hypnotic Language: Its Structure and Use, Volume I* and is the sole author of *Mastering Blocking and Stuttering: A Cognitive Approach to Achieving Fluency*. He and his wife, Linda, make their home in Gastonia, North Carolina.

email: bobbybodenhamer@yahoo.com
web: www.renewingyourmind.com
      www.masteringstuttering.com

# 15  What Triggers Stuttering?
## A Model for Achieving Fluency

*Bobby G. Bodenhamer*

Do you know someone who stutters? Only 1% of the population stutters, so you may live your entire life and never meet a PWS (person who stutters). Because of the small percentage, stuttering has not received a great deal of attention. The movie *The King's Speech* introduced many to the problem revealing both the struggles as well as the difficulty in treating a PWS.

Regrettably, those charged with treating the disorder, Speech Language Pathologists, are taught that stuttering isn't a psychological problem, but a physiological problem with the primary cause being genetics. However, how does such a theory explain that the vast majority is fluent in certain circumstances, such as when they are alone, but block and stutter at other times, such as in social occasions?

Using Neuro-Semantics and NLP I began by asking: "How does this circumstantial stuttering happen?" It isn't physiological, for it can only be explained as a function of cognition. A PWS has two strategies for speaking: (1) fluently and (2) blocking and stuttering. After years of working with PWS, I discovered that *fear* and *anxiety* are the two primal emotions that trigger the stuttering strategy. Until these are dealt with, a person will just keep on stuttering when the triggers present themselves.

Fear is a primitive emotion processed in our limbic system, primarily in the amygdala, and so can be challenging to re-imprint. The good news is that layering negative emotions with resourceful thoughts activates the cerebral cortex. The cerebral cortex both literally and functionally is above our limbic system. Therefore, systematic meta-stating, which utilizes the power of our cerebral cortex, can eliminate those negative emotions. Neuro-Scientists refer to this process as the "plasticity" of the brain.[1]

It is possible for the PWS to create new neural pathways for old triggers. All successful reframing involves linking old un-useful triggers to new and useful responses. This creates new neural synapses, neurons and neural pathways. We are never too old to learn.

## NLP and Stuttering

After I led an "Introduction to NLP" sales seminar, a man came up to me and inquired, "Can you help people who stutter? I have a grown son who stutters. He doesn't do it all the time but he does it enough to cause him difficulty. Do you think you can help him?"

I really didn't know if I could. Approximately ten years earlier, when I first started learning NLP and using it therapeutically, one of my Gaston College students stuttered and wanted to know if I could help him. After a good effort, I wasn't able to help him. Later, after learning about Meta-States, he came back and we eliminated his stuttering habit.

I now faced the same question but with two major differences. First, through several years of training NLP, writing NLP training manuals, and practicing NLP, I felt much more confident about my ability. Second, the really big confidence booster was learning the Meta-States Model and working with Michael Hall. Through this model and the subsequent developments in Neuro-Semantics, I had discovered what worked in NLP and why it worked.

When asked if I could help his son, I replied, "I'm not sure, but I want to try and if I can't help, there will be no charge." When he told me that his son didn't stutter all the time, a question immediately popped into my mind, "How does he know when to stutter and when not to stutter?"

This question comes directly from the meta-model of language, but my understanding of the *how* of this question took a giant leap forward with the Meta-States Model. The fact that he didn't stutter all the time confirmed that his stuttering was not a physical problem but rather a psychological problem.

## Psychological vs. Physiological

When someone stutters in certain contexts, but not in others, and the person does this consistently day after day, week after week, year after year, there is something going on in the mind–body system and "choice" as a cognitive process is at play. The person who stutters is unconsciously "choosing" when to stutter. This has been true for every PWS with whom I have worked over the past eight years.

I was sure my client had a "cognitive" problem and that suggested a good chance of him getting some results. In my office, he shared how this speech problem had bothered him his entire life. I inquired, "Well, how do you know *when* to stutter?" That sent him into trance. When he came out, he said, *"I stutter when I am around authority figures."*

In examining this we found out that the root of his problem was in his childhood. His father was a very busy man and didn't go to his son's ballgames to watch him play. As a child watching the stands from the ball field, he longed to see his father sitting there, cheering him on. It never happened. The meaning he gave to that is: "My father doesn't love me. If he did, he would come to watch me play."

How did this develop into a stutter? He very much wanted to tell his father about his disappointment, but he couldn't bring himself to do so. Indeed, he was *fearful* of telling his father he felt so unloved because he was not supported in doing something he loved—playing ball. He was fearful that his father would get angry and the relationship would deteriorate. So, he blocked his emotions even though he desperately wanted to share them with his dad. Then he generalized from his father to *everybody in authority*. When around authority figures, he would tighten up and have a mild panic attack, which often became a full-blown panic attack.

## Does the Map Match the Territory?

The trigger of meeting an authority figure sent my client back to the ball field. As with most emotional issues, such as post-traumatic stress disorder, the client flashes back to the moment of trauma which created the fear/anxiety. No wonder one becomes fearful of speaking! My client was an adult; yet in conversing with an authority figure, he became a fearful child operating from the fearful child's mental map. His map was confused with the territory.

Ask a PWS what they are *feeling* when they are blocking and you will discover that the person has the very feelings that the DSM-IV-TR (2000) describes as a panic attack. In addition, the PWS will often isolate himself from social settings. Many of them are "loners" by choice. Their psychological profile tends to reveal a person suffering from a social anxiety disorder. Indeed, the disorder labeled shy bladder syndrome or paruresis (whose symptoms include the inability to urinate in public) is recognized as a social anxiety disorder and the recommended treatment is cognitive-behavioral therapy.

Both stuttering and shy bladder syndrome are structurally the same; the only difference is where in the body the client feels the anxiety/fear? The stutterer is fearful of speaking in certain contexts and so will *block* their speech. The person suffering from *Shy Bladder Syndrome* is fearful of being seen urinating so they *block* their urination.

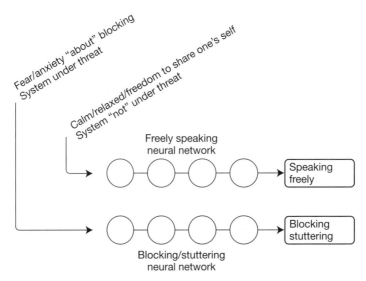

**Figure 1:** *Two ways of speaking*

An easy way to understand stuttering is illustrated in Figure 1. The PWS has learned two ways of speaking. One mind–body strategy leads to fluency; the other mind–body strategy leads to blocking and stuttering. What determines which strategy is operative? When the PWS is calm, relaxed, confident and safe, he will speak out of his "fluency strategy." It is as if the brain says, "You can relax now. There is nothing here that threatens you. There is no fear of others judging you." However, when the PWS is in a context where he feels anxious and is fearful that he may be judged should he stutter, then that person's "stuttering strategy" will be activated and he will block and stutter.

When he realized that he "causes" his own stutter, my client asked, "You mean I do this to myself?" I said, "Yes, you are doing it to yourself. Are you tired of doing this?" "Yes." Only one hour had passed and he was clear—he didn't want any more therapy. He'd had enough. When he discovered that he was doing this to himself, something clicked inside him. His head jerked backwards. This knowledge really struck home. I followed up with him over a number of years and during that time he was stutter free. As far as I know, he never reverted back to stuttering.

I wish I could say that it always ends like this and this quickly, but it doesn't. Working with adult stutterers will humble most NLP therapists. The behavior is often so locked in, through years of negative layering and habituation, that many hours of therapy plus several years of practice are often required before they can begin to gain control of their speech.

However, if the PWS stays with therapy sufficiently long enough and practices the strategies, then there is real hope for improvement.

## How Does the Model Work?

There are some physical strategies that assist PWS in being more fluent, and I encourage the severe stutterer to take advantage of them. The reason is because therapeutic work usually involves a great deal of time and effort and the PWS will probably need immediate assistance. Some of these physical strategies can be taught quite quickly, but the root problem isn't fixed until the person reframes their multi-layered fear that triggers the stuttering.

Be warned that these physical strategies may lead the PWS to speak like a "robot"— it isn't "natural speech." However, they do help them get started on the road to fluency because they can at least begin to communicate. My concern is that the PWS becomes addicted to the physiological intervention and never moves forward to change their mental frames around stuttering. If you do this, you are robbing yourself of experiencing the richness of living life without fear and anxiety as well as diminishing and even destroying the need to ever block again. Why block when it no longer serves a positive purpose for the PWS?

With the exception of a stutter caused by a brain injury, the Meta-States Model is appropriate to use with every PWS.

## Phases of Therapy for PWS

### Phase 1: Identify the Client's Strategy for Stuttering

What is the client seeing, hearing, and feeling and how is the client talking to himself in order to trigger the stuttering behavior? In this step you want to identify what the client is doing inside their head in order to trigger their blocking strategy.

### Phase 2: Lead the Client to "Step outside" of their fear of stuttering

The PWS will probably believe that they have no other choice but to block and stutter in every fearful situation. By teaching the client how to *step outside* those multiple negative frames that trigger fear and anxiety, you are beginning the process of teaching them how to run their own brain.

### Phase 3: Discover the Client's Resource(s)

Ask, "What resource(s) do you now have that once you *apply* it/them to the fear and anxiety, the fear and anxiety will diminish and eventually to go away?" Suggest resources if they find it difficult, e.g., spiritual beliefs, courage, faith, contentment, relaxed, unity, universal love, connectiveness.

In the Drop-Down-Through Pattern, resources are discovered as the client moves "down" and "out of" their negative mental frames and into more positive mental frames. As you lead the client to drop down through these positive meanings, they will eventually (usually three or four mental frames at the most) reach their "highest" state of meaning. This will provide the resource(s) necessary for the healing of the uncovered negative mental frames.

### Phase 4: Applying the Resources

"What is the *purpose* of the fear about speaking?" Most PWS struggle with the thought that behind every behavior is a positive intent, most often *protection*. In my experience when chunking up from the fear we discover not only the unconscious painful frames, usually few in number, but also great resources for applying to the fear/anxiety, and to reframing the negative frames.

### Phase 5: Testing your Work

Lead the client to step back inside the blocking experience that you ran the pattern on. Check to see if the client has any negative feelings left. If they do, have them step inside the negative feeling that remains and run the pattern through again. Keep repeating until all of the negative emotions are gone.

### Phase 6: Future Pace

Ask the client while they are *really feeling* being inside their highest resource state to go out into their future maintaining that state but this time to experience future similar situations where they formerly would have blocked to experience them with this new resource.

## The Drop-Down-Through Process

I use this more than any other pattern because of its effectiveness and simplicity. Here are the steps:

1.  Ask the client to recall a recent time that they experienced a bad block and lead them to step inside it.

2.  Inquire, "What are you feeling and where in your body are you feeling it?" Write down each state elicited, for you are going to bring healing to those negative states shortly.

    In these first two steps we are leading the client through **Phase 1** by inviting them to "step inside" a bad block thus "associating" them into the problem state.

In Step #1 by asking the client to recall and to experience a recent bad block, we are inviting them to be "inside" an experience of blocking. We are *associating* the client into what it feels like when they block. In order to elicit a proper strategy for the act of blocking, the client must be *inside* the experience and really feeling it.

In Step #2 we are inviting the client to mentally *step outside* the problem state by asking them to identify what they are experiencing in order to block. When you ask them, "what are you seeing, hearing, and feeling and how are you talking to yourself in order to experience that blocking state?" the client has to momentarily *step back* from the blocking state in order to identify what he is experiencing in that state.

Thus Step #2 begins **Phase 2** for we have invited the client to mentally *step outside* that blocking state and experience it from a *dissociated* state. Many love to refer to this Phase of therapy as a process of gaining *distance* from the problem. As mentioned above, **Phase 2** is critical for the client to learn how to manage their own states by running their own brain and experience a sense of control.

3. Instruct them to *drop-down-through* the feeling (use their name for the feeling). Ask them to imagine themselves inside an elevator and dropping down from one level to the next. "Imagine that you are peeling off that thought-feeling (name it). What thought-feeling is under it?" Repeat this line of direction until the client reaches a cognitive space of "nothingness"—a place of "no meaning."[2]

   **Phase 2** continues as you lead the client to *step outside* each negative state into the next and out of it and into the next, and so on. Write down each mind–body state they experience as they drop from one level to the next. You will need this information when you lead them to apply their higher resource state to each of the negative frames elicited from the pattern.

4. Once inside the nothingness, say to the client, "Great. Now imagine that you are dropping-down-through the 'nothingness,' going down through the nothingness and *out the other side, out beyond* all those negative thoughts-feelings that you had."

   (Here I mention all the negative frames elicited as I direct them to move beyond their negative mind–body states.)

5.  Pace them and when you detect that they have accessed a more positive state, ask them, "What are you thinking and feeling *out beyond* all that negative pain?"

6.  Continue the process leading them to drop-down-through each positive state until they reach their very *"highest state."* You will know they are there when they reach a state of being that has no other more important state. To make sure simply inquire: "Is there anything more important to you than (name their highest state)?"

    **Phase 2** continues as you step outside one state and into another and you lead the client into **Phase 3**, where they discover resources that you will use in bringing healing to the negative frames.

7.  Lead the client to apply their highest state to each negative state beginning from the top. "Now, being in your highest state (name it), bring your highest state to bear upon the negative state (name it). Ask, "What happens as you apply your highest state to the pain of that negative state? How does (name the resource) transform and enrich (name the negative state)." Give the client time to process the shift and to describe to you what is happening to them.

    **Phase 4** is completed here, along with the addition of uncovering those mostly unconscious negative meanings that trigger their strategy for stuttering. As the client moves on down through negative layer after negative layer, eventually they will find their most powerful mental resources. They will either drop into a cognitive place where there are no meanings and from there move on into their resource state or they will simply flip into positive resource frames. In that cognitive space, the client will often experience a mental resource that they never dreamed possible. It is with these resources that healing will come as they learn how to apply their resource state to all the negative frames that were uncovered on the way down.

8.  Repeat this meta-stating process applying their highest state to each negative state.

    *How To Meta-State:*

    In meta-stating we apply one thought onto and into another thought. A great example of how this works is the way we mentally process adjectives and adverbs.

By definition adjectives *modify* nouns and by so doing they *set the frame* or determine the meaning of the noun being modified. Take the word "love" which has many meanings depending on its context. When we layer the adjective "brotherly" onto the noun "love" we have "brotherly love". You will experience that in one way but notice what happens when you choose another adjective, such as, "erotic"? You will note that when you apply a different adjective to the word "love" you will have a totally different meaning. That is how we meta-state—we apply; we change; we modify one thought with another thought.

Consider the thought "I am fearful that I will block when I am in a job interview." Notice how fearing blocking feels in your body. Now, take the phrase, "I am a courageous adult. I am not a child. I know how to speak fluently and I am going to do just that." What happens when you apply the second thought to the first thought? What happens when you apply "courage" to "fear"?

You may ask, "How specifically do I do that?" You can do it visually—by imagining a visual representation of what "fear of blocking" looks like and another visual representation of what "courageous adult" looks like. Now, take those two images and visually move "fear of blocking" into the same location as "courageous adult". Do this *with your eyes only* and not with your head. You can also do this with "feelings" and "sounds".

9.  To test your work, ask the client to step back into that time of blocking and ask them what they are now thinking-feeling. If they still have negative feelings, repeat the process until there is no longer a negative kinesthetic when they access that time of blocking.

10. Future pace the client by asking them to imagine themselves going out into the future when they would normally block but now with these added resources. Take note how it goes.

## Case Study: Having to Prove Myself

David had been a client for a year and a half. During this time we had done a great deal of work surrounding the limiting beliefs he had learned in childhood and that had triggered him as an adult to hold back and block.

It had been a long and tedious journey, but David had remained persistent and determined to change his thinking about his speech. Since he was perfectly fluent by himself, David surmised that his *thinking* was a major driver that triggered him to block.

As you read the following transcript, focus on my use of language and questions and how they lead David to discover (1) the roots of his problem and (2) how he can use the resources of his religious faith to reframe his experiences. Since David maintained strong religious beliefs, we used those to change how he thought and felt. Other people might apply other kinds of resources. In David's case, reframing his fears led to a reduction of stress and holding back since he was now seeing his relationships differently.

**BB:** What is all this about, David?

**David:** There is a place inside of me that drives me. This place wants me to do well.

**BB:** Okay, David, imagine yourself entering into and becoming one with that part.

(David slips into a relaxed state as he accesses the experience. Once he is inside himself and experiencing that part, I ask him a question.)

**BB:** David, what is the purpose of this part for you? No doubt this part has been there a very long time, so it must be doing something or it would have left years ago. Just what does this part want for you?

**D:** Its purpose is to dominate, to win, to be the best that I can be.

**BB:** And what is the purpose of being the best that you can be?

**D:** By being and doing my very best, I get praise and recognition. This part craves praise and recognition.

**BB:** And by having praise and recognition, what does that give you that is even more important?

**D:** It makes me feel significant. It makes me feel like my life and my efforts are worthwhile.

**BB:** Let's keep going with this sense of higher purpose. By feeling worthwhile, what does that give you?

**D:** It makes me feel like my existence means something.

**BB:** And David, what is the purpose of having your existence mean something?

**D:** If I am doing something worthwhile, making my existence mean something, I get this strong internal sense that I have accomplished something. It lets me know that I am "good enough." But it doesn't work. It's not coming from a peaceful place. It comes from a restless place. It's all for my ego.

**BB:** So when did you learn that you were not good enough?

**D:** (Long pause) I just had a few thoughts pop into my mind. I remember one time in the ninth grade that I went out for football. I was passed over for the first string. Another time when I was younger—maybe I was in about the fifth or sixth grade—I asked this girl out. I had wanted to do this for a long time as I had my eye on her. When I asked her to go out with me, she refused. That really hurt. It was the first time that I had ever asked a girl out.

**BB:** What did all of this mean to you, David?

**D:** It meant that I was not good enough. There were a lot of times that I experienced rejection. I remember in the fifth grade I was bullied by a kid. I couldn't fight back. I was too afraid. Again, I was not good enough.

On another occasion I wanted to start a club. So I wrote up this document of rules, but I couldn't get anybody to join. I didn't feel like I was good enough to start a club that anyone would want to join. The urge to constantly prove myself is always there.

**BB:** You feel this urge all the time?

**D:** Yes. It is always leading me to try to prove myself. It feeds into the stuttering, for without the urge I wouldn't care if I stuttered, and it wouldn't matter. This competitive drive to be fluent, to be right, to feel like I am good enough would not matter if I didn't have this urge.

**BB:** How do you experience the urge? Is it something you see, feel or hear?

**D:** When I have it, I become obsessed with it. I can't focus on anything else but what I want. It has served me well but what drives it is an ego thing. If I applied it toward a higher purpose rather than being an egotistical type thing, it would be far better. But I am always trying to win. I am addicted to that feeling. I have to have it, and it is all about my wanting to belong.

**BB:** So if I understand correctly, you have a feeling that you call an "urge." It is a feeling that focuses your mind on what you want. It is like an "addiction" to a drug, only for you it is an "urge" that constantly drives you to "prove yourself."

**D:** Yes, that is correct. It focuses me totally on proving myself.

**BB:** I want you to now step inside that urge and allow yourself to feel it strongly.

(I pause as David accesses the mind–body state. I know when he is inside that state of mind by subtle changes in his physiology. At that point I ask a question— David, where in your body do you feel this urge?

**D:** It is high in my chest. It is up into my throat, my face, and into my neck.

**BB:** So be with that urge, that feeling in your chest, throat, face and neck. Now, I want you to imagine dropping down through that urge. What thought or feeling is underneath the urge?

**D:** I have to win! I have to get my point across. (Long pause) It's a weird feeling— almost like a nauseous feeling. It's like a nervous, edgy feeling in the pit of my stomach. I can feel a panic attack attached to this feeling. I believe that a speech block is a panic attack. It starts in the pit of my stomach and works its way up.

**BB:** So the "urge" is down in the pit of your stomach? Drop down through that nauseous panicky feeling that is in the pit of your stomach. What is underneath that feeling?

**D:** There is just more of the sick feeling.

**BB:** Good. Just move that sick feeling aside and drop down underneath all of that. What do you experience underneath the sick feeling?

**D:** More of the same but there is a heaviness on my chest, and my breathing is short and shallow.

**BB:** You're doing really well, David. Now just imagine yourself dropping down through the heaviness. What is underneath that?

**D:** I want to outsmart everybody.

**BB:** And as you drop down through outsmarting everybody, what will get you what you want?

**D:** I will feel better than everybody else.

**BB:** And what supports that?

**D:** I am special. I am smart.

**BB:** And David, by being special and smart, what does that provide for you that is so important to you?

**D:** I am chosen. Just like it is not good enough to be like everybody else, I have to be special. I have to be gifted.

**BB:** And being special and gifted, what supports that and gives it meaning?

**D:** I am the special chosen one by God. Then I would be wittier, more clever, and smarter than everybody else. When God created me, it took Him longer to make me than it took Him to make all other people. I don't know why I believe this so strongly ... maybe my parents who kept repeating it when I was young. They kept saying how good I was and how gifted I was.

**BB:** So, during those impressionable years your parents just kept on layering in how special, smart, and gifted you were. And because of this, as we have learned from other sessions, you grew up believing that you had to perform at such a high level so as to keep fulfilling these high expectations. Because if you didn't, your parents might cease loving and caring for you. And the fear of not living up to their high expectations led to your holding back in speaking as your thoughts might not live up to what was expected of you?

**D:** Yes, that is correct. I developed a complex about it. When I do something, I have to do better because I am chosen. You have to work hard and do well so that you can support your parents' beliefs about you. I kept on being told this until I believed it. Then I took over and started telling myself how special, smart, and gifted I was. But as I grew older, I started having experiences that were the exception to my rule about being special. The ideal is still there driving me, yet reality tells me that I am not so special. I have to get reality to be congruent with what I believe about myself.

(David has shifted the context from childhood beliefs to adult realities.)

**BB:** You believed that you were the best. What did that do for you?

**D:** I was created for this to do my best. I am fulfilling what God wanted me to do. If I am doing all these things, I am doing what He wants me to do. If I am not doing these things, then I would be denying what I am created for.

**BB:** Is this the same incongruent part?

**D:** All of this stuff has taken hold of the natural gifts that I have. It leaves me restless when I don't achieve things. I keep pushing and pushing trying to get there. Even when everybody tells me about what a great job that I am doing, it still doesn't fill me up. Something on the inside doesn't satisfy me. I always feel like I am not achieving what I should.

(Note: It is here where the client is ready to access his/her highest resource.)

**BB:** As we know from past work, you've described as your purpose the need to fulfill what you believe to be the divine calling for your life. Now, imagine yourself in God's presence and ask Him what He has to say about this obsession and need to prove yourself smarter and better than anybody else.

**D:** (Very long pause) He says I can't get this sense of being special by just doing. I can only achieve peace and the feeling that I am special by being in His presence. The only way for me to go is to let God lead me. This incessant need to perform to be something is not the way to go. This realization came to me three days ago. So when I get the desire to be somebody, I will immediately be in His presence.

**BB:** So this means that any time this old "urge" to be somebody special pops up, you immediately place yourself in the presence of God?

**D:** Yes, I have to. I can't keep on like this. I have to and I will do this.

**BB:** Just keep doing this and over a period of time the urge to be better than others will get less and less, and being in the presence of the Lord will be as natural as breathing. You will no longer have to be better. You already are where you want to be. By living in God's presence, you are fulfilling the higher purpose of your life which is helping people.

**D:** Yes, that is correct. It is funny how the unconscious mind takes these things and drives your life and you don't have a clue that you're doing it.

This session was a turning point in David's ultimate resolution of his stuttering. It removed a set of beliefs that had stood as a block to progress; beliefs that had kept him stuck. He ended up reframing both his sense of himself and his relationship with other people. The need to hold back and block dissolved of its own accord.

## Warnings and Caveats

The one major caveat with PWS is that for most adult sufferers, they have run those multi-layered negative frames for so long and they have blocked and stuttered so many times that the habit is most often ingrained deeply in the unconscious mind. You will rarely find a "quick therapy" with PWS. Be careful to have an agreement with your client about the necessity of entering into a multi-month or even a multi-year process. The brain has to be retrained.

As discussed earlier, hearing about "quick fixes" can sometimes create a problem for PWS who have read about other examples and expect just as quick a fix for them. However, for most gaining a good degree of fluency requires several hours of therapy and a great deal of practice. Many people need to practice, not only for several months but quite often for several years. Yet the changes are permanent. The one who "pays the price comes to enjoy the rewards."

### Notes

1. Schwartz and Begley (2002); Dodge (2007).

2. Korzybski, A. (1933).

### References

American Psychiatric Association (APA). (2000). *Diagnostic and Statistical Manual of Mental Disorders, Fourth Edition, Text Revision* (DSM-IV-TR). Washington, DC: American Psychiatric Association.

Bodenhamer, B. G. (2004). *Mastering Blocking and Stuttering: A Cognitive Approach to Achieving Fluency*. Carmarthen, UK: Crown House Publishing.

Bodenhamer, B. G. and Hall, L. M. (1999). *The User's Manual for the Brain, Vol. 1*. Carmarthen, UK: Crown House Publishing.

Dodge, N. (2007). *The Brain that Changes Itself*. New York: Penguin.

Hall, L. M. (2000a). *Secrets of Personal Mastery*. Carmarthen, UK: Crown House Publishing.

Hall, L. M. (2000b). *Winning the Inner Game: Mastering the Inner Game for Peak Performance*. Grand Junction, CO: Neuro-Semantic Publications.

Korzybski, A. (1933). *Science and Sanity: An Introduction to Non-Aristotelian Systems and General Semantics*. Englewood, NJ: Institute of General Semantics.

Schwartz, J. and Begley, S. (2002). *The Mind and the Brain: Neuroplasticity and the Power of Mental Force*. New York: HarperCollins.

For more information on PWS please visit our website www.masteringstuttering.com.

# Part III
# Innovative Tools

From Models and patterns emerge tools—technologies and assessment scales that can be used as an expression of the model or pattern. Traditionally NLP has not had many tools. We could look upon the lists of meta-model linguistic distinctions and questions as a tool, or the list of meta-programs and their elicitation questions as a tool, and so on.

But fully formulated tools are much more. One of the first NLP tools was the LAB Profile® by Rodger Bailey.

 **H. Arne Maus** is an experienced management trainer and coach and works as a consultant to major corporations in industry and commerce. In 1994, he founded Identity Compass International, a network of consultants that utilise the Identity Compass® system. H. Arne Maus continues to be a member of Identity Compass International and devotes himself primarily to the research on meta-programs and related fields. H. Arne Maus is author of the book *Forget About Motivation*, (May 2011) published in English by KONA Publishing, North Carolina, USA.

email: info@identitycompass.com
web: www.identitycompass.com

# 16 The Identity Compass®
## Mapping Meta-Programs for Business Success

*Arne Maus*

The Identity Compass is a software-based tool that measures meta-programs in the context of work. It also reveals the perception of employee engagement within the organization.

## Why the Identity Compass?

I was intrigued, in 1995, to find myself unable to answer certain questions about the meta-programs. When I asked myself, "How can one organize meta-programs like meta-model questions?" and "How do meta-programs influence each other?" I didn't really know. When I asked other trainers for answers they couldn't answer either. Interestingly, only Robert Dilts showed an interest in finding the answers, so together we began our quest.

Robert provided material[1] from which I developed the first version of the Identity Compass. From this I met Bert Feustel and together we developed the Professional Edition of the Identity Compass.

### *What is the Identity Compass?*

The Identity Compass is mainly used for recruiting and coaching. Experienced coaches, trained in the use of meta-programs, quickly recognize how certain patterns create typical problems (e.g., self-sabotage, burn-out). One profile with the Identity Compass often reduces the number of coaching sessions necessary to help the client define the result they want and identify the leverage points to achieve their outcome.

The Identity Compass is a computer-based tool designed to make practical use of meta-programs. This tool offers individuals and organizations an opportunity to measure and display:

1. Fifty single meta-program preferences and many interesting combinations.

2. How an employee uses those meta-programs in the work context.

3. A view of employee engagement within the organization.

4. Meta-program profiles for both individuals and their teams.

The benefits of the Identity Compass include:

• A deeper understanding of how different people are thinking and how they are motivated; a valuable insight for all leaders and managers.

• An insight into the way individuals perceive and assess themselves, differentiating self-perception from the perception of others.

• Faster and more precise data at much lower cost than an assessment center.

• A support tool for coaches helping their clients to find work–life balance.

### *Using the Identity Compass in Organizations*

In 1997, I tested the Identity Compass in a company with 8,000 employees. The organization had a serious problem in one of its divisions and with an annual revenue of US$34 million. The sales department and the service department were at war and customers were complaining directly to the chairman. I was invited in to resolve the conflict and I was given two days to do it! This would be the crucial test for Identity Compass. Could it really identify the cause of such an intractable problem and offer a sustainable solution? I accepted the challenge.

Before the two-day training session, I asked participants to complete the meta-program questionnaire. Sales, being open to learning something new about themselves, did this with enthusiasm. Not so for the service team, who objected to the concept of "psychological testing" on principle and sent their representative to stop the process. Offering no resistance, only information about my intention and the integrity of the proposed process, I left them to decide whether to take part. Fortunately, everyone agreed to complete the questionnaire.

The results were revealing: they showed the service employees had a procedural and highly detailed way of thinking. Because of this, they failed to hear the clients' problems accurately enough or to respond with enough flexibility. Over time, this had led to a strategy of quickly resolving problems that they knew about, but which didn't exactly fix the clients' problems. On the contrary, the sales people were very option-oriented and global.

We displayed both sets of results anonymously for all participants to see, and began to explain the various meta-program differences such as Options/Procedures, Global/Details, Abstract/Concrete, and so on. Where the differences were significant, I went into more detail on how differences between people's meta-programs can result in mutual misunderstanding. The sales people made global statements which the service people judged as "very superficial." They wanted all the details. This was irritating to the sales people. They also judged the sales people as "peanut counters." Soon both teams could readily identify their own thinking preferences, realizing that, although they had a common aim of solving customer problems, each team had a different way of thinking about how to resolve them.

After a few exercises to show them the value of each meta-program and the equal value of its counterpart, the division between the two teams quickly diminished as each came to understood how the other could offer a valuable complement to their own preferred way of thinking.

To get the service team to understand the advantage of the global pattern I told them a story of a person with a weird behavior and asked for the cause of this behavior. One of the stories (of the joke story type we used as kids to challenge each other) I told them was:

> A man came home from his four-week holiday. He used the lift to the sixteenth level and walked the last two staircases to the eighteenth level, where he had his flat. He entered his flat, and went into the kitchen. When standing beside the table he did not see the chipped wood on the floor. Then he opened the window and jumped. Why?

The only way to get to an answer is to ask very global questions and then to get step by step into the details. All my responses were just "yes" or "no" or, if irrelevant, I responded with "apple pie." When they started with wild guesses like, "The man was crazy" or "He was ill," all they got was a "no," and it gave them no more clues about what happened. But when they started to ask more global questions like: "The reason for using the lift only to the sixteenth level had to do with the lift," they also got a "no," but this time they could easily conclude it had to do with the man. Then the question they might ask themselves was, what could be the cause for such a behavior? This might have them led to the next question: "Was he too small to reach for the button of the eighteenth floor?" and got a "yes." If someone is that small he may even be earning money because of this. When asked, the answer was "yes" again. In fact, he was the smallest man in town. Thinking over why he would jump out of the window, while overlooking the chipped wood, it seems someone had shortened the table legs. After returning from his holiday he stood beside the table, where he had stood often before, but this time the table appeared smaller to him. So he assumed he had grown during the last four weeks while on holiday. Therefore he believed he was not the smallest man anymore and could not make any money, so he jumped.

The original "war" was reduced to a healthy working "friction." This happened without a formal agreement. It became simply obvious to everybody that respecting each other was the only way to get ahead. Even the company's employee representative acknowledged the value of the exercise and endorsed the future use of the Identity Compass in the company.

To address the service and complaints issues another workshop was planned with just two goals:

1. Service employees were tasked to develop a procedure for responding to complaints, by first getting an overview of the customer's situation and only then seeking greater detail.

2. To develop the best way to deal with potentially hostile customers on the telephone.

We did this because the service people were claiming some customers were "idiots." By checking the details of the problems, we found that the service people were offering solutions too quickly. So some solutions did not fit the problems.

Within weeks, there were no more complaints from customers and the service and marketing departments were cooperating better. The service people had already learned to start with global questions and to go step by step into the details to find out the most appropriate solution for the customer. It can be very revealing to repeat the Identity Compass profiles six months after such an intervention. This follow-up can help determine to what extent the objectives were achieved, assess how well the changes were integrated, and provide a sound basis for further discussions.

In another example, employees at a company in Hamburg, Germany were also very detail oriented. By using exercises such as the one described above, we trained them to use also their global thinking. Half a year later we rechecked them with the Identity Compass. The result was that they still preferred thinking in details, but they were substantially more flexible in switching to global thinking when necessary.

## How Does the Identity Compass Work?

### *What Is Measured?*

*Meta-Programs*

#### Perception
*Sensory channel*: seeing/hearing/feeling
*Primary interest*: people/places/activity/information/things
*Perspective*: own/partner/observer

#### Motivation Factors
*Values*: target values/sustaining values
*Motives*: influence/affiliation/achievement
*Direction*: away from/towards
*Reference*: internal/external
*Planning style*: options/procedures
*Primary attention*: caring for self/caring for others

#### Motivation Processing
*Level of activity*: pre-active/re-active
*Comparison*: sameness/difference
*Primary reaction*: consensus/polar

*Success strategy*: vision/realization/quality control
*Work orientation*: relationship/task

## Information Processing

*Information size*: global/details
*Thinking style*: abstract/concrete
*Working style*: team player/group player/individualist
*Time orientation*: past/present/future
*Time frame*: long term/short term
*Convincer channel*: looking/listening/reading/doing
*Convincer strategy*: skeptic/trustful
*Management style*: managing/self-reflective/instructing/not managing/
non-reflective

## Combined Patterns

*Four sides of a message*: facts/request/relationship/self-revelation
*Assertiveness*: assertiveness
*Speed in thinking*: thinks slowly/thinks fast
*Speed in decision-making*: decides slowly/decides quickly
*Riemann-Thomann: space axis*: closeness/distance; *time axis*: permanence/
change

## Working Climate

*Autonomy*: influence/significance of the job/identification/network of social
relationships/opportunities of promotion
*Dependency*: negative stress
*Security*: opportunities of development/recognition/community
*Absence of prospects*: lack of support/lack of communication/social coldness
*Challenge*: positive stress/strategic skills/interpersonal skills/focus on
service
*Pointlessness*: pointlessness
*Engagement*: resigned/destructive/inert/productive

## *What Is Inspirational about This Model?*

In learning NLP I was introduced to individual meta-programs, whereas the Identity Compass system addresses the systemic complexity of multiple meta-programs. The Identity Compass takes the results of single meta-programs and adds them up to display combined patterns.

## *An Example of Complexity In Action*

From spontaneous to unpredictable behavior in simple steps. Spontaneity is fundamentally rooted in these three preferences:

1. Options: people who hesitate to take decisions—because taking decisions means to drop all options except one.

2. Active: people who decide spontaneously in the moment.

3. Present: people who are very much in the present—the "here and now."

If all three of these meta-programs are found together, the result will be employees who behave spontaneously. If we add in a preference for "difference" (who like change) we can expect employees with such a high level of spontaneity they will then take on the new quality of "variety." Add a further preference, "polar" (first reaction is to disagree with other people), and these employees gain the ability to assert controversial points of view and, when necessary, oppose the operational mainstream.

From the same base preferences of "options," "present," and "active," if a person shows a balance between "consensus" (first reaction is to agree with other people) and "polar," others will find this person to be completely unpredictable because they are likely to agree at some times and to disagree at other times with no rational reason or justification.

# Measuring the Context

The reliability and accuracy of the meta-programs depends entirely on defining the context of work with clarity and consistency. Ten years of experience and empirical testing also teaches us that if we explore how effectively a client can use their meta-programs in that work, then we also get a measure of their "job satisfaction." Example: an option-oriented person who has to follow a lot of procedures most likely will be unhappy in the job. This will result in low job satisfaction.

The measure of a person's job satisfaction is strongly related to their motives. The three basic motives, as defined by David McClelland[2] (MIT Boston) and Norbert Bischof[3] (University of Zurich) are: power, affiliation, and achievement. (In Germany, "power" has complex connotations so in the Identity Compass it has been relabeled "influence.")

Consider three strongly motivated people, each having a different motivation. The first is motivated by influence, the second by affiliation, and the third by achievement. Each of them will evaluate the same work context differently, according to their own meta-programs; their unconscious biases.

According to Norbert Bischof[4] and David Scheffer,[5] the context of work may be divided into three parts, each with a correlation to motivation.

1.  Autonomy vs. dependency (related to the motive influence).
2.  Security vs. absence of prospects (related to the motive affiliation).
3.  Challenge vs. pointlessness (related to the motive achievement).

Based on this, we can measure how much a person can utilize their particular meta-programs in their professional context to allow us to understand how well they fit their work and how well their work fits them. The Identity Compass system measures both sides of each motivational context, the positive and negative attributes, differentiating motivation and de-motivation and acknowledging that both can be present at the same time.

Research by Professor David Scheffer on the working climate in companies proved the correlation between people's meta-programs and their job profiles.[6]

By looking at hundreds of profiles we found that the scale of "autonomy" measures and displays how much a person can experience the motive "influence" in their work. Low scores on the influence scale indicate that the company does not give them the power they need to do their work.

The scale of challenge vs. pointlessness measures and displays how much a person can experience the motive "achievement" in their work. People who show high scores on "pointlessness" are likely have an external reference, meaning they are likely to get insufficient feedback from the organization, with the result that they can't tell what difference they make through their work—hence a sense of futility or pointlessness.

## Motivation Is Good—Productive Engagement Is Better

Watson Wyatt Heissmann conducted a survey of 1,525 professionals, and found that 86% of all employees, either openly or secretly, are in the process of looking for a new job, and 52.14% of them said they would accept lower wages if they could find a position that really suited them. At the same time, two thirds of personnel department heads believed that the employees in that same company felt good about working there.[7]

Obviously, to simply believe that all is well within one's organization without testing the hypothesis is insufficient. No controller merely believes the figures without thorough testing and inspection to validate their accuracy.

Interviewing more than 100 managers in German-speaking countries we found that although managers themselves are rarely motivated by money, when asked, "What motivates you?" and "How can you best motivate your employees?" most managers rank money as the best way of motivating others.

What then, do employees really expect from a good job and from their company in order to feel not just motivated but *engaged*? According to Professor Bernhard Bandura (University of Bielefeld, Germany, in a live presentation) there are in principle five items:

> Job security
> + Significance of the work
> + Opportunities for advancement
> + Cooperative and supportive social relationships
> + Fair pay
> _____
> = causes **high engagement**

All of these factors are subjective and will, of course, be evaluated by each employee on the basis of their own meta-programs. For each person, their meta-programs and their position must be compatible with each other. Until now, far too little attention has been paid to this when recruiting employees for positions. Previously, the focus in selecting applicants has been on professional training and experience. We now understand that this process is seriously flawed in matching people to jobs for optimal motivation and engagement. An English personnel manager summed it up when he said, "We hire people because of their knowledge and professional experience, but we fire them because of their behaviour."

Employee engagement has two attributes to be measured: quality (type of engagement) and quantity (low to high). Together, these attributes define the type of engagement and give us clues to the behaviors we can expect (see Figure 1).

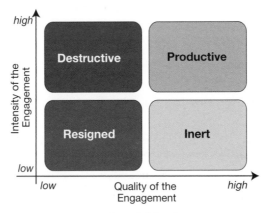

**Figure 1:** *The four fields of engagement*

Where the level of engagement and the quality of engagement are both low, the people have *resigned*. The employees have given up and the top performers are looking for new jobs. The employees have lost faith in the organization and that anything can be changed.

The *destructive* zone is indicated by a high level of poor quality engagement. There is significant opposition to the goals of the organization. Instead of pursuing these goals, many employees compete against each other.

People are judged *inert* when the quality of engagement is high but the level of engagement is low. Employees accept the goals of the organization. There is a sense of unity and a feeling of invulnerability. Along with a general complacency and carelessness, employees display a reluctance to change.

What organizations really want is *productive* engagement, where both the level of and the quality of the engagement is high. Employees align themselves with the goals of the company and in a way that is oriented toward progress. Employees generally have a high level of work satisfaction; they take pleasure in their work (the work is said to "flow").

Motivation forms the foundation for engagement. Although the engagement in a company can be deduced directly from its economic performance,[8] the reasons for low engagement are more complex[9] and need to be measured in different ways. If engagement is poor, the Identity Compass can be used to measure the motivational factors in the workplace by measuring the motivational and de-motivational factors of their job.

Historically motivation has been assumed to have a relatively linear scale, with people being either highly motivated or completely unmotivated,[10] or falling somewhere between the two. Motivation, like meta-programs, is now proving to be much more complex.[11]

When the workplace holds neither motivating nor de-motivating factors, employees experience emotional distress, anxiety, and other psychosomatic symptoms that initially reduce efficiency and eventually lead to ill-health.[12] Burn-out and bore-out are both extreme forms of stress with potentially dramatic consequences for any organization.[13] Costs related to burn-out will often be directly attributable and manifest as illness or absenteeism.[14] Bore-out will more often lead to behavioral changes, with indirect costs resulting from employees reducing their commitment and working strictly to their terms and conditions of employment, as if inwardly they have quit their jobs.

If those same managers were to ask questions such as:

- How do we get the best employee for each position?
- How well do we understand each employee and optimize their job fit?

- How do we make our jobs both enjoyable and productive so that employees engage fully?
- How do we develop best culture for all stakeholders and the organization as a whole?
- What does the organization stand for—what are its enduring characteristics and values?

the Identity Compass can give them an answer.

## *Recruiting Example*

In the middle of 2009, a job candidate had his thinking preferences measured. According to his profile, he was unequivocally a team player. The head of personnel said that could not be because this applicant had already been working for the company for seventeen years as a so-called "nomad" (company jargon). He had always been traveling on behalf of the company, and always on his own. A week later he called me and said this applicant had indeed been on the road alone from the viewpoint of the company, but he had always been working with suppliers to ensure the level of quality required by the firm. So while he was on the road, he had plenty of people around him. The job he was now applying for, however, called for someone who really would be always traveling alone. He was to maintain free-standing technical facilities which were located in the countryside. There would be no people around. After this was made clear to the applicant he voluntarily withdrew his application. Without the profile that had been created previously, this fact would not have come to anyone's attention until after he was hired, and then there would have been great costs on both sides.

Meta-programs are the link between values and beliefs[15] (e.g., If two people have the same value, "peace," but one is "towards" and the other is "away from," they will develop different beliefs on how to reach or maintain "peace").

All meta-programs influence the quality and efficiency of an individual's work. If the person's work criteria correspond to their personal meta-programs, then the likelihood of job satisfaction and employee engagement is increased.

To bring sustainable changes to a company it is helpful to measure how engaged the employees are. Add to this an assessment of "flow" in the work context and all that is left to identify are the levers for change. People are in "flow" when the requirements of the job match their meta-programs, for example, options-oriented people can set up procedures and procedures-oriented people can follow them. This is true for every single meta-program. The Identity Compass reveals those leverage points by highlighting the meta-programs most likely to initiate and maintain the change for individuals and groups in their particular context.

Early in 2011 my partner from Finland, Timo Katajamaa, revisited a client from the previous year. He was excited to show his client the latest development of the Identity Compass system—the measurement of "employee engagement"—in order to enhance their ongoing relationship and explore how the feature might add value. Using the existing profiles completed in June 2010, Timo examined employee engagement for the previous year, finding that a high score on "resigned" was clearly measured. On seeing the results, the client immediately commented: "If I had this information last June, I would have saved at least €200,000!" It showed that the whole sales team had resigned already in June. This was because the new sales manager (who had not been profiled with the Identity Compass) was not able to manage the team. Therefore the sales figures went down and the sales team resigned more and more.

## Identity Compass Consultants

Identity Compass licenses consultants to use this profiling system with their clients. Certification is dependent upon the successful completion of three days of comprehensive training. After certification, consultants get access to the full version of the software with which they can generate and score online interviews. For their clients, answering such an interview usually takes 45–55 minutes. The results show an impressive fifty thinking preferences in the meta-programs plus seventeen motivating and de-motivating factors at the workplace. Additionally, each profile now shows how that person perceives employee engagement within the organization.

Companies that have used the Identity Compass to enhance their existing recruitment and assessment processes produced more precise and cost-effective results. Retrospective analysis confirmed that, when Identity Compass delivered results that conflicted with their conventional assessment process, invariably Identity Compass was the more accurate and reliable system. With the cost of an assessment center in Germany at around €2,000 per participant, and a profile with Identity Compass only a fraction of this, which is the most cost effective?

## Caveats

The Identity Compass has been designed so far for the professional context. Even though some people also find it valuable for the private context, I do not think this is appropriate as people may think and behave differently in various contexts.

### Notes

1. Dilts (1995).

2. McClelland (1961).

3. Bischof (1985).

4. Bischof (1985).

5. Scheffer and Kuhl (2006).

6. Scheffer and Kuhl (2006).

7. CSC Deutschland Akademie (2003).

8. Towers Perrin (2007).

9. Sprenger (1997).

10. Bischof (1985); Towers Perrin (2007).

11. Techniker Kasse (2010).

12. Petermann and Studer (2003); Towers Perrin (2007).

13. Techniker Kasse (2010).

14. Petermann and Studer (2003).

15. Techniker Kasse (2010).

## Bibliography

Bischof, N. (1985). *Das Rätsel Ödipus*. Munich: Piper.

Bruch, H. and Vogel, B. (2005). *Organisationale Energie*. Wiesbaden: Gabler.

CSC Deutschland Akademie and Dr. Heissmann (now Watson Wyatt Heissmann). (2003). Fiebes in Company. Welche Spuren hat die Krise hinterlassen. Study, Wiesbaden.

Dilts, R. (1995). Unpublished manuscript.

Gritschneider, I. (2009). *Burn-out: Schuften bis zum Umfallen*. Documentary. Arte. 17.11.2009, 21.00h.

Hackman, J. R. and Oldham, G. R. (1975). Development of the Job Diagnostic Survey. *Journal of Applied Psychology* 60: 159–170.

Hackman, J. R. and Oldham, G. R. (1976). Motivation through the design of work: test of a theory. *Organizational Behavior and Human Performance* 16: 250–279.

Hackman, J. R. and Oldham, G. R. (1980). *Work Redesign*. Reading, MA: Addison Wesley.

Hall, L. M. and Bodenhamer, B. G. (2005). *Figuring Out People*. Clifton, CO: Neuro-Semantic Publications.

Herzberg, F. (2003). Was Mitarbeiter in Schwung bringt. *Harvard Business Manager*, April, pp. 50–62.

Herzberg, F., Mausner, B., and Snyderman, B. B. (1976). *The Motivation to Work* (2nd edn). New York: John Wiley and Sons.

Kofler, W. and Kalte, H. (2004). Vienna: *Deutike*.

Korzybski, A. (1948). *Science and Sanity: An Introduction to Non-Aristotelian Systems and General Semantics*. Lakeville, CT: Non-Aristotelian Library Publishing Company.

McClelland, D. (1961). *The Achieving Society*. Princeton, NJ: Van Nostrand.

Maus, H. A. (2011). *Forget About Motivation: Focus on Productive Engagement*. Charlotte, NC: KONA Publishing & Media.

Myers, D. G. (2008). *Psychologie*. Berlin: Springer.

Petermann, F. Th. and Studer, D. (2003). Burnout: Herausforderung an die anwaltliche Beratung. *Aktuelle Juristische Praxis* (7): 761–767.

Rose Charvet, S. (1997). *Words that Change Minds*. Dubuque, IO: Kendall/Hunt Publishing.

Rost, K. and Osterloh, M. (2008). Management Fashion Pay-for-Performance for CEOs. In M. Vartiainen, C. Antoni, X. Baeten, N. Hakonen, R. Lucas, and H. Thierry (eds), *Reward Management: Facts and Trends in Europe*. Lengerich: Pabst Science Publishers, pp. 139–163.

Scheffer, D. and Kuhl, J. (2006). *Erfolgreich motivieren*. Göttingen: Hogrefe.

Sprenger, R. (1997). *Mythos Motivation*. Frankfurt/New York: Campus.

Strack, D. (2009). *Kulturelle Implikationen der Internationalisierung im Lebensmittel-Einzelhandel*. Lengerich: Pabst Science Publishers.

Stummer, H. (2008). Nebenwirkungen schlechten Managements. *Harvard Business Manager* (7): 16–17.

Techniker Kasse (2010). *Gesundheitsreport 2010*. Band 25, Hamburg: Techniker Kasse.

Towers Perrin. (2007). *Global Workforce Study 2007*. Available at http://www.towersperrin.com/tp/getwebcachedoc?webc=HRS/DEU/2007/200701/GWS.pdf (accessed September 03, 2011).

Walker, W. (1996). *Abenteuer Kommunikation*. Stuttgart: Klett-Cotta.

Weinert, A. B. (2004). *Organisations- und Personalpsychologie: Textbook*. Weinheim: Beltz Psychologie Verlags Union.

Whitehead, A. N. and Russell, B. (1910–1913). *Principia Mathematica*, 3 vols. Cambridge: Cambridge University Press.

Woodsmall, M. and Woodsmall, W. (1999). *People Pattern Power: P3*. Washington, DC: Next Step Press.

Woodsmall, W. (1988). Metaprograms. Unpublished manuscript.

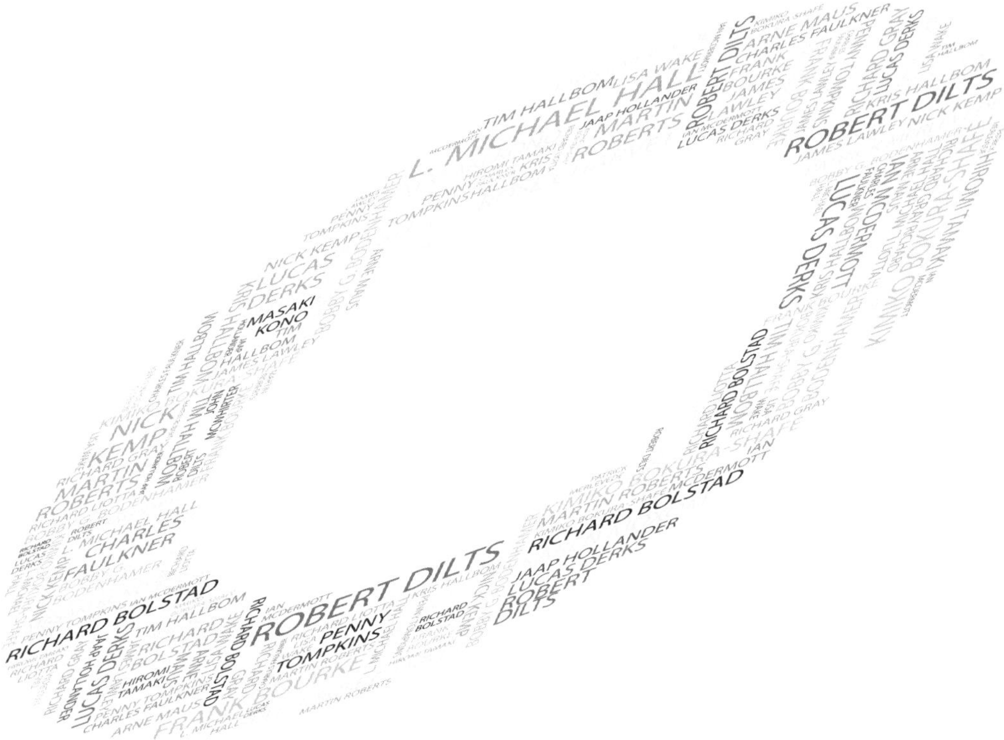
L. MICHAEL HALL
TIM HALLBOM
LISA WAKE
JAAP HOLLANDER
ROBERT DILTS
ARNE MAUS
CHARLES FAULKNER
LUCAS DERKS
KRIS HALLBOM
NICK KEMP
JAMES LAWLEY
IAN MCDERMOTT
KIMIKO BOKURA-SHAFE
HIROMI TAMAKI
RICHARD BOLSTAD
RICHARD GRAY
MARTIN ROBERTS
MASAKI KONO
PENNY TOMPKINS
FRANK BOURKE
RICHARD LIOTTA
BOBBY G. BODENHAMER

 **Jaap Hollander** (1952) lives in Nijmegen, Holland. He started his career as a clinical psychologist in a large mental hospital. From the middle eighties on he specialized in hypnosis, NLP (Neuro-Linguistic Programming) and Provocative Therapy. Together with his wife and colleague Anneke Meijer he introduced NLP in the Netherlands in 1984 and founded the IEP (the Institute for Eclectic Psychology). Today the IEP trains hundreds of professionals each year, mostly in NLP and Provocative Coaching. The IEP's goal is to contribute to a world where people take time to reflect upon themselves and to advance their inner potential, becoming more flexible in their work, more sensitive in their communication and stronger as individuals.

Jaap Hollander has written ten books, amongst them *Essentials of NLP*, the Dutch standard text on NLP, *Trance and Magic*, about trance rituals in Brazil and *Success isn't everything*, about provocative coaching. His latest book *Provocative Coaching* (in English) will be published in 2012. He developed "MPA MindSonar®" and the "Nano Tech Power Deck," an NLP card game. He was chosen five years in a row by *Quote* magazine as one of the top 500 professionals in Holland.

# 17

## MPA MindSonar®
An NLP Tool for Coaching, Team Building, Personnel Management, and Marketing

*Jaap Hollander*

*Vir prudens non contra ventum mingit.*
(A wise man does not urinate against the wind.)

Roman proverb

## An X-Ray Machine for the Mind

If you had a machine that could measure how people think, how would you use it? MPA MindSonar is a psychological test that measures people's meta-programs, their criteria (what they find important), the hierarchy in their criteria, and what type of criteria they are. MPA MindSonar is like an x-ray machine for the mind.

In MPA, thinking refers to a combination of self-talk, images, and feelings (emotions and sensations), what is important (criteria and values), and what is true (beliefs or convictions). It is assumed—and this is different from most other psychological tests—that someone's meta-programs and criteria will be different in different situations. For instance, when someone is leading a team, he or she may be thinking completely differently from when they are playing with their children. Therefore MPA MindSonar always measures someone's thinking style for *a specific context.*

## What Is MPA MindSonar Used For?

MPA MindSonar can be used wherever it is important to understand how people think. Applications may be personal (e.g., helping a coaching client be a better parent) or business-related (e.g., selecting effective salespeople). By and large, MPA MindSonar is used for the following purposes:

1. **Improving communication:** Adapting messages to the thinking style of the people receiving the message. This improves both reception and acceptance of the message.

2. **Effective coaching:** Helping people understand why they get stuck (e.g., experience unpleasant emotions and behavioral limitations) in certain situations and why they thrive (e.g., experience pleasant emotions and behavioral freedom) in other situations.

3. **Adapting working and learning situations to people:** Adapting the dominant thinking styles in working and learning situations to the thinking styles of the people involved. This makes it easier for individuals to work and learn.

4. **Modeling excellence:** Mapping out the thinking style that enables certain people to accomplish extraordinary things, in order to make that capability (more) learnable for others.

5. **Developing psychological capital:** Enhancing the valuable elements in people's thinking styles and thereby increasing the psychological capital of a group or an organization.

6. **Selecting candidates:** Determining the thinking style that predominates among people who function well in a particular position. Selecting people who have a similar thinking style.

7. **Understanding competencies:** Mapping out the underlying structure, in terms of meta-programs and criteria, of a particular skill-set or competency.

8. **Changing culture:** Identifying the dominant thinking style in a group to determine which meta-programs could be adapted to change the culture in a desired direction.

## Examples of MindSonar Projects

- **Developing leadership in the Dutch military**
  When an officer in the Dutch military is being prepared for a high ranking position, they start a leadership development training of approximately one year. In this year they work on their communication, strategic, and leadership competencies. At the beginning of the course an MPA profile is made and the candidate defines their own strengths and weaknesses as a potential high ranking officer.

Their MPA profile is related to the competencies they want to develop (they choose five from a list of twelve competencies defined by the military). Their meta-programs and criteria are seen as a "lever" to better enable them to develop these competencies. An officer might, for instance, want to develop a thinking style that has stronger "towards," "general," people," and "structure" aspects, combined with more "yellow" criteria (personal development and systems overview). During the year the officer has several conversations with a coach. At the end of the course, another measurement is done to determine if the target competencies have indeed been developed.

- **Selling automobiles**
  Selling automobiles in the top segment of the market usually involves several hours of personal contact between a sales person and the customer. In this segment personal relationships are an important factor influencing sales. All Dutch salespeople of one of the top automobile brands were profiled with MPA MindSonar. Their meta-programs and criteria were related to the number of cars they sold per year. In this way, the desired profile for a salesperson—with this brand—was calculated. The desired profile—where different meta-programs were given different weights—correlated highly with the number of cars sold. From then on, all candidates for sales positions were profiled with MindSonar. How similar their profile is to the desired profile partly determines whether or not they are hired. Also, in the current sales force, salespeople who diverted from the desired profile were offered a training course, tailored to develop their underdeveloped meta-programs.

- **Selecting jury members for freestyle horse riding**
  A Dutch association for horse riding sports wanted to develop an objective basis for the selection of jury members for their freestyle competitions (*concours hippique*). The monetary value of a horse depends on its score in this competition. So, for horse owners, there are both emotional and financial interests at stake. The score, unlike that in other competitions like barrier jumping, depends entirely upon the subjective evaluation of the jury. The association hired two MPA professionals who profiled twelve outstanding jury members. They calculated an average profile and formulated a psychological explanation of why this profile described the thinking of a good jury member. The excellent jury members recognized both the profile and the explanation. This resulted in a desired

profile with relative weights for different meta-programs. Since then, every year hundreds of people wanting to become freestyle jury members are profiled with MPA MindSonar. The MPA professionals present the selecting committee with a matching percentage for each candidate and they specify the meta-programs on which the candidate matches or mismatches the desired profile. The committee then coordinates their impressions from interviews with the MPA results to decide.

- **Helping pedagogy interns adapt to their professional environment**
  Before pedagogy students of a Dutch university start their internship, for instance in an educational institution, they are profiled with MPA MindSonar. Their supervisor, knowing the culture of the institutions where the students do their internships, can express that culture in terms of meta-programs and values. The supervisor, comparing the profile of the student with the culture of the institution, then predicts the kinds of obstacles that particular student is likely to encounter in that particular institution. Let's say the institution's culture is reactive, specific, and information-oriented and the student has a proactive, global, and activity-oriented profile. The supervisor can then predict that some people in the institution may experience the student as rash, uncontrollable, vague, and inaccurate. The supervisor discusses this with the student and also how the student can respond, should this problem occur. This has advantages both for students and for the institution. If the predicted problems occur, the student is ready to respond adequately and this tends to prevent escalation and drop-out.

- **Keeping people involved in a volunteer organization**
  A Dutch volunteer organization, promoting inter-ethnic understanding in schools, was having trouble retaining volunteers. MPA professionals profiled both the volunteers and the people recruiting them. They noticed that the recruiters and the older volunteers, as well as the new volunteers, all scored high on the meta-program "together." Recruiters often enlist people with meta-programs similar to their own. In and of itself this seemed like a good strategy because similarity tends to enhance rapport. Within the dynamics of this organization, however, it had a contrary effect. Older volunteers, valuing togetherness and having had the experience that new people would leave the organization rather quickly, did not invest in the new people socially. Precisely because of their preference for togetherness, it was an emotional strain for them to see

people leave. So they would focus on their in-group of older volunteers and more or less neglect the newcomers for the first few months. The newcomers, on the other hand, did not feel welcomed. This was a major setback, precisely because they too had a strong preference for togetherness. Their response was to leave the organization, which in turn consolidated the belief of the older volunteers that there was no use in investing in newcomers. To break this vicious cycle, all the MPA professionals had to do was to explain this to the older volunteers. As soon as they started giving more attention to the newcomers, the problem gradually disappeared.

- **Banking and entrepreneurial attitude**
  A large Belgian insurance bank defined a new corporate strategy in which it was important for their insurance brokers to develop a more entrepreneurial attitude. A central factor in this development was the relationship between the insurance brokers and the local insurance agents in the community. The company defined a list of key competencies for their brokers related to dealing with these agents. All brokers were profiled by MPA professionals. Surprisingly, after a statistical analysis, it turned out that there was no significant relationship between thinking style, criteria, and key competencies on the one hand and sales volume on the other hand. Further analysis revealed that this had to do with the targets that were being set. Because targets were set at a relatively low level, it did not matter much how brokers thought, what they found important, and which competencies they had. The volume of sales was determined mostly by demand from the local insurance agents and the efforts of the brokers seemed to have little to do with it. This finding led the company to change the system of setting targets. After targets were adjusted, thinking style did make a difference. A training program was developed in which brokers were trained in those competencies that their MPA profile showed them to be lacking in. For this project the company won a prestigious training award.

## Where Does the Name Come From?

MPA stands for Meta Profile Analysis. The term "MindSonar" uses physical sonar technology as an analogy. Sonar shows us objects that cannot be seen by observing the surface of the water, and sonar requires an expert to understand the exact nature of those objects.

**Figure 1:** *MPA MindSonar logo*

MPA MindSonar uses distinctions taken mainly from NLP.[1] Most people taking the MPA certification training are master practitioners of NLP.

## How Does It Work?

MPA MindSonar presents the respondent with seventy-six questions and two tasks (criteria sorting and criteria categorization). It also registers the time it takes the respondent to finish each test item. The English text is 95% "Globish" (a simplified international version of English).

The program starts by explaining (in text and audio) how the system works, what the respondent may expect, and the importance of answering the questions based on how they think rather than how they would like to think or ought to think. Next, the program asks the respondent to identify the context in which he or she wants their meta-profile to be measured. Alternatively, this context may be predefined by the professional using the system, in which case the program simply states the context.

Once the context has been defined, the respondent is asked to concentrate on that context for a few moments while a piece of music is played. This process is repeated twice later on, thereby anchoring awareness of the context to that particular piece of music. The respondent can change the music if they wish. A wide range of music styles is offered to choose from. Later on during the questionnaire, the program will play the same music ("fire" the anchor) to stimulate continued awareness of the context.

Next, the program asks for identifying and demographic information: name, birth date, educational level, work area, work function level, and marital status.

Then the program asks the respondent to define four things they find important in the chosen context (four criteria) and then to order their criteria from most to least important (hierarchy of criteria). He or she is then shown the four criteria and asked to define the opposites (e.g., the opposite of "vigor" might be "weakness" for a given respondent). Different respondents will define different opposites for the same criteria, thereby clarifying the meaning (complex equivalence) of that criterion.

The hierarchy (top two positions) is tested in the following way. The respondent is asked whether or not he or she would accept a *small loss* of criterion #2 in return for a *large gain* in criterion #1. For example: is he or she willing to accept *a little* loneliness in return for *a lot of* creativity? If the respondent does not accept the offer, they are directed back to their list of criteria and encouraged to make changes. Sometimes criteria are components of or conditions for other criteria. MindSonar resolves this by encouraging respondents to combine criteria. For instance, if a respondent believes that they can only be creative together with other people, they cannot accept some loneliness to get a lot more creativity, because the loneliness will in turn decrease their creativity. The respondent is then advised to combine "creativity" and "communication" into one new criterion (e.g., "creative communication"). This enables the respondent to create a "clean" set of criteria (without direct dependencies) which can then be sorted.

Next, the respondent is shown one criterion and seven groups of two words representing seven Graves categories. After doing the Graves categorization, the respondent is presented with seventy-six questions related to meta-programs. The number of questions per meta-program varies between four and seven, depending on how many questions are needed to achieve the desired statistical reliability (Cronbach's Alpha = 0.7 or higher).

There are six types of test items for meta-programs:

1. **Identification items:** Photographs showing people thinking different things (in text balloons). The respondents indicate which person thinks most like them.

2. **Symbolic items:** The respondent chooses from a set of symbols.

3. **Avoidance items:** An avoidance question is asked ("What do you want to *prevent*?").

4. **Key word items:** The respondent chooses from different key word combinations.

5. **Proverb items:** The respondent chooses from two or three proverbs.

6. **Straightforward items:** The respondent is asked directly about the meta-program in question ("Do you think more like this or more like this?").

MPA MindSonar also measures response times (i.e., how long it takes the respondent to answer the questions).

## Meta-Programs Measured

Meta-programs[2] are patterns in people's thinking. In the term *neuro-linguistic programming*, the term "programming" refers to mental strategies (sequences of inner images, sounds, and feelings). Meta-programs are "meta" to these strategies; they describe general trends in the content of these strategies. Since most NLP-readers will be familiar with meta-programs, they will be described here only briefly. The following meta-programs are measured by MPA MindSonar:

- Proactive (preference for acting quickly and taking the initiative) versus
- Reactive (preference for waiting, considering, and reflecting).

- Toward (focus on achieving goals) versus
- Away From (focus on avoiding problems).

- Internal Reference (using one's own standards in evaluations) versus
- External Reference (using other people's standards in evaluations).

- Options (preference for many different possibilities) versus
- Procedures (preference for step-by-step plans).

- Maintenance (preference for things staying the same) versus
- Development (preference for gradual change) versus
- Change (preference for fast and radical change).

(In overviews of meta-programs, the *desire* for stability/sameness or change/difference is often assumed to coincide with its *perception*. Someone with a desire for change is thought to also perceive more change. However, people often desire change precisely because they do *not* perceive enough change and often desire stability when they perceive *too much* change. We have therefore chosen in MPA MindSonar to focus on the desire for—and not the perception of—stability or change.)

- Global (focus on broad overview) versus
- Specific (focus on details).

- People (focus on people) versus
- Activities (focus on activities) versus
- Information (focus on information).

- Concept (focus on concepts and principles) versus
- Structure (focus on relationships between elements) versus
- Use (focus on practical applications).

- Together (preference for working closely together with shared responsibility) versus
- Proximity (preference for mutual support with individual responsibility) versus
- Solo (preference for working alone).

- Matching (focus on what is good and correct) versus
- Mismatching (focus on what is bad and incorrect).

- Internal locus of control (focus on how someone influences their circumstances) versus
- External locus of control (focus on how someone's circumstances influence them).

- Past (focus on the past) versus
- Present (focus on the "here and now") versus
- Future (focus on the future).

- Visual (focus on images and movies) versus
- Auditory (focus on sounds and words) versus
- Kinesthetic (focus on feelings and movement).

(These last three distinctions are sensory modalities rather than meta-programs. They are measured together with the meta-programs for the sake of convenience.)

## Criteria

Criteria are values. They indicate what someone finds important in a given context. In the TOTE (Test–Operate–Test–Exit) Model of goal-directed behavior, the present situation is compared with a criterion to determine whether operations (actions) are necessary.[3] Meta-programs can be understood as ways in which people handle their criteria. MPA MindSonar asks the respondent to define:

- Four criteria (four things they find important in the context their profile is measured for).

- A meta-criterion (what happens when the first four criteria are met).

- The opposites of all criteria (e.g., for a particular person, the opposite of "inspiration" might be "dullness").

- The hierarchy of the criteria (their order of importance).

## Categorizing Criteria

Originally, MPA MindSonar simply took stock of people's criteria by storing their verbal descriptions. This made it difficult to compare criteria, since different people attach different meanings to the same words. We wanted to be able to accurately define and compare criteria based on numbers. To achieve this, we needed a typology of values, and we chose the Graves (Spiral Dynamics®) model. Graves theorized that there are eight value systems which evolved over the course of human history.[4] He assumed that each value system flows from the previous one as a response to ever more complex living circumstances and the problems which are inherent in the last system. MPA MindSonar now measures the extent to which criteria are associated with seven of the eight Graves categories, using colors derived from Spiral Dynamics[5] theory:

## Purple Drive

When someone has a strong purple drive, their criteria in that particular context have to do primarily with security and safety. Other key words for this drive are: belonging, tradition, feeling at home, togetherness, and seniority.

## Red Drive

When someone has a strong red drive, their criteria primarily relate to power and respect—to getting respect in particular, but also to showing respect. They act impulsively, quickly, and forcefully without thinking of the consequences. Other key words for this drive are: reputation, power, strength, honor, and courage.

## Blue Drive

When someone has a strong blue drive, their criteria have to do primarily with order and security. Other key words for this drive are: discipline, reliability, duty, and control.

## Orange Drive

When someone has a strong orange drive, their criteria have to do primarily with competition and winning. Other key words for this drive are: success, achievement, results, progress, and influence.

## Green Drive

When someone has a strong green drive, their criteria have to do primarily with ideals and loyalty to the group. Other key words for this drive are: harmony, community, connectedness, love, social contact, and consensus.

### Yellow Drive

When someone has a strong yellow drive, their criteria have to do primarily with learning and independence. Other key words for this drive are: creativity, analysis, and personal growth.

### Turquoise Drive

When someone has a strong turquoise drive, their criteria primarily have to do with the big picture and a holistic vision. Other key words for this drive are: responsibility for the earth as a whole, spirituality, balance, and integration.

## Gradual Responding

MPA MindSonar works with a gradual responding system, meaning that the respondent does not have to make absolute yes-or-no choices. He or she indicates *to what extent* an alternative applies to him or herself by moving a ball (see Figure 2).

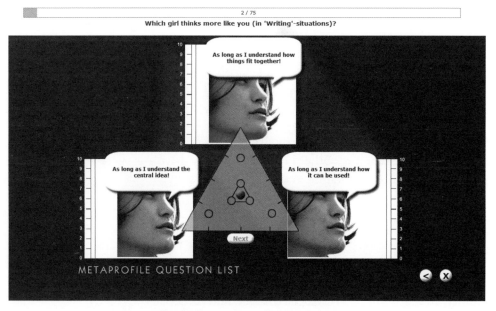

**Figure 2:** *Gradual scoring system*

## Online Administration

Respondents take the test via a website on the Internet. The report is available to the professional administering the test one minute after the respondent finishes the test. No reports are sent to respondents directly.

## MPA MindSonar Report

The report describes thirty-two elements distributed over thirteen meta-programs and seven criteria dimensions (Graves categories). The scores are expressed in numbers, graphs, and interpretive texts.

### Sonar Diagram

The Sonar diagram provides a quick overview of the most dominant meta-programs and value systems.

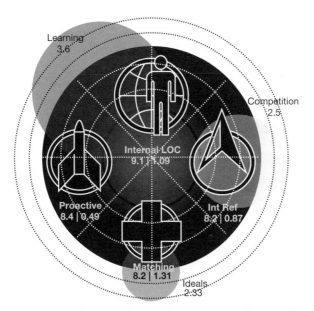

**Figure 3:** *Cognitive style diagram (Sonar diagram) with "internal locus of control," "proactive," "internal reference," and "matching" as dominant meta-programs (in that order), and "learning" (yellow), "competition" (orange), and "ideals" (turquoise) as dominant value systems.*

## *Bar Chart*

The bar chart provides a complete overview of all meta-programs and value systems measured. The higher the bar, the higher the score. Behind the colored bars, lighter "shadows" are shown, representing the averages of all profiles in the MPA database (currently containing 4,000+ profiles).

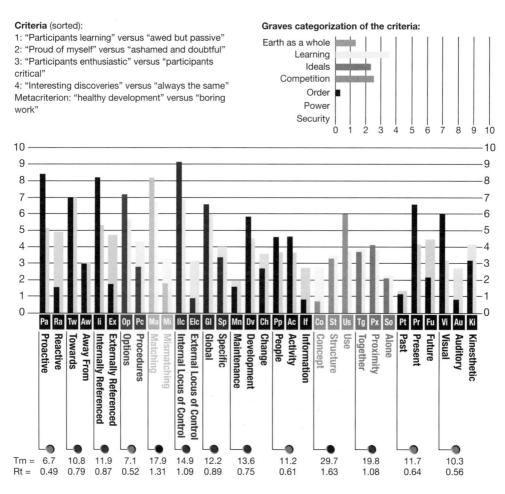

**Figure 4:** *Bar chart (for the same profile as shown in Figure 3)*

### Relative Response Times

The response times are listed below the bars. They are corrected to the respondent's average response time for all meta-programs and compensated for items containing three choices (which take longer to understand). Long response times indicate hesitation; short response times indicate certainty.

### Interpretative Text

An interpretative text of more than thirty pages describes all the results verbally.

## Licensing and Certification

MPA MindSonar is exclusively available to licensed professionals who have obtained a certification by completing a seven-day training course. MPA certification training covers subjects such as: coaching and team building with MPA MindSonar, teaching MPA workshops, non-verbal expression of meta-program clusters, basic psychological testing theory, and calculating return on investment on MPA-projects.

An international registry of MPA MindSonar professionals is maintained by the Institute for Eclectic Psychology in Nijmegen, The Netherlands. This registry is publicly available at www.mindsonar.info. MPA MindSonar is available in English, French, and Dutch.

**Figure 5:** *MPA license seal*

## Notes

1. Bandler and Grinder (1975, 1979).

2. Cameron-Bandler et al. (1985); Rose Charvet (1997).

3. Miller et al. (1960).

4. Graves (1970).

5. Beck and Cowan (1996).

## References

Bandler, R. and Grinder, J. (1975). *The Structure of Magic I: A Book about Language and Therapy*. Palo Alto, CA: Science and Behavior Books.

Bandler, R. and Grinder, J. (1979). *Frogs into Princes: Neuro-Linguistic Programming*. Moab, UT: Real People Press.

Beck, D. and Cowan, C. (1996). *Spiral Dynamics: Mastering Values, Leadership and Change*. Cambridge: Blackwell.

Brown, N. (2004). What makes a good educator? The relevance of meta programmes. *Assessment & Evaluation in Higher Education* 29(5): 515–533.

Cameron-Bandler, L., Gordon, D., and LeBeau, M. (1985). *The Emprint Method: A Guide to Reproducing Competence*. San Rafael, CA: Future Pace.

Graves, C. W. (1970). Levels of existence: an open systems theory of values levels of human existence. *Journal of Humanistic Psychology* 10(2): 131–155.

Hollander, J. (2005). *Handboek MetaprofielAnlayse 6.1*. Nijmegen: Metaprofiel b.v.

Hustinx, G. and Durlinger-van der Horst, A. (2005). *Voorbij je eigen wijze: effectief communiceren met metaprogramma's in professionele relaties*. Soest: Nelissen.

Kompagne, J. (2008). Samenhang tussen MPA MindSonar® en Spiral Dynamics. Artikel in het kader van MPA-certificering, Instituut voor Eclectische Psychologie.

Miller, G. A., Galanter, E., and Pribram. K. H. (1960). *Plans and the Structure of Behavior*. New York: Henry Holt & Co.

Nijskens, J. (2002). Onderzoek naar de validiteit van MPA, deel 1. Available at www.iepdoc.nl/biblio/artikel_detail.asp?ID=71 (accessed August 11, 2011).

Nijskens, J. (2003). Onderzoek naar de validiteit van MPA, deel 2. Available at www.iepdoc.nl/biblio/artikel_detail.asp?ID=71 (accessed August 11, 2011).

Nijskens, J. (2004). Onderzoek naar de validiteit van MPA, deel 3. Available at www.iepdoc.nl/biblio/artikel_detail.asp?ID=71 (accessed August 11, 2011).

Rose Charvet, S. (1997). *Words that Change Minds: Mastering the Language of Influence* (2nd edn). Dubuque, IO: Kendall/Hunt.

Wielders, L. and Burghard, J. (2009). *Samenhang tussen MPA & de selectie en opleiding van juryleden voor de KNHS*. Internal publication.

Woodsmall, M. and Woodsmall, W. (1998). *People Pattern Power: The Nine Keys to Business Success*. Washington, DC: Next Step Press.

 **Patrick Merlevede**'s mission is to help people find the job of their lives. With this purpose in mind, he created jobEQ.com and a network of trainers, coaches, and consultants to work according this philosophy. He co-authored several books, including *7 Steps to Emotional Intelligence* and *Mastering Mentoring and Coaching with Emotional Intelligence*. In 2010, he launched a series of books in a Tips format (see www.105tips.com).

After completing the NLP trainer's training at NLP University in 1996, Patrick set out to integrate models such as the meta-programs and the value systems of Graves with emotional intelligence, focusing on applications in the field of human resources management. Patrick has been called "The World's Expert on the Integration of Emotional Intelligence and NLP."

If you want to know more or reach Patrick, check out www.merlevede.biz.

# 18 jobEQ
## Profiling Meta-Programs to Improve Emotional Intelligence

*Patrick Merlevede*

## Why JobEQ?

The promise NLP makes when it is used in a business context is that it enables people to obtain more from the individuals they work with by:

- Gaining a better mutual understanding.
- Being more efficient at communication.
- Having fewer conflicts and negative emotions.
- Making better use of complementary characteristics and skills.

In this NLP has had a mixed reception. Skeptics often point to the lack of "scientific evidence" regarding NLP. The result is that some human resources or organizational development personnel may dismiss NLP. Starting from this observation, jobEQ grew out of a "scientific" project in 1999, similar to the NLP Research and Recognition Project.

We focused on applications in the work environment, such as recruitment, assessment, yearly performance reviews, coaching, training, management and leadership, retention, outplacement, and so on. Our questions were: What does NLP have to add? How can we do better than the current "state of the art" in those areas? How can we prove our results are better?

JobEQ's main innovations are:

- Integrating NLP models and presuppositions in all of these approaches.
- Linking NLP to Daniel Goleman's "Emotional Intelligence."
- Linking all of the above to NLP's modeling excellence.
- Using more "scientific" and statistical ways of working, and using these approaches to ensure NLP gets the credibility and scientific recognition it deserves.

The framework we have designed combines several NLP models and links them to all areas of human resources management. Further information about jobEQ can be found in the books 7 *Steps to Emotional Intelligence*[1] and *Mastering Mentoring and Coaching with Emotional Intelligence*,[2] as well as Marilyn Powell's 2009 Ph.D. thesis, which uses jobEQ's tools and approaches to study which meta-programs make a difference in selecting and training medical doctors.[3] Furthermore, jobEQ's tools have been translated into more than sixteen languages and used for projects in organizations in over thirty countries.

## The Performance Framework and Supporting Toolset

Suppose you enter a supermarket looking for your favorite chocolates. If you do not find what you are looking for, you approach the clerk who is restocking items further down the aisle. At first you wait a bit, hoping to catch their attention. This doesn't seem to work. So you grow a bit impatient and speak up, "Excuse me, sir."

This example can be deconstructed into the cognitive processes that are going on between the moment an external stimulus invites the person to react and the actual observable behavior that results. The first requirement is that the event passes the filters of the person. Then the individual needs to evaluate the event and decide what action to take. Only if the actions are appropriate will he get the desired results. If any one of these building blocks is missing, the result will not be obtained. Figure 1 shows how these steps are linked.

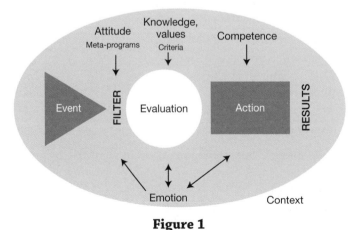

**Figure 1**

In the supermarket instance we went through this cycle twice. First, you are the "stimulus" to the clerk; however, no reaction follows. This means the individual has either filtered out your presence, or evaluated it and decided he would continue with his own work. Second, noticing he does not respond (second event), you grew impatient (emotion) and decided you wouldn't wait any longer (evaluation), and so you took action and spoke up.

Let's summarize the different elements of the example in the following table:

|  | Cycle 1 | Cycle 2 |
|---|---|---|
| Context | You in a supermarket, waiting for a clerk who is at work. | You in a supermarket, impatient and wanting information. |
| Event | You approach the clerk. | You notice the clerk doesn't pay attention to you. |
| Filter | The clerk may not notice you or your non-verbal call for attention because he concentrates on the task at hand, instead of the people in the store. | You wanting information and noticing that you are waiting. |
| Evaluation | The clerk could be thinking that customer friendliness is less important than stocking the shelves (doing my job). | You feel that being helped is more important than restocking a shelf, so you decide to take action. |
| Action | He keeps restocking ... | You ask for attention by saying "Excuse me, sir." |
| Emotion | From neutral to impatience. | From impatient to confident. |

Note that in the second context (Cycle 2), if you'd had different filters at play, or if you'd evaluated the situation differently, your emotion would be different. If your impatience grows, and if you interpret the lack of attention from the sales clerk as "impolite," you could get angry instead of speaking up.

In the Performance Framework, it is our presupposition that if a person's metaprograms, values, and actions are aligned with what works in a given context, then that person will face fewer negative emotions and will have an increased chance of being in a flow state. JobEQ's aim is for organizations to build workplaces which are more "emotionally intelligent," where people get the chance to do a job they like and which they are good at.

The following "formula for success" summarizes the three building blocks of our Performance Framework:

$$\text{Results} = \text{Attitude} \times \text{Values} \times \text{Competence}$$

The Performance Framework can be used as a diagnostic model when evaluating or coaching people. If a staff member doesn't obtain the desired results, the question is: In which step of the process is the problem situated? Maybe the person wasn't aware that something needed to be done. Or maybe the person dismissed the whole issue (e.g., seeing it as "not important" or "not their problem"). Or perhaps the person didn't know what to do to get to the desired outcome.

The Performance Framework can also be used as a predictive model. Here we ask: Which are the attitudes, values, and competencies needed so that we will get the results we want?

Because we wanted to be able to model excellence and work with larger groups of people, we soon ran into the problem that having to interview people one by one to figure out their attitude (or meta-programs), value systems, and competencies was a serious constraint. So we developed a toolset to support the Performance Framework, which consists of several families of questionnaires, one for each of the three building blocks:

1. **iWAM**: Inventory for Work, Attitude, and Motivation. This measures various categories of meta-programs and can be considered a computerized version of the LAB Profile®. In fact, Rodger Bailey, one of the creators of the LAB Profile, also made the first prototypes of what is now iWAM.[4]

2. **VSQ**: Value Systems Questionnaire. This measures individual values as well as the value systems as they were defined by Clare Graves and further developed by Beck & Cowan into the Spiral Dynamics model. Because the VSQ is also used as a tool to evaluate organizational culture, it complements the iWAM by adding several additional filters.[5]

3. **COMET**, a methodology to design custom competence (or capability) models based on the behaviors of top performers, and the software for administering questionnaires which are based on these competence models, either for self-assessment or for 360 degree feedback evaluations. JobEQ also makes available specific questionnaires to measure emotional Intelligence (COMET/EQ) as well as coaching and mentoring skills (COMET/mentor). These specific questionnaires are designed to complement 7 *Steps to Emotional Intelligence* and *Mastering Mentoring and Coaching with Emotional Intelligence.*

These tools can be used "out of the box" to support projects ranging from hiring and assessment, to training and coaching, and management and leadership. On an individual level reports teach people more about themselves: What makes them tick? What are their strengths? What are development areas? For people who need to work together, jobEQ offers reports to compare two people in order to learn where there may be potential areas of misunderstanding and how people can learn to make better use of their complementarities, rather than conflicting. Other reports show how we can do the same type of analysis for a team, for example: What are the typical communication patterns of the team? What are the team weaknesses? How well does the leader match the team? On an even larger scale, we can measure the organization's culture or compare cultures between departments and take these findings into account when developing organizational change initiatives. All these applications have merit on their own and offer a good place to start for many organizations.

## How Does jobEQ Work?

The iWAM and VSQ are so called "forced ranking" questionnaires, in which the test-takers have to put the test items/statements in order of preference. On the paper and pencil version, the test-taker writes a number in front of the test items to indicate ranking. The online user interface allows test-takers to place the items in the right order on the screen. Each of the statements has been designed to test one specific pattern and most have a positive formulation. The patterns of a particular category are mostly tested together, but in other questions they will be combined with other meta-program categories. Here are two examples of iWAM questions, with an indication as to which patterns are being measured.

At work, I like to:

| | | |
|---|---|---|
| ____ | achieve the outcome | *towards* |
| ____ | be responsive | *reflecting and patience* |
| ____ | initiate tasks | *initiate (proactive)* |
| ____ | avoid problems | *away from* |
| ____ | observe the systems | *interest filter: systems* |

At work, one should be rewarded for:

| | | |
|---|---|---|
| ____ | finding problems | *away from* |
| ____ | deciding for oneself | *internal reference* |
| ____ | reaching the goals | *towards* |
| ____ | doing what others ask | *external reference* |
| ____ | having the information | *interest filter: information* |

The answers are then computed in relationship to how other people have completed the questionnaire. The resulting scores are then used as a basis for a variety of reports.

One of the iWAM reports is shown opposite: this one sorts the patterns in the order from "most preferred" (starting at 12 o'clock) to "least preferred." In this case, the patterns are listed in relation to the business culture in Malaysia and Singapore.

## JobEQ's Approach to Modeling Excellence

Suppose you enter a store where they sell mobile phones and all kinds of subscriptions for telecoms, the Internet, and so on. At first sight, you might think: "Oh, all these stores are the same." In reality the organizational cultures can be quite different and the motivational drivers of a successful salesperson may differ a lot from one shop to the next. A store from a traditional telecoms operator may have evolved into a shop where they sell mobile phones. The store next door is maybe just a couple of years old and is run by a franchisee of a newer mobile phone operator. The staff you find in the first store may have been working there for years, while the staff in the second store are allocated on a daily basis, depending on the expected number of visitors. People in the first store might earn a group bonus, depending on how well the whole store does in a specific month, while the salespeople in the second store

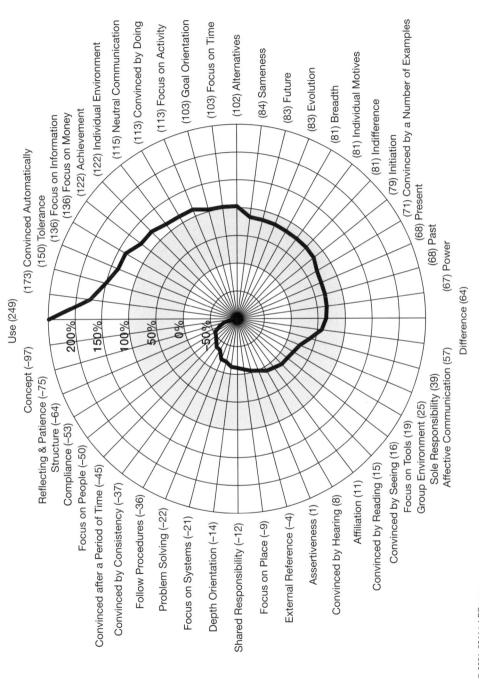

Use (249)
(173) Convinced Automatically
(150) Tolerance
(136) Focus on Information
(136) Focus on Money
(122) Achievement
(122) Individual Environment
(115) Neutral Communication
(113) Convinced by Doing
(113) Focus on Activity
(103) Goal Orientation
(103) Focus on Time
(102) Alternatives
(84) Sameness
(83) Future
(83) Evolution
(81) Breadth
(81) Individual Motives
(81) Indifference
(79) Initiation
(71) Convinced by a Number of Examples
(68) Present
(68) Past
(67) Power
Difference (64)
Affective Communication (57)
Sole Responsibility (39)
Group Environment (25)
Focus on Tools (19)
Convinced by Seeing (16)
Convinced by Reading (15)
Affiliation (11)
Convinced by Hearing (8)
Assertiveness (1)
External Reference (−4)
Focus on Place (−9)
Shared Responsibility (−12)
Depth Orientation (−14)
Focus on Systems (−21)
Problem Solving (−22)
Follow Procedures (−36)
Convinced by Consistency (−37)
Convinced after a Period of Time (−45)
Focus on People (−50)
Compliance (−53)
Structure (−64)
Reflecting & Patience (−75)
Concept (−97)

200%
150%
100%
50%
0%
−50%

only get a personal bonus. The result of these differences will be that the patterns (meta-programs, values, etc.) to be successful in the first store may be quite different from what it takes to be a great salesperson in the second store.

Many tools outside NLP claim they have a "model" of "telecom salespeople" (or even more generally "salespeople for shops"). Other tool-builders almost leave it to their users to "guess" which would be the most appropriate patterns for doing the job. From an NLP perspective, it makes much more sense to make a specific model for a specific job in a specific organization, based on the real performance of real top performers, by modeling these exemplars. That's the only way you can be sure that your model will find "the difference which makes a difference" for that specific organization.

When making a model for a job profile, we ask organizations to point out who are the high performers for that position and compare them to counter-examples. This is done by using a blend of questionnaires as well as interviews. Ideally, to have a full model, we will study the meta-programs, values, and competencies linked to the position. On some occasions a model will be limited to just one of those aspects, and then we often recommend focusing on work, attitude and motivation, based on the notion of "hiring for attitude." If one starts from the premise that meta-programs are the filters shown in the performance model, then if an employee is using the wrong filters, not much can happen downstream.

The resulting model will be validated by comparing the prediction of the model with the performance data of the people currently doing the job. A good model will have a correlation of 60% or more. Given that function and reality may change, we recommend organizations check after a year to see whether the predicted performance still matches the reality.

There are three main steps to doing this in practice.

**Step 1:** Model the top performers of the organization performing a specific role by having them take the iWAM and VSQ.

a) Decide together with the organization which individuals can be considered the top performers and why. Which criteria are to be chosen? How do people score on these criteria?

b) Determine which are the key meta-programs—the important empowering beliefs, key values, and capabilities which are making "the difference which makes a difference." We recommend modeling three or more top performers to identify a pattern. The first example is an anecdote. The second example allows you to formulate a hypothesis. The third and following examples confirm the hypothesis and suggest there may be a pattern.

**Step 2:** Refine and test your model of excellence:

a) Compare the model with the performance of people who are doing less well. Which meta-programs are they lacking or not using? Which beliefs do they reject? Which capabilities and behaviors aren't observed?

b) Check how well the model predicts performance. If you have a performance ranking of the sample, to what extent do the patterns you have modeled explain the difference between top performers and lower performers?

**Step 3:** Apply your model. Once a model is formulated, ideally all human resources processes should aligned with it. As illustrated in Figure 2, a model of excellence can be used to improve each step of the employee life cycle—from attracting the right candidates to the moment we decide whether it's important to retain staff members or let them go.

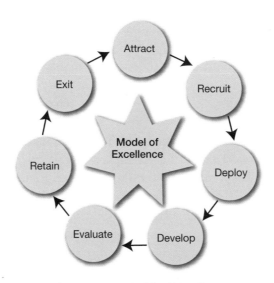

**Figure 2:** *A Model of Excellence*

This third step is reflected by jobEQ's mantra: *Hire for attitude, train for competence, coach for performance, and manage to retain.* Let's consider the role these four elements play in an organization.

a) Recruiting: How can we design a campaign to attract the right type of candidates? To what extent does the candidate have the desired meta-programs, values, and competencies? If they are not present, can we expect to can train/coach the person to quickly bridge the gap?

b) Training: Which are the important competencies for the role? Which skills does the person already have and which ones do we need to train? In some cases, doing a 360 degree evaluation can be appropriate to assess the current situation before enrolling people onto a training program.

c) Coaching: Nobody is perfect. Even after hiring the right person and training them, there will be issues to deal with. A coach can help the person to make better use of their skills and to develop better coping strategies.

d) Management and retention: Does management use the right motivational language? What can we do so that employees will stay longer?

Once a jobEQ modeling project has identified the differences which make a difference, customers use our questionnaires—such as the iWAM—for large-scale recruiting applications, sometimes testing thousands of candidates to find the individuals who are the closest to the model for a certain job. Other customers use the model to adjust their coaching approach and/or the way their managers handle staff members.

Whether the modeling project is about a specific job function or a larger scale research project, we always combine the notions of NLP modeling with the statistical model used in psychology and medicine. In an NLP-based modeling approach you often focus on a select number of exemplars and use a contrastive analysis to figure out the differences which make a difference. In statistics, one often looks at larger samples, with the risk of "modeling averages," as John Grinder has pointed out. Unfortunately, by dismissing statistics as a valid modeling approach, NLP has invited skeptics to dismiss our approaches as "unscientific." JobEQ's modeling approach bridges this gap by marrying the strong points of both approaches.

# Limitations

As the name jobEQ implies, the toolset focuses on the workplace, with questionnaires optimized for a work context. This means that the biggest limitation of jobEQ's
solutions at this time is that our tools are currently not available for other contexts.
However, we are looking for partners to expand our methodology into other areas.

Although models of excellence offer organizations an important competitive advantage, jobEQ's questionnaires can also be applied "out of the box," without models
of excellence. For instance, coaches draw on the meta-programs based in the iWAM
as a coaching tool to help people find another job or to work with executive teams
(e.g., team-building or resolving conflicts between team members). Universities and
training institutes employ the iWAM for classes about work motivation and interpersonal communication. COMET/EQ is helpful as a questionnaire for classes on
emotional intelligence as well as for various research projects.

Next to the formulation of models of excellence for a specific job role, jobEQ's tools
can help to create cultural models for an organization or division. In these cases
the approach is more statistical—sometimes a stratified sample of 500 or more
people are tested using the iWAM and/or VSQ. Such modeling will highlight which
meta-programs or value systems are typical for the organization, the range of value
systems and how they interact. When the organization also wants to identify typical behaviors, this will be complemented with behavior-based interviews (using the
COMET methodology).

On an even larger scale we can look at entire countries. The iWAM comes with "standard groups" which show how meta-programs and value systems differ between cultures. A typical example might be comparing President Bush Jnr. with President
Sarkozy. In absolute terms, the management style of the former was probably as
proactive as the second, but while Bush might be seen as only "slightly above average" on proactivity in the United States, Sarkozy is considered to be "too proactive"
or even "hyperactive" in France. The French population seems to think he takes too
many initiatives and that he involves himself in everything.[6]

## Conclusion

Even used on their own, there is a lot of value in using jobEQ's tools in coaching, recruiting, or training in order to measure meta-programs, value systems, and competencies. This chapter stresses two factors:

1. A combination of tools will give a more complete picture and will better predict performance.

2. One of NLP's great contributions is the principle of modeling excellence. There is a lot to gain by including that notion in projects—because something which may work in one organization may not work in another.

### Notes

1. Merlevede et al. (2001).

2. Merlevede and Bridoux (2004).

3. Powell (2009).

4. For more about meta-program categories measured by the iWAM, see www.jobEQ.com/categories.php.

5. For the patterns measured by VSQ, see www.jobeq.com/vsq_patterns.php.

6. Some other jobEQ related research projects include: a study of over 800 Chinese leaders who were tested to analyze how the Chinese business culture differs from the managerial culture to be found in the United States. The findings of this study were published in *Fortune Magazine China*, October 2008. For more information visit www.newleaders.com.cn. In the USA, Malcolm Baldrige Award winners were tested to identify which meta-programs are typical for a leader who manages to build an organization where quality management is key. See Appleby et al. (2009).

### References

Appleby, C. A., Harshman, C. L., and Latham, J. R. (2009). *Baldrige CEO Attitudes and Motivations: Developing a Model of Excellence*. Research Report. Greeley, CO: Monfort Institute at the University of Northern Colorado. Available at www.monfortinstitute.org/pdf/iWAMBaldrigeCEOReport091015.pdf (accessed August 25, 2011).

Beck, D. and Cowan, C. (1996). *Spiral Dynamics: Mastering Values, Leadership and Change*. Oxford, UK: Blackwell Publishing.

Goleman, D. (1995). *Emotional Intelligence: Why it Can Matter More Than IQ*. London: Bloomsbury.

Hall, L. M. and Bodenhamer, B. (2005). *Figuring Out People: Reading People Using Meta-Programs*. Clifton, CO: Neuro-Semantic Publications.

Harshman, C. (2011). *Modeling Excellence with the iWAM*. St Louis, MO: Institute for Work Attitude and Motivation.

Harshman, C., Merlevede, P., and Moran, E. (2009). *iWAM Resource Guide*. St Louis, MO: Institute for Work Attitude and Motivation.

Merlevede, P. and Bridoux, D. (2004). *Mastering Mentoring and Coaching with Emotional Intelligence*. Carmarthen, UK: Crown House Publishing.

Merlevede, P., Bridoux, D., and Vandamme, R. (2001). *7 Steps to Emotional Intelligence*. Carmarthen, UK: Crown House Publishing.

Merlevede, P. and Vurnum, G. (eds) (2011). *105 Tips for Creating an Emotionally Intelligent Organization: More Success by Focusing On Work Attitude and Motivation*. Seattle, WA: CreateSpace.

Powell, M. F. (2009). Work motivations as predictors of academic and clinical performance and satisfaction with career choice in medical students. Unpublished Ph.D. thesis. University of Newcastle, Australia.

Rose Charvet, S. (1997). *Words that Change Minds: Mastering the Language of Influence*. 2nd rev. edn. Dubuque, IA: Kendall/Hunt.

Vurnum, G. and Merlevede, P. (2010). *Choose A Career And Discover Your Perfect Job: 105 Tips on Work Attitude and Motivation*. Seattle, WA: CreateSpace.

Test out jobEQ's questionnaires for free at www.jobEQ.com/SelfTest.

# Part IV
## Innovative Communities

From Models, patterns, and tools come communities. A community is a group of individuals who have a particular commitment to the use of a Model, pattern, or tool—a community which has a vested interest in using or developing an aspect of a model or pattern. In NLP the first communities of interest were the NLP associations that arose in various states and countries. While sometimes these involved people who were or became close friends and associates, they were mostly business associations. In fact, while business associations can become communities, usually they do not.

Communities typically require a personal commitment from people because they are volunteer organizations and operate from a common vision that unites individuals. This has actually been a weakness in the field of NLP and so we here identify some of the current communities that are operating as an innovative contribution to the field.

What is required for a community? What are the prerequisites and criteria?

- **A vision and mission that unites the community:** There is a sense of vision that creates a direction for people. What is the vision and mission of this particular community?

- **An inner group of committed people:** Communities do not seem to thrive or grow or sustain without one or more people who are committed to them and invest the time, energy, money, and heart to make them succeed. Who are the committed people within this community?

- **A clear organizational structure:** Communities that are successful have worked out its culture including how it is organized, how it operates, its rituals, values, beliefs, and so on. How is this community organized? What are its processes for communicating, gathering, generating services, and so on?

**James Lawley and Penny Tompkins**

NLP has been a significant part of James and Penny's lives since 1991 when they met on a practitioner training course in London. They were even married by Todd Epstein at NLP University in Santa Cruz at the end of their trainer's training!

Their lives took an unexpected turn when they decided to model David Grove. It took them four years and resulted in *Metaphors in Mind: Transformation through Symbolic Modelling* and a training DVD *A Strange and Strong Sensation*. They've also produced "Modelling Robert Dilts Modelling" which includes nine short videos. This and many more articles are available on their website.

They have been neurolinguistic psychotherapists registered with the United Kingdom Council for Psychotherapy (UKCP) since 1993 and recognized Neuro-Linguistic Psychotherapy and Counselling Association (NLPtCA) supervisors since 1995. Recently the Association of Coaching Supervisors (AOCS) made them honorary members. They have a private practice in London—except in winter when they slip off to the sunshine of Australia and New Zealand. In recognition of their contribution to the field, Penny and James have been awarded lifetime memberships of the Canadian Association of NLP (CANLP), and were the first to be appointed Honorary Certified Trainers of the International NLP Trainers Association (INLPTA). In addition to their work with individuals, they have provided consultancy and conducted modelling projects for organizations as diverse as GlaxoSmithKline, Yale University Child Study Center, NASA Goddard Space Center and the Findhorn Spiritual Community. They are leaders in the field of using metaphor, modelling and Clean Language.

email: james@cleanlanguage.co.uk
      penny@cleanlanguage.co.uk
web: www.cleanlanguage.co.uk

# 19 The Clean Community

*James Lawley and Penny Tompkins*

The clean community is a "community of practice."[1] Such communities are created by people gravitating to like-minded people who have a passion for something they do, the desire to learn how to do it better, and the motivation to interact regularly.

## The Community

Our community is connected by a shared belief that a clean approach is a highly respectful way to facilitate individual systems and systems of individuals to learn from themselves. The community is made up of people and companies who have developed a variety of clean approaches for personal development, health, education, research, commerce, organizations, and a host of other fields. We are fascinated by our own and others' interior worlds, we like learning by doing, and we have a high value of working collaboratively. If we had our own Temple of Apollo the sign over the door would not read "Know thyself" but "Learn from thyself."

In researching this chapter we asked the community a clean question: The clean community is like what? A sample of the responses were:

- A barbecue.

- A cooperative gardening club.

- A most enlightening, unfinished, unbound manuscript.

- A fruit machine that pays a jackpot nearly every time you pull the handle.

- A network of points of light that send out shafts of brightness that connect across and around the world, sparking together as they meet, forming fireworks, small and large, for the delight and insight of those involved.

## Source of the Community

The clean community exists because of David Grove, creator of Clean Language, Clean Space, and Emergent Knowledge.[2] David imbued his work with a spirit of generosity. He did not put boundaries and constraints on the use of his innovations; instead he operated from an "open source" and "creative commons" approach long before these became well known. All his life he "chased ideas" and he was still innovating at the time of his death in 2008.

David thought of himself as "a launch pad" enabling others to take his ideas to different worlds. His lack of fixity and delight in discovery rubbed off on those who traveled with him. David was a leader in terms of ideas and methodologies, and the community sprang up around him. He supported it and it supported him, but he never considered himself its head.

## How the Community Came Together

When we modeled David Grove and introduced his ideas into the NLP community people began to organize themselves into practice groups.[3] Our personal metaphors at the time were "sowing seeds" and "spreading the word." Even at this embryonic stage it seemed natural to adopt Gregory Bateson's idea of "code congruence."[4] This meant the way the community went about establishing itself needed to be congruent with a clean philosophy. Traditional metaphors of competition, hierarchy, and centralized control were rejected in favor of metaphors of cooperation and "co-inspiration."[5]

## Self-Organization

Self-organization and emergence are at the heart of a clean approach so it made sense that the clean community network would be flat and open. As a result there is no centralized control, chair, or head. Anyone can join simply by participating. In this way the network grows organically.

The community has no vision or mission statement, no plan, and no strategy. What emerges is what happens, and what happens gets responded to. Ideas and events that survive thrive until they cease to have sufficient participation and then they fade away. For example, while there is no standard training syllabus, demand from students resulted in a "criteria for foundation skills competency" being produced and widely adopted.[6]

But how does a community that is non-hierarchical, has no formal association, no committees, no constitution, and is continually evolving, regulate itself? Mostly through internal feedback where community members informally canvas others for their opinions, support and advice before embarking on new ventures and receive feedback on their actions. How that feedback is given, received, and incorporated is key to strengthening the bond between members. One way we do this is with the Clean Feedback Model which helps people to get really clear about the difference between behavior and interpretation.[7]

## Shared Events

A community is an abstract concept that becomes embodied in institutions and shared events. There are few clean community institutions, but there are plenty of events where community values and practices are embodied. These have emerged from small groups working together to achieve a common objective and are sustained by the active participation of those who attend. For example:

- Practice Groups have sprung up in many places throughout the world—like the one in London started by Caitlin Walker and Dee Berridge in 1996.[8] Practice exercises are passed around like old-style football cards. Marian Way has documented all of her group's practice exercises on her website.[9]

- The Developing Group consists of a core of long-standing members of the community as well as highly-trained newcomers who want be part of the latest developments and applications of Symbolic Modelling—our model of David Grove's work.[10]

- The Clean and Emergent Research Group, initiated by Philip Harland, has met regularly since 1999. It has covered such diverse topics as: landscapes of time, sin and evil, death, memory, and group dynamics, to name but a few.[11]

- The Paris Salon, set up by Jennifer de Gandt and her loyal French colleagues, organized the first cross-channel gathering of like-minded researchers.[12]

- The Clean Business Exchange where people who work commercially and in organizations discuss applications in a business context, receive feedback on their work-in-progress, and develop themselves professionally.[13]

- The annual Clean Conference run by Wendy Sullivan and colleagues at the Clean Change Company has hosted international keynote speakers such as cognitive neuroscientist Daniel Casasanto, author James Geary, and NLP developer Charles Faulkner.[14]

An important factor in the formation of our community was the advent of the Internet. We jumped on the bandwagon both as a metaphor for the kind of community we wanted to be part of, and as a practical means for making the ideas of David Grove and others publicly available. We started the first Clean Language website in 1995 and now there are dozens. The cleanforum.com was established by Phil Swallow and has been hosting discussions since 2003. It provides a free service where announcements of events are collated and fed into calendars of events on other websites. In this way, anyone can support everyone.

The clean community is not just internally focused. Individuals and companies have joined together to support other communities living in the midst of our troubled world. These have included developing a learning environment in a failing secondary school, visioning for a spiritual community, a multi-country environmental regeneration project, and building resourcefulness among those living in a deprived area.

## And Currently ...

There are now hubs in the UK, France, Holland, Italy, the USA, Australia, and New Zealand with smaller nodes in other countries. These groups are beginning to cross-fertilize as the network extends across national boundaries. As increasing numbers become involved in the clean community the complexity of the network will grow, necessitating new and innovative systems. In whichever way this happens and whatever direction it takes us, we aim to remember our origins are rooted in the legacy left by David Grove—to be congruent, cooperative, and co-inspiring.

## Notes

1. Wenger (1999).

2. Articles by David Grove are available at www.cleanlanguage.co.uk/articles/authors/7/.

3. A number of dedicated people in the United States, New Zealand, and UK were already supporting David and his work before we met him 1995.

4. Bateson (1972).

5. Maturana and Bunnell (1998).

6. See www.cleanforum.com/forums/showthread.php?570-Level-1-Criteria.

7. Doyle and Walker (2008).

8. See www.cleanforum.com/forums/forumdisplay.php?10-Practice-Groups.

9. See www.cleanlearning.co.uk/blog/category/practice-group/.

10. Notes and articles associated with all the Developing Group days since 2001 are available at www.cleanlanguage.co.uk/articles/categories/The-Developing-Group/.

11. A list of all the topics presented at the Clean and Emergent Research Group are available at www.cleanlanguage.co.uk/articles/articles/267/.

12. See www.cleanlanguage.fr/.

13. Sponsored by the Clean Change Company (www.cleanchange.co.uk/cleanlanguage/clean-business-exchange/).

14. See International Clean Conference 2010 Report by Jackie Calderwood at www.cleanchange.co.uk/cleanlanguage/2010/12/21/internationalcleanconference2010report-by-jackie-calderwood-clean-conference-2010/.

## References

Bateson, G. (1972). *Steps to an Ecology of Mind: Collected Essays in Anthropology, Psychiatry, Evolution, and Epistemology*. Chicago, IL: University of Chicago Press.

Doyle, N. and Walker, C. (2008). Cleaning up the F-word in coaching. *Rapport* (Nov.). Available at www.cleanlanguage.co.uk/articles/articles/272/.

Wenger, E. (1999). *Communities of Practice: Learning, Meaning, and Identity*. Cambridge: Cambridge University Press.

Maturana, H. and Bunnell, P. (1998). The biology of business: love expands intelligence. *Reflections* 1(2). Available at www.mitpress.mit.edu/journals/SOLJ/Maturana.pdf (accessed August 12, 2011).

 **Shelle Rose Charvet** has been learning NLP since 1983 and became a Certified NLP Trainer in 1992. She has been exploring Rodger Bailey's Language and Behavior Profile (LAB Profile®) since she encountered it at Institut Repère in Paris in the mid-1980s. Today she is known in the NLP community as the "Queen of LAB Profile" because of her books—*Words That Change Minds* (1997) and *The Customer is Bothering Me* (2010)—and the LAB Profile training she delivers to NLP institutes around the world. She also works with businesses and organizations to help them transform communication with customers and solve other influencing and persuasion challenges. Shelle speaks English, French and Spanish and is currently learning German.

email: shelle@wordsthatchangeminds.com
web: www.WordsThatChangeMinds.com
     www.labprofilecertification.com

# 20 The LAB Profile® Community

*Shelle Rose Charvet*

The LAB Profile community is a "community of interest" pulled together by the involvement that numerous people have in the LAB Profile—using it, training it, and developing it. The community is more of a virtual community as it operates through various social media—a Yahoo Group forum for certified trainers, the LinkedIn Language and Behaviour Group (which is open to everyone), and so on. People from the community meet in person occasionally, coinciding with training I am conducting in different places around the world. To this date, LAB Profile aficionados communicate to ask questions, share knowledge, and explore the uses of the LAB Profile in various contexts. The community has so far not evolved to the point where there is a formal structure with a vision and mission, or even a clearly defined set of values, although that may happen in the future. It is the practical applications of the LAB Profile that pull people together to create the LAB Profile community, particularly discussions on how to effectively use it for recruiting, change management in organizations, understanding and coaching people with different profiles, marketing, and sales.

Currently the community operates mostly on an informal basis as LAB Profile trainers and consultants stay in touch with me to let me know what they are working on. Facebook and LinkedIn allow me to keep people informed about what is happening and new events coming up. In Japan, the trainers, practitioners, master practitioners, and others will soon be able join the Japanese LAB Profile Association, which is being created.

The LAB Profile community will evolve as needed by the people who are passionate about it.

 **L. Michael Hall, Ph.D.** is an international speaker and consultant who focuses primarily on modeling and researching self-actualization excellence. He worked for several years with Richard Bandler and wrote a number of books for and about him including *The Spirit of NLP* (1996) and *Becoming a More Ferocious Presenter* (1996). He co-founded the International Society of Neuro-Semantics with Bob Bodenhamer and the Meta-Coaching Foundation with Michelle Duval. Known for his prolific creativity, Michael has published over forty books on NLP, including eight on meta-coaching, and he has created more than a dozen NLP models. As a visionary leader, Michael pioneered the founding of neuro-semantics to "take NLP to a higher professional and ethical level."

email: meta@acsol.net
web: www.neurosemantics.com
     www.meta-coaching.org
     www.self-actualizing.org

# 21 The Neuro-Semantic Community

L. Michael Hall

## The Story of the Why

The International Society of Neuro-Semantics (ISNS) originated as a reaction to the problems that I saw in the field of NLP. With Dr. Bob Bodenhamer I launched the Society of Neuro-Semantics due to two factors. First, in 1996 Richard Bandler filed a US$90 million law suit against the field of NLP in the USA. Having been a NLP trainer under Bandler and Associates since 1990 I had always sent my US$200 for every person I certified, but in 1996 I received a new "contract." I crossed out two paragraphs and included US$4,000 for twenty participants who had just completed practitioner training. One paragraph said that anything I developed would be "the intellectual property of Richard Bandler," the other said that I agreed to pay all legal bills if Richard decided to sue me. Neither seemed reasonable so I crossed them out, initialed them, signed the contract, and mailed it in with the money. But the money and contract were returned a few days later with a note that I was no longer recognized as an NLP trainer.

We became aware that if Bandler wins a lawsuit and NLP becomes his private domain, we would need something to fall back on. So Bob and I filed for the trademark of "Neuro-Semantics" and launched a website (www.neurosemantics.com). Bob created the website and asked me for a vision statement. So I dashed off a simple statement:

> Vision: To take NLP to a higher ethical and professional level, to operate from collaboration, abundance, acknowledgment of sources, respect of others, and the congruence of applying NLP to oneself by using the Meta-States Model of reflexivity.

The other factor was the ongoing development of the Meta-States Model (1994). My studies of Alfred Korzybski led to new meta-model distinctions, new distinctions for modeling, new patterns, and many of the distinctions that now make up the field of Neuro-Semantics. I wanted to continue that exploration as a way of extending NLP.

The day after the vision statement went on the website, somebody called and asked to join. "What shall I tell him?" Bob asked me. I didn't know. I had not thought that far ahead! "Well, tell him that he has joined!" "And what has he joined?" Bob asked. And with that we launched the National (and later, International) Society of Neuro-Semantics. Within a few weeks we had lots of people who wanted to be a part of it.

## The What

The design of the International Society was to provide ongoing support and encouragement for those who had received training. It was also to provide an umbrella of credibility and support for their training of Neuro-Semantic NLP. And the understanding was and continues to be that *we can do so much more together than alone or apart*.

Today the International Society of Neuro-Semantics has 270 trainers, 1,400 licensed meta-coaches, 17 institutes in different countries, and over 25,000 who have been trained and certified in the Meta-States Model. We have websites in Spanish, French, Chinese, Italian, Swedish, and many other languages. And to support the community we have an egroup devoted exclusively to the trainers, another exclusive one for the meta-coaches, and an international egroup (Neurons) for anyone who is interested. Funds collected are used for the websites, for scholarships for people wanting to attend trainings, and for what we consider that will support the trainers and coaches.

## The How

To avoid the problems so common in NLP, we established the Neuro-Semantic Community as a volunteer association linked to no single person's website or vested interest. We further established Neuro-Semantics as a non-profit charitable educational corporation designed to promote Neuro-Semantic NLP everywhere as an umbrella of credibility.

From the beginning I wanted the community to be self-directed, but quickly found that if I did not provide leadership, there would be no sense of direction or focus. So I established a co-leadership with Bob. Later I experimented with bringing others onboard to create a leadership team. As a volunteer organization, anyone who volunteered was designated a "leader," but that didn't work out very well. Eventually we had a group of people who loved to talk and talk and plan and dream, but who never did anything! Perhaps telling, I had designated the first leadership group, "The Dreamers." And that name came true with a vengeance that I never planned for.

As the community grew, we began training and certifying trainers around the world. I began looking for those who were actually running a training center and training people. I wanted people leading who were *doers*—who actually acted on what they talked about. They were the ones I invited to assist in trainers' training. But another problem emerged. Some of them liked being in front and given a platform but did not know how to support others, groom other trainers and leaders, co-lead, or take a supportive role off-stage. We also had conflicts arise due to the "ego" investments of some of them. That led to yet another distinction beyond actively doing—that of contributing to the community.

That led in 2009 to the first leadership team made up of trainers, coaches, and consultants who were successful in self-leadership, who were making a difference in their communities, and who had a heart for others—for contributing their time, energy, money, and so on for the larger community. Today we have thirteen on the leadership team from eight countries, an equal number of men and women. We have a private egroup for this team and a requirement that everybody agrees to be actively involved and respond to the conversations within twenty-four hours. Serving on the leadership team is entirely voluntary and no one is paid in their leadership roles. Currently, I am the executive director.

In January 2010, we gathered in San Francisco for a Leadership Summit and to plan for the future of this community. We made decisions about the training of NLP and Neuro-Semantics and we made decisions on how to set and guide ethical considerations in members. We decided to launch international conferences every other year beginning in July 2011. The next conferences are scheduled in Malaysia in 2013 and Hong Kong in 2015. We established criteria and benchmarks for the competency of trainers and master trainers.

For the trainers' egroup, there are a number of us who write weekly posts: myself, Omar Salom in Mexico, Colin Cox and Alan Fayter in New Zealand, and Lene Fjellheim in Norway. Currently we have seven websites in various languages and to demonstrate collaboration and abundance, training manuals are made available to everyone for a minimum fee (US$5 royalty) as well as advertisement pieces. It is an open community in terms of resources.

With the licensed meta-coaches, we have the Meta-Coaching Foundation (MCF) (a non-profit organization) established in Australia and the two English websites are replicated in Spanish, French, Chinese, and other languages. The MCF provides governance for meta-coaches, receiving complaints and working through any disagreements. It provides a professional "board of examiners" that hold members accountable to the ethical and professional standards.

### Resources

International Meta-Coach Foundation: www.metacoachfoundation.org

International Society of Neuro-Semantics: www.neurosemantics.com

Meta-Coach System: www.meta-coaching.org

Self-Actualization: www.self-actualizing.org

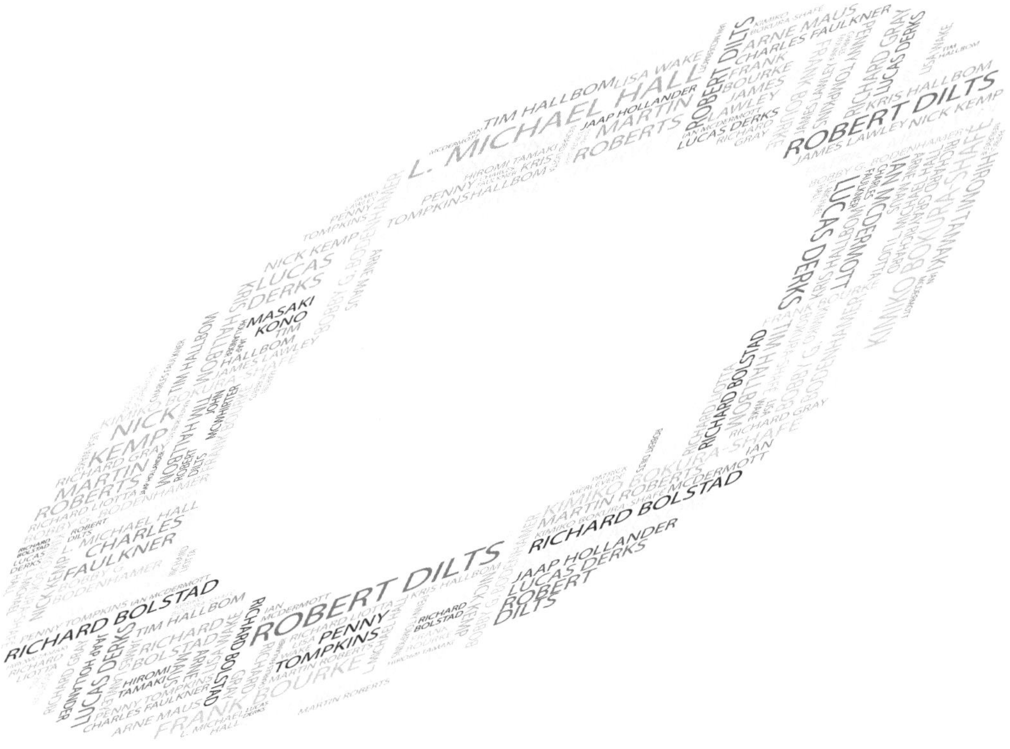

L. MICHAEL HALL
TIM HALLBOM
LISA WAKE
ROBERT DILTS
ARNE MAUS
CHARLES FAULKNER
JAAP HOLLANDER
MARTIN ROBERTS
LUCAS DERKS
NICK KEMP
KRIS HALLBOM
JAMES LAWLEY
IAN MCDERMOTT
HIROMI TAMAKI
KIMIKO BOKURA-SHAFE
PENNY TOMPKINS
MASAKI KONO
RICHARD BOLSTAD
RICHARD GRAY
FRANK BOURKE
BOBBY G. RODENHAMER
RICHARD LIOTTA
JOHN MCWHIRTER

 **Rich Liotta, Ph.D.** is a psychologist in private practice in the Adirondack region of upstate New York. Rich was introduced to NLP while in graduate school in 1983 and immediately recognized how it could expand his options as a cognitive behavioral therapist, family therapist, and human potential enthusiast. In the late 1990s he pursued more training in NLP and is now a Certified Trainer of NLP, Neuro-Semantics, and Ericksonian Hypnosis. Rich has worked closely with Frank Bourke on the NLP Research and Recognition Project in the areas of website development, organizational communication, fundraising, and the efforts of the research committee. He has also co-authored an article with Richard Gray (PTSD: Extinction, Reconsolidation and the Visual-Kinesthetic Dissociation Protocol) for the journal *Traumatology* (in press).

email: rfliotta@gmail.com
web: www.enrichmentact.com
      www.changepathsblog.com

 **Frank Bourke** first encountered NLP in the mid-1970s after 15 years of studies in psychology including a Ph.D. at the Institute of Psychiatry in London. He taught at Cornell University for a number of years but left to grow his private practice—with NLP techniques an essential part of his clinical skill-set. His work with World Trade Center survivors after 9/11 and overcoming a terminally diagnosed case of cancer led to his founding of the NLP Research and Recognition Project, which aims to support, coordinate, and fund rigorous scientific research in the field of NLP.

email: fpmc1000@hotmail.com
web: www.nlprandr.org

# 22 The NLP Research and Recognition Project

*Richard Liotta and Frank Bourke*

Many NLP practitioners have long wanted NLP to achieve its full potential to contribute to human welfare by establishing itself as an accepted change technology. The recognized academic and professional criteria for this necessitate scientific proof of its effectiveness. The NLP Research and Recognition Project was incorporated in 2008 to help accomplish this. Since its inception, it has gained swift recognition and is working hard to network a well formed, international NLP research movement. It appears to be an idea whose time has come.

We will overview here the timeliness, accomplishments, difficulties, and importance of the NLP Research Project as well as explain why it is so close to our hearts.

## Why This Project Is Relevant Now

The Research and Recognition Project seeks to put validation and credibility at the forefront of NLP as it develops in the future. We believe that the only way to accomplish this is to have sound clinical research that demonstrates the efficacy of NLP processes and procedures and an organizational structure that ensures integrity and high performance standards.

While many NLP institutes and organizations have recognized and have been working on research and performance standards, especially in Europe, much more expertise, energy, time, and money will have to be dedicated to this end if it is to be successful. The NLP Research Project is dedicated to helping spread worldwide the NLP developments that have begun to demonstrate the efficacy of NLP processes and to help bolster those efforts until NLP is fully recognized and accepted.

Presently, only NLP practitioners fully understand and value NLP interventions. Those of us who are practitioners know that NLP interventions can help ease human suffering and assist people to function more effectively in their lives. But those of us with this knowledge are often frustrated because we realize that NLP and its processes are not accepted or understood by millions of people who could benefit from them. When people ask, "What is the evidence that NLP works?" the only answers, for the moment, are anecdotal.

The fact that NLP does not have enough scientific evidence to demonstrate that it works is by far the largest issue preventing wider dissemination of these valuable tools. NLP is not an "evidence-based" technology and, as such, it will be dismissed in all those quarters that require evidence until it is. That is not to belittle other problems, internal and external, that will also have to be resolved before NLP receives wider acceptance, but to place constructive efforts for more widespread recognition where they will do the most good.

We find the prospect of having NLP validated by research inspirational! Those of us working on the Project know from experience the value that NLP adds to mental health-oriented therapy, treatment of medical conditions, coaching, health, and education. We know in our hearts and minds that NLP can address many symptoms more effectively than the "respected" models. What inspires us is the vision of these NLP treatment and practice possibilities being realized for all the people that could benefit.

## How the Project Began

Frank Bourke launched the NLP Research and Recognition Project formally with a presentation at the Institute for Advanced Studies of Health (IASH) conference in San Francisco in September 2006. He believed that the *idea* of the Research and Recognition Project for NLP was an idea whose time had come. From the outset, energy and support has been forthcoming, reflecting the widespread frustration with the lack of scientific evidence both within and outside the NLP community. He felt this frustration keenly himself during the year he worked clinically in New York City after 9/11 and saw the thousands of people who could have been helped with NLP protocols for the treatment of post-traumatic stress disorder (PTSD) and were not.

His personal mission became "establishing NLP as having value to the larger community." The NLP Research and Recognition Project was born from the vision of what New York could have looked like had the NLP tools been known and used by the hundreds of mental health professionals beside whom he labored during that difficult year.

Frank first encountered NLP in the mid-1970s after fifteen years of studies in psychology including a Ph.D. at the Institute of Psychiatry in London. Six months after his first NLP readings and workshops, he was convinced that NLP was the largest advance in psychotherapy in the previous fifty years. Very quickly, researching it became his career passion and obsession. After three years of hard work, however, neither NLP nor Cornell University would support his research proposals. At that time NLP community members did not think it should be scientifically researched, and Cornell University and his academic peers did not believe that he could continue in a serious academic career and be associated with NLP. Eventually, as a consequence, in 1979, he left the NLP community and Cornell University feeling like a tribe of one.

Two occurrences brought Frank back to NLP and to the founding of the NLP Research and Recognition Project. The first was nine months of clinical work with World Trade Center survivors after 9/11 when he found his NLP-derived protocols could eradicate the incapacitating symptoms of PTSD in two to four hours. The second was his own terminally diagnosed case of cancer, in which he used NLP tools for a year and a half to deal with the pain and produce a daily physiological state, which in Chinese medicine is called "an inner smile." Suffice it to say, his recovery was labeled medically remarkable.

When he realized he had "survived" the cancer and did a life re-evaluation, he took an oath to do what he could to get NLP researched, recognized, and used to its full capabilities. In discussions with other NLP leaders, especially Judith DeLozier and Steve Andreas, the NLP Research and Recognition Project was born and we have been nurturing it ever since.

## What is the Project?

The overall mission of the NLP Research and Recognition Project is to support, coordinate, and fund rigorous scientific research in the field of NLP. Our mission statement is as follows:

> Our individual and collective experiences helping others with NLP technologies demonstrates that NLP methods are effective in facilitating change, enrichment, and symptom relief. Multitudes of suffering clients don't presently have access to the effective methods and skills that practitioners of NLP use regularly. Only by researching and validating the efficacy of NLP as an effective treatment and change technology will it achieve the wider recognition among therapy, education, and health care professionals that it warrants. The NLP Research and Recognition Project is dedicated to advancing the science of Neuro-Linguistic Programming and all related technologies. Only by advancing the science of NLP through research and scholarly work will NLP's potential to help more people live more fulfilling and productive lives be realized.

We are aspiring to advance NLP as a science and technology so more people can be helped. To accomplish these goals, various objectives have been identified and an active community which sees the need for NLP research is emerging.

## Goals

Some of the current research and organizational goals for the Research and Recognition Project include the following:

1. Pace current outcome research in psychotherapy. NLP must submit its materials to the same rigorous testing that Western health systems demand for all approved treatments. It must first adapt some of its protocols to the formats amenable to random control trials and conduct research that will establish their validity outside the NLP community. While this in no way constitutes research of NLP practice, using all the basic skills, protocols, and advanced skills, the effectiveness of the protocols will prompt the research-based establishment to look further.

2.  The scientific results need to be published in prestigious peer-reviewed journals and presented at national conferences. Over the years this omission has left NLP out in the academic and professional cold as an unproven and highly suspect set of exaggerated clinical claims. Professor Richard Gray of Fairleigh Dickinson University and Richard Liotta, Ph.D. have modeled this goal in an article written for the journal *Traumatology*.[1]

3.  Lead the field of clinical outcome research in new directions. Conduct random controlled trial research designs to establish the effectiveness of NLP clinical protocols; but also innovate with new designs that lend themselves to the individual client-oriented approach of full NLP practice.

4.  Develop cost-effective outcome measures that can be integrated into regular clinical practice and add an element of evaluation and measurement to regular NLP clinical practice. Such computer-generated outcome evaluations done by practitioners of NLP could also serve as pilot research and establish a databank of measured clinical NLP performance as well as help practitioners improve their clinical performance. Scott Miller's work in the US[2] and Clinical Outcomes for Routine Evaluation (CORE) evaluations in the UK exemplify such approaches.

5.  Help develop certification and training materials that consistently teach competency in the application of the researched NLP protocols.

    In Europe, the Research and Recognition Project is working closely with the Association for NLP (ANLP) and the European Association for Neuro-Linguistic Psychotherapy (EANLPt) in the UK and on the Continent to learn from, refine, and coordinate the development of their training and certification techniques, which are far ahead of US developments. The establishment of NLPt, with its clearly defined trainings and certifications for clinical practice, has separated NLPt from fly-by-night trainings and allowed professional and government health agency recognition.

    In regard to specific protocols, this model is being developed in conjunction with the PTSD treatment research with the Reconsolidation of Traumatic Memories (RTM) protocol. Once the treatment protocols for PTSD have been scientifically validated the training and certification materials that produce the well-established scientific results can be made available and ensure continued clinical effectiveness.

6.  Develop and/or network with organizations, especially a department within a university, which can support continuing research, training certification, and effective clinical performance. This would essentially help establish a credibility base for those utilizing NLP.

7.  License institutions, universities, and professional organizations to use training materials and certification procedures which also follow up clinical training with outcome measures in a fashion that ensures clinical effectiveness.

While this is not something that many NLP practitioners have been exposed to, especially in the United States, it is a direction that must be pursued if NLP is going to be recognized not only for having effective materials, but for having a system that can teach people to utilize the materials with integrity and skill. European practitioners are far ahead of Americans with the development of certification organizations like EANLPt. In addition to the development work being done by the Research and Recognition Project in the United States, Dr. Michael Hall has recently finished work on a book regarding benchmarking and has been utilizing benchmarking in his trainers training and coaches training.[3] An extension of a benchmarking model to assess the competency of professionals utilizing validated profiles would be a useful addition to all effective clinical practice.

## Challenges and Caveats

Certainly there are challenges to accomplishing these goals. First and foremost is the terrible reputation NLP has accrued over the years among the professionals and academics who would have to approve the research grants and provide the foundation support necessary to research NLP. Over the last three years the Research and Recognition Project has had US$17 million worth of university-sponsored grants denied. Based on our interactions across ten to fifteen meetings with the members of the reviewing organizations, our best guess is that most of these grants were never read or reviewed because of their association with NLP.

Research into the effectiveness of NLP was never a goal of the founders of NLP and often the little research done in the early years was poorly conceived and designed. This has resulted in a pervasive criticism that NLP has made grandiose and exaggerated claims of clinical efficacy, and that where research has been done it has not supported those claims. NLP's failure to take responsibility for these failed studies and the lack of research substantiating its "grandiose clinical claims" is seen, by most academics, as the final proof of its disingenuous nature.

We have to reverse these perceptions. In a recent example to establish a university presence from which research could be conducted, the Research and Recognition Project's initial proposal to establish an NLP university department was well-received. However, critics using NLP's negative professional reputation and the negative Internet reviews of NLP's disingenuous nature convinced the university in question to withdraw its invitation.

Here is a sample of the opposition from a tenured faculty member: "NLP is a hoax. The guy coming to speak claims he can cure post-traumatic stress disorder in two to four hours. The entire profession of counseling and psychology has long condemned this nonsense … What shall we have next, a speaker from the Flat Earth Society?"

In our opinion, many critics of NLP overstate their contentions with exaggerations and misunderstandings in the same "quasi-scientific" fashion they accuse NLP of employing. Members of the NLP community, unfortunately, have often given them more than sufficient material to warrant continuing criticism. Historically, many NLP practitioners have grossly exaggerated the capabilities of NLP for obvious personal gain and behaved with clients and one another in fashions that are far from professional.

The NLP community itself has been fragmented instead of appropriately responding to constructive criticisms and seeking recognized legitimacy in accordance with its own basic tenet—the meaning of a communication to another person (or organization) is the response it elicits in that person (or organization), regardless of the intent of the communicator.

Perhaps this negative label will necessitate a completely new labeling of the field to something like "Full Spectrum Cognitive-Behavioral Therapy" before a widespread transition to professional and academic acceptance can be accomplished. Perhaps a research-oriented NLP2, built upon more clearly defined training and practice guidelines, would be a better solution. Without rebranding NLP in the minds of its professional and academic critics, it will not achieve widespread utilization or have the chance to help all those who could be helped.

## Progress and Trends

Despite these challenges, there is also reason for optimism. There are many in the NLP community who share the vision of evidence-supported NLP delivered with competence and integrity. The Project has made significant progress in many areas. Communication with the greater NLP community has also highlighted the fact that there are positive developments occurring around the world that bode well for the future of NLP applications. "Progress" is defined not just by the accomplishments of the NLP Research and Recognition Project itself, but also by developments evident in the greater community.

Progress and accomplishments can be summarized as being in two major categories, *community development* and *research progress*. Only some highlights will be reported here—a more complete presentation of the Project's accomplishments can be viewed at www.nlprandr.org.

## Community Development

Our community of supporters includes leadership from experienced personnel encompassing business, academic, NLP, research, and politics. To date we have gained the formal support of over forty NLP institutes, several university departments, and hundreds of multi-talented volunteers. We have many volunteers already involved in program development and more waiting to be mobilized. Our research committee has offered consultation to over thirty graduates designing their Ph.D. dissertations.

In the NLP community the Project has helped galvanize discussion regarding establishing a research base for NLP and the need for integrity to gain broader support. We have been heartened by the fact that these issues are being considered in many NLP camps; and they are now starting to communicate more with each other!

Integrative projects have begun in a strong spirit of collaboration. This book is an example, respecting and highlighting the diversity of innovation in NLP and related disciplines. The NLP Research and Recognition Project is also coordinating the writing of a book on NLP research, aimed at health professionals, which organizes and presents research evidence supporting the clinical effectiveness of NLP. The format will be congruent with the professional presentation of research studies in the field of therapeutic outcome studies with the goal being to present the clear evidence of a well-grounded and committed NLP research movement.

## Research and Scholarly Progress

- NLP research conferences have now been held in Europe for the past two years. These were co-hosted by ANLP and a UK university, and organized by a steering committee consisting of Charles Faulkner, Visiting Senior Fellow, University of Surrey; Dr. Suzanne Henwood, independent practitioner; Karen Moxom, independent practitioner and Chair of ANLP; Dr. Paul Tosey, University of Surrey; and Lisa Wake, independent practitioner. Dr. Bourke delivered the keynote address in Wales in 2010 (the address can be viewed on the Project website). The Research and Recognition Project remains a key supporter in the continuing development and enlargement of the conference.

- The *NLP Research Journal* was launched in the Houses of Parliament in the UK in 2010. It is edited by Dr. Paul Tosey and published by ANLP. This is a peer-reviewed journal, the first of its kind for NLP, and a milestone, along with the conference, in the formation of the infrastructure necessary for NLP research.

- On the European mainland, Peter Schutz and members of EANLPt have modeled the development and integration of NLP as a therapeutic modality into a nationally recognized professional and mental health organization. Their conferences, members' research articles, and functioning within the European Association for Psychotherapy (EAP), their psychotherapeutic mother organization, are years ahead of most of the world in bringing NLP the integrity and recognition its techniques deserve.

- Integrative and scholarly examination of NLP is critical to set the groundwork for formal research. Several authors have published books in this spirit in recent years. Lisa Wake wrote *Neurolinguistic Psychotherapy* in 2008. She connected NLP to many of its roots in psychotherapy. She aptly discusses how the practice and teaching of NLP is often disconnected from those roots (including its orthodox clinical foundations) and that those scholarly supports for NLP are not sufficiently acknowledged. Richard Bolstad's book on the RESOLVE Model (2002) notes the similarity of some NLP interventions to those in more accepted areas of psychotherapy (see also Chapter 5).

- Some 1,200 American Psychological Association formatted NLP research articles have been referenced and put on the Project website, far surpassing the number of articles thought to exist only a few years ago. The expansion of this database into a library of NLP and related research articles in four or five languages is a high project priority. Between the Project website and other NLP article bibliographies such as EANLPt, Inspirative, and NLP.de there is the basis for the development of a comprehensive NLP research library. Utilizing and categorizing this research base will help us know what has been done and inform future research. While most of the research to date is not of the quality needed to establish the evidence-based practice of NLP, the studies would compare favorably with the evidence for many established therapies.

- NLP Research and Recognition Project researchers have developed a state-of-the-art research sequence from initial pilot studies to certified training programs of the NLP derived treatment protocol for post-traumatic stress syndrome labeled Reconsolidation of Traumatic Memories. The RTM protocol was developed to provide a standardized and researchable version of the visual–kinesthetic dissociation (V/KD) intervention, integrating the core processes that have been described in various ways in the literature. Pilot research has begun which will increase the likelihood of acquiring funding for the complete research sequence.

- Wayne Perry, a member of the Project Research Committee, with the help of eight other members, has developed an online research study to begin the measurement of long-held NLP assumptions about the cognitive representation of pictures, words, and feelings internally.

- Professor Richard Gray of Fairleigh Dickinson University and Richard Liotta, Ph.D. have written an article which has been accepted by the journal *Traumatology*. The article, based on recent discoveries about the neurology of traumatic memories, is able to postulate the mechanisms by which an NLP derived protocol (RTM) may function in relieving and transforming traumatic memory.

- Various evidence-based papers and research in NLP have been done in recent years. Susie Linder-Pelz has examined the use of NLP in evidence-based coaching practice.[4] In Mexico, Juan Francisco Ramírez Martínez (Paco) has led efforts through the Centro Mexicano de Programación Neurolingüística (CMPNL) to offer a master's degree in NLP. Since its inception in 1999 they have been leading qualitative research dissertations on NLP (thirty-seven so far). In the UK, Richard Churches and colleagues have produced research around the impact of

NLP in education and done the first complete literature review covering NLP and education.[5]

## Summary

The Research and Recognition Project is a voice advocating working together to improve both NLP's professional acceptance and its clinical functioning, in a fashion that benefits all who utilize NLP in an ecologically sound fashion and all who can be helped by it.

There are many who share the mission of developing evidence-supported NLP, delivered with competence and integrity. Mobilizing a genuine movement for the field of NLP and working together is the vision for this NLP Research Project.

It is our contention that researching, validating, and supporting integrity and standards in the field of NLP would help move it forward as a field. It is the goal of the NLP Research and Recognition Project to bring the clinically effective methods from NLP to a broader population. NLP has broad applications that can be transformative for many people and for a troubled world. Helping individuals helps the whole system.

The impact we could have is extraordinary! Consider how NLP excites you or makes you feel truly passionate, seeing, hearing, and feeling your responses when you think about the growth of NLP. The future success of the NLP research movement may well reside in your internal representations—and in our collective representations of them!

We urge you to take your strong feelings about NLP seriously. Ultimately it is all of us, as a community, who will realize the vision of the NLP Research and Recognition Project. With your help, we will continue our efforts to make this happen.

### Notes

1.  Gray and Liotta (forthcoming).

2.  Duncan and Miller (2003); Miller (2003); Miller et al. (2004).

3.  Hall (forthcoming).

4. Linder-Pelz (2010).

5. Carey et al. (2010).

## References

Bolstad, R. (2002). *RESOLVE: A New Model of Therapy*. Carmarthen, UK: Crown House Publishing.

Carey, J., Churches, R., Hutchinson, G., Jones, J., and Tosey, P. (2010). Neuro-linguistic programming and learning: teacher case studies on the impact of NLP in education. CfBT Education Trust. Available at http://www.cfbt.com/evidenceforeducation/pdf/NLP%20and%20learning%20full%20report.pdf (accessed August 12, 2011).

Duncan, B. and Miller, S. (2003). The Session Rating Scale: preliminary psychometric properties of a "working" alliance measure. *Journal of Brief Therapy* 3(1): 3–12.

Gray, R. and Liotta, R. (forthcoming). PTSD: Extinction, reconsolidation and the visual-kinesthetic dissociation protocol. *Traumatology*.

Hall, L. Michael. (forthcoming). *Benchmarking Intangibles: The Art of Measuring Quality*. Clifton, CO: Neuro-Semantic Publications.

Linder-Pelz, S. (2010). *NLP Coaching: An Evidence-Based Approach for Coaches, Leaders and Individuals*. London: Kogan Page.

Linder-Pelz, S. and Hall, L. M. (2007). The theoretical roots of NLP-based coaching. *Coaching Psychologist* 3(1): 12–17.

Miller, S. (2003). The Outcome Rating Scale: a preliminary study of the reliability, validity, and feasibility of a brief visual analog measure. *Journal of Brief Therapy* 2(2): 91–100.

Miller, S., Duncan, B., and Hubble, M. (2004). Beyond integration: the triumph of outcome over process in clinical practice. *Psychotherapy in Australia* 10(2): 2–19.

Wake, L. (2008). *Neurolinguistic Psychotherapy: A Postmodern Perspective*. London: Routledge.

**Resources**

European Association of Neuro-Linguistic Psychotherapy: www.eanlpt.org/
    research.html

Inspirative Database: www.inspiritive.com.au/nlp-research/database.htm

NLP Research and Recognition Project: www.nlprandr.org

NLP.de: www.nlp.de/cgi-bin/research/nlp-rdb.cgi?action=res_entries

**Lisa Wake** is a former nurse and NHS manager. She is a Master Trainer of NLP, UKCP accredited psychotherapist and at the time of writing is a Ph.D. candidate at the University of Surrey. She has served as Chair and Vice Chair of the UKCP, and has long been a proponent of the effectiveness of brief therapy, actively campaigning for rigor of standards, ethics, and research in psychotherapy. She has contributed to the neurolinguistic psychotherapy field with the publication of her groundbreaking book for the Advancing Theory in Therapy series for Routledge, *Neurolinguistic Psychotherapy: A Postmodern Perspective*, followed by *The Role of Brief Therapy in Attachment Disorders* for Karnac.

Lisa also has extensive experience as a training and change management consultant with a diverse range of organizations. As part of her consultancy work she has published an evidence based book on the applications of NLP in a wide range of contexts—*NLP Principles in Practice* (Ecademy Press).

email: lisa@awakenconsulting.co.uk
web: www.awakenconsulting.co.uk

**Karen Moxom** is CEO of the Association for NLP (ANLP), a founder member of the International Research Conference Steering Committee, editor of *Rapport*, the magazine for NLP Professionals, and publisher of *Acuity* (the anthology of shared findings and learnings in NLP) and current research in NLP. In conjunction with a well respected university, ANLP co-hosts the International NLP Research Conference every two years.

Karen is driven by her passion to ensure that NLP professionals can deliver their NLP with more confidence, professionalism and confidence so that NLP can establish itself and become more credible and widely accepted in society.

email: vision@anlp.org
web: www.anlp.org

# 23 The International NLP Research Conference

*Lisa Wake and Karen Moxom*

## Why Is It Important to Develop the NLP Research Conference?

The vision and purpose of the NLP Research Conference is to gather together academics, practitioner researchers, and others interested in furthering inquiry into NLP, and through this to build and support a global research community.

Developed in the UK in 2007 by a group of academics, practitioners of NLP, and the Association for NLP in the UK (ANLP), the International NLP Research Conference arose in response to increasing calls for research-based evidence in NLP.

Such evidence is called for in areas such as psychotherapy and psychology, where NLP has only a limited place amongst mainstream and more orthodox modalities. Within Europe there is some recognition of NLP as a valid form of psychotherapy, notably through the European Association for Neurolinguistic Psychotherapy (EANLPt), with some European countries having statutory regulation for psychotherapy. Austria was the first country to gain a national psychotherapy law in 1990.

Healthcare sectors within the UK and globally will frequently only support expenditure on an approach where there is demonstrable evidence base of effective treatment interventions. Businesses are carefully considering how and where they invest funds for personal development, coaching, and soft skills interventions and want them to be directly related to outcomes or key performance indicators. A similar situation exists in education. Organizations of all kinds are increasingly asking for evidence to justify expenditure, and in the public sector there is an increasing need for training programs to demonstrate learning outcomes that meet the needs of various professions; one example is the Knowledge and Skills Framework for the National Health Service in the UK.

Beyond these specific contemporary calls for evidence, many practitioners express a wish for NLP to be perceived as respectable. Yet NLP has mostly developed as a field of practice that has lacked a research ethos, leaving it over-reliant on claims that self-evidently "it works." The value of theory has often been rejected by many, and some of the ideas used within NLP are outdated. For such reasons, it has low credibility in academic circles. To date, only a handful of universities in the UK offer opportunities for master and doctoral level study in NLP, including Surrey, the home of the inaugural International NLP Research Conference.

In our experience, organizations and individuals are looking for evidence to support NLP and its application. Lisa's consultancy work often includes working with people from technical or scientific backgrounds, most of whom require references for any sources that are used, including the wider relationship of NLP to other fields of applied psychology.

There is a challenge for the NLP field in moving toward a more evidence-based way of working. Does this destroy or demean the essence of what is NLP? Paul Tosey and Jane Mathison argue that if NLP does not move forward by developing research activity, its future could be in doubt.[1] They suggest that NLP may experience entropy whereby the energy of individuals who have kept NLP going will dissipate and there will be a lack of new ideas and fresh material being brought into the field to keep it alive.

Our view is that if NLP is to be taken seriously by clinicians, coaches, practitioners, and commissioners in both the public and private sectors, it needs to develop an evidence base and critical reflection of its efficacy and effectiveness. While there is a recognition of the value of non-empirical research studies in the wider and associated fields of psychology, psychotherapy and counseling, these studies need to be conducted to support the development of more empirical randomized control trials—considered to be the "gold standard." This does not necessarily mean that the essence of NLP becomes demeaned through the research process; rather, as a model of performance excellence that reflects the subjective nature of experience, NLP can be used as both a research tool and a way of reflecting the heuristic nature of meaning.

Tosey and Mathison also suggest that the increasing diversity of opinion in the field may result in NLP destroying itself or being taken over by emerging theories in neuroscience and cognitive semantics. The third scenario proposed by Tosey and Mathison is one of renaissance within the field, where new and emerging theories are included within the body of knowledge of NLP. This can only happen through research and critical questioning of the efficacy of NLP and its composite elements. Some steps are already being made in this area through the Research Conference, the NLP Research and Recognition Project, and evidence-based writings.[2]

It is challenging to marry the "typical" NLP practitioner with the rigor required in academic research. Most individuals who pursue an interest in NLP tend to have an opposite set of meta-programs to those who pursue an academic career, with a preference for global, difference, and options in thinking styles, whereas academic researchers tend to have a preference for detail, sameness, and procedures. Empirical research is also appropriately time consuming which is counter-intuitive to the model of working presented by NLP. Additionally because most NLP training programs exist outside of mainstream education facilities globally, there are a number of hurdles to be overcome to facilitate a substantial evidence base in this field.

## How the Conference Works

The inaugural conference was held at the University of Surrey, UK, in July 2008, attracting more than seventy participants from across the world. Its steering group consisted of Charles Faulkner, independent practitioner, USA, and Visiting Senior Fellow, University of Surrey, UK; Dr. Suzanne Henwood, UniTec, Auckland, New Zealand; Karen Moxom, independent practitioner and Chair ANLP, UK; Dr. Paul Tosey, University of Surrey, UK; and Lisa Wake, independent practitioner, UK.

The conference has been taken forward by ANLP International, with the second event being hosted at Cardiff University in Wales in 2010, and a third is planned for the University of Hertfordshire in 2012.

The conference is designed to share research-based and scholarly developments relating to NLP; it is intentionally not a forum for demonstrations of practice, for which NLP is already well-served. It is multidisciplinary, and the fields of psychotherapy, business, and education have been those most strongly represented in contributions to date.

Selected conference proceedings are published in a new journal established for this purpose, *Current Research in NLP*. The journal is peer-reviewed, which means that only those papers that meet the stringent standards for academic publication are accepted. Copies of the journal are available from ANLP.

## The Innovation of the Conference

The principal outcome for the conference is an increase in the quantity and quality of research activity relating to NLP of all kinds, including practitioner-led research as well as independent studies, and using qualitative as well as quantitative methods. The aim is to show that NLP is committed to the type of questioning and evaluation that characterizes all established professional practices. As the community of researchers continues to grow we anticipate and hope that we will see a growth in the body of evidence and, depending on the nature of that evidence, that this may lead to greater acceptance of NLP as an effective model for change management, therapy, social, and personal development. Research can only add to the range of effective tools, techniques, and philosophies required by a troubled and changing world.

The steering group identifies keynote speakers for the conference. Each speaker is chosen on the basis of their critique and inquiry of NLP rather than their advocacy of NLP. This reflects the critical nature of the conference—a forum for serious study and exploration of what does and does not work in NLP, what evidence there is, and what principles or tools have no evidence base to support them.

This innovation has a core vision and aspiration to become the number one internationally recognized research platform for NLP, and through this to establish NLP as a more accessible, credible, and evidence-based profession.

## The Intentions and Vision of the Conference

The conference is international by design, and its aims include:

- To further develop the discipline of NLP as a field of theory, research, and practice.

- To provide a credible platform for supporting and promoting NLP research across the globe.

- To establish *Current Research in NLP* as an internationally recognized, credible, and academically peer-reviewed journal for NLP research, and to disseminate research through this publication.

- To provide a dissemination forum for empirical and practical research in NLP.

- To facilitate a partnership between NLP practitioners and academics and enable research to take place across the field of NLP.

The conference is open to anyone interested in NLP, and papers and presentations are invited from practitioner researchers, educators, and academic researchers.

## How Does the NLP Research Conference Work?

The NLP Research Conference is a practitioner-led conference that is co-hosted in alternate years by a university and ANLP International.

Practitioners from a variety of contexts are invited to present papers or presentations in an abstract format. Papers are either research or practice-based evidence of the applications of NLP across a range of contexts from business, coaching, therapy, sports, education, and health. Examples of the types of research that are accepted include single case studies and research that has been conducted as part of a practitioner's continuing education (e.g., Diploma in Management Studies, master's degree, Ph.D.).

Others are practice-based evidence papers, such as simple reviews of interventions that a practitioner has conducted with one or a number of their clients. Each paper is required to include a literature review ensuring that earlier research in the field is considered in the light of ongoing research, and also requires practitioners to make links between the known body of knowledge of NLP and wider psychological theories and constructs. This is an essential element of the writings that are accepted, all of which will add to the credibility of NLP.

Each paper is expected to include conclusions from the findings and in many instances this has included recommendations for practice and further research. It is hoped that this will encourage others in the field to continue to model the model of NLP and develop the model further.

Each paper is peer reviewed by a group of experienced academic writers and research-ers, all of whom are at NLP practitioner level as a minimum. Papers are either accepted as submitted, returned to the author(s) for amendment, or rejected. Some papers are considered for workshop presentations and others are offered the oppor-tunity for poster presentations.

The standard of papers presented at both conferences has been high and the steer-ing group, with ANLP's support, has chosen to create a journal that is published in the year following the conference. Each presenter is invited to submit a full version of their research paper and these are again peer reviewed prior to being accepted for publication. The publication is available either online via ANLP or as a paper-based journal.

## How to Become a Part of the NLP Research Community

Individual practitioners who want to submit research articles for the next confer-ence should visit the Research Conference pages on the ANLP website for up-to-date information about the procedures for submitting papers and details of future con-ferences (www.anlp.org/the-international-nlp-research-conference).

ANLP is an active player within the NLP research conference community and, as such, reports regularly on the activities of the conference and wider research through its quarterly journal, *Rapport*. Practitioners who want to read about or report on their action-based research are encouraged to submit articles to the ANLP journal *Acuity* (www.anlp.org/acuity).

There is now also a strong and growing group of practitioner and academic research-ers, linked via the NLP Research and Recognition Project (see Chapter 22 or www.nlprandr.org). Individuals can sign up to the project to receive newsletters and updates on research activity.

One of the aims of the project is to provide support to clinical practitioners who wish to further their research. Some of the projects currently being supported include innovations using NLP in countries where there are high levels of trauma through war and conflict.

## Notes

1. Tosey and Mathison (2009).

2. Linder-Pelz (2008); Wake (2010).

## References

Linder-Pelz, S. (2008). Meta-coaching: a methodology grounded in psychological theory. *International Journal of Evidence Based Coaching and Mentoring* 6(1): 43–56.

Tosey, P. and Mathison, J. (2009). *Neuro-Linguistic Programming: A Critical Appreciation for Managers and Developers*. Basingstoke: Palgrave Macmillan.

Wake, L. (2010). *NLP: Principles in Practice*. St Albans: Ecademy Press

---

Our grateful thanks go to Paul Tosey who has offered his thoughts and suggestions to this chapter, and whose ethics, integrity, commitment, and passion for research makes this innovation such a success.

# Appendices

# Book Design

## Chapter Formats

In order to create some similarity in structure, each chapter in this book is formatted similarly with six parts. We created this template so that the chapters would fit a basic structure and guide you in your reading. To do that we used a basic format—the 4-mat structure of what, why, how, and what if.

For Models and patterns, the chapters are structured in the following way:

1. *What* is the Model or pattern? What does it do? How does it work? What does it innovate in NLP?

2. *Why* was this Model or pattern developed? What are the benefits of the Model? What advantages will a person gain through using it? Why is it important for the field of NLP?

3. *How* does it work? What is the process or method by which a person uses it (a step-by-step description of how to actually use the Model)? What are the indicators for using this Model? When to use it and with whom?

4. *What if/Where else*: Identify warnings and/or caveats about the use of the Model or pattern. Where does it not work? Where does one have to be careful? What are some of the ways it can be misused? What are other purposes/uses for the Model?

5. *Make it personal*: To make it more personal, the story of how the Model/pattern was found or created.

6. *References and resources*: Further information on sources (books/websites), plus where the full Model can be obtained.

For tools, we have asked that contributors offer a description of their innovation in the following way:

1.  *Why:* What is the tool designed to do? What is its purpose and why is it important?

2.  *What:* A description of the form/presentation of the tool. What does it look like? What form or media does it involve?

3.  *How:* A brief description of how it works and how the tool could be used.

4.  *Experience:* What results have already been attained by the use of the tool?

For communities, we have asked that contributors offer the following information:

1.  *What:* What community of people have you brought together? What unifies and connects the people?

2.  *Why:* What is the purpose of the community? What is its vision and mission?

3.  *Form and expression:* Is the community a research community, an NLP association, conference, Internet community, and so on?

# Appendix B

# Requirements for a Model

What is required for something to be called a "model?" If we are open to new models in the field of NLP and if we anticipate that additional models will be added to NLP that were not part of the models that existed in 1975 or 1985, then by what criteria do we determine if something meets the conditions necessary to be considered a new model? In the sections within each chapter, there is a lot of talk about *models*, *patterns (applications)*, *tools*, and *communities*. With each of these, we have attempted to offer a description and criteria so as to define with some precision what we mean.

In the field of NLP, there is no consistent use of the terms model, patterns, techniques, etc. In this volume we have attempted to use the following as a way to distinguish a small-caps model and a big-caps Model (a Model with a capital M).

1. **A Theory:**
   First there has to be a theory which establishes the theoretical descriptions, background, foundation, hypothesis, etc. and which offers an explanatory model for how the model or a system works. An explanatory model will involve the governing ideas of the model and how to test and refine the ideas that will then lead to the creation of new applications. A model will present an idea (an hypothesis) that can be tested and falsified and can answer the *why*-does-this-work questions. What explains this experience or process? Does the model have construct validity?

   A theory functions as a way of bringing together a multitude of facts into a comprehensive order and when it does, it allows us to make reasonably precise predictions. A theory then is a tentative expression of a regular pattern.

   Now, in spite of possible protests to the contrary, NLP does have a theory. Declaring that NLP was a model and not a theory was perhaps good public relations, but it doesn't exclude the model from having a theory behind it. The hidden theory in NLP can be seen in the "NLP Presuppositions" and as such establishes NLP on the premises of constructionism, phenomenology, and on cognitive psychology. Interestingly enough, George Miller, Eugene Gallanter, and Karl Pribram along with Noam Chomsky are recognized as the founders of Cognitive Psychology (1956). From them NLP created the Meta-Model, the Representational Model, and the Strategy Model.

## 2. Variables and Elements:

If a theory comprises an over-arching frame for an experience, process, or skill, then the variables and elements of the theory are the pieces and parts that make up the components of the model. This answers the questions:

> *What* makes up this model?
> *What* elements are absolutely necessary and sufficient to make the model work?
> *What* processes are involved, what mechanisms does the model rely upon?

Variables of a model enable us to then experiment, to observe, to identify key factors, to create factorial designs in research projects. And from variables we can then generate operational definitions, theoretical constructs stated in terms of concrete, observable procedures. Now we can answer the question: what can be observed and tested?

So for the field of NLP, what are the variables of the NLP model? As a communication model, the variables are the sensory systems, the representations (VAK) and language, sub-modalities, meta-programs, etc. The variables would be the linguistic distinctions of the Meta-Model, the specific details within the list of sub-modalities, and so on.

## 3. The Guiding and Operational Principles:

After the theory and variables, next comes the guiding principles or the operational principles of a model. The laws or principles define and articulate the mechanisms that make it work and how to use them in a methodological, systematic, and systemic way. This gives a person the ability to keep refining the model. Principles answer the how questions:

*How* does the model work?
*What* processes and mechanisms govern the operation of the model?
How can I use this model?

In the NLP model, there are guidelines for how the various models work. For example, for the linguistic Communication Model, there are the Meta-Model questions for our to explore and challenge an ill-formed linguistic expression. For the Representation System Model there are principles for how to detect and use the representational systems, how to listen for predicates, how to use eye-accessing cues, etc. For the Strategy Model for modeling an experience, there are the processes for working with the TOTE model, with sequencing a set of representational steps, with using the hypnotic language patterns of the Milton Model, for example, "pace, pace, pace, lead."

In addition, in NLP training, participants generally learn the operational principles for how to "run" or use a pattern like the Swish Pattern, Circle of Excellence, The Phobia Cure pattern. This usually takes the form of step-by-step instructions.

### 4. The Technologies or Patterns:

This refers to the specific tools that provide immediate application for using the model to achieve something. Patterns answer the questions about *how to: how* do you anchor a state, calibrate to a person's non-verbals, reframe meaning? Etc.

In the NLP model, there are some 200 to 300 distinct patterns. Each one provides direction for how to do something in order to achieve a specific outcome. With patterns, always look for information about its context — where it is useful and effective and where it is not, and the elicitation questions that a person can use to begin the process. Typically also, there are usually conditions that are noted as times for caution in using the pattern.

### References

Hall, L. Michael; Bodenhamer, Bob. (1999, 2001). *User's Manual of the Brain, Volumes I and II*. Wales, UK: Crown House Publications.

Kelly, George A. (1955). *The Psychology of Personal Constructs*. London: W. W. Norton.

Pelham, Brett. W. (1999). *Conducting research in psychology: Measuring the weight of smoke*. Pacific Grove: Brooks/Cole Publishing Company, ITP: An International Thomson Publishing Co.

# Innovations in NLP, Volume II

This book is obviously not exhaustive about the innovations that have been occurring in the field of NLP from the 1990s onwards. Our hope is that as this volume goes out, we will hear from many people about lots of other innovations that we have not been aware of and that we will be able to include in the volumes that follow. In this way, we hope that we can recognize and acknowledge the innovations and the individuals who are creating and innovating new things for this field—innovations as additional models, patterns, tools, and communities. And perhaps this will facilitate more collaboration among us.

NLP, by its very nature and content, is a highly creative field; it invites creativity and innovation. Because it is all about modeling human excellence and the structure of experience, NLP calls for continuous improvement of the original models that launched this field and further discovery about the structure of experience and excellence. This is a field that will not become entrenched as a belief system with a creed, but will always be evolving and developing, so we can expect new innovations with each new generation of trainers and thinkers.

If you have used your creativity to invent something or know someone who has, contact us using the contact information below.

*L. Michael Hall, Ph.D.*
Neuro-Semantics International, P.O. Box 8, Clifton, CO. 81520, USA
email: meta@acsol.net; usa@meta-coaching.org
web: www.neurosemantics.com

*Shelle Rose Charvet*
1264 Lemonville Road, Burlington, Ontario, Canada L7R 3X5
email: shelle@wordsthatchangeminds.com
web: www.WordsThatChangeMinds.com
　　　www.labprofilecertification.com

# Index

ROBERT DILTS
L. MICHAEL HALL
TIM HALLBOM
LISA WAKE
JAAP HOLLANDER
MARTIN ROBERTS
ARNE MAUS
CHARLES FAULKNER
FRANK BOURKE
JAMES LAWLEY
LUCAS DERKS
RICHARD GRAY
KRIS HALLBOM
NICK KEMP
JAMES LAWLEY
BOBBY G. BODENHAMER
IAN MCDERMOTT
KIMIKO BOKURA-SHAFE
HIROMI TAMAKI
PENNY TOMPKINS
MASAKI KONO
RICHARD BOLSTAD
RICHARD LIOTTA